JESSE LIBERTY'S

from scratch

PROGRAMMING SERIES

XML Web Documents *from* scratch

Jesse Liberty and Mike Kraley

D1401814

A Division of Macmillan USA
201 West 103rd Street,
Indianapolis, Indiana 46290

XML Web Documents from Scratch

Copyright © 2000 by Que Corporation

International Standard Book Number: 0-7897-2316-6

Library of Congress Catalog Card Number: 00-100250

Printed in the United States of America

First Printing: March 2000

02   01   00   4   3   2

Trademarks

Warning and Disclaimer

Associate Publisher
Tracy Dunkelberger

Acquisitions Editor
Holly Allender

Development Editor
Jeff Durham

Managing Editor
Matt Purcell

Senior Editor
Susan Ross Moore

Copy Editor
Cynthia Fields

Indexer
Cheryl Landes

Proofreader
Benjamin Berg

Technical Editor
Dallas Releford

Team Coordinator
Cindy Teeters

Media Developer
Jay Payne

Interior Design
Sandra Schroeder

Cover Design
Anne Jones
Maureen McCarty

Copy Writer
Eric Borgert

Production
Stacey Richwine-DeRome
Ayanna Lacey
Heather Hiatt Miller

Overview

Contents

About the Authors

Jesse Liberty is the author of *WebClasses from Scratch*, as well as a dozen other books on Web applications development, C++, and object-oriented programming. Jesse is the president of Liberty Associates, Inc., where he provides custom Web applications development, training, mentoring, and consulting. He is a former vice president of electronic delivery for Citibank and a distinguished software engineer at AT&T. Jesse also serves as the series editor of Que's *Programming from Scratch* books. He supports his books at http://www.LibertyAssociates.com.

Mike Kraley has been developing hardware and software for 30 years. In college, he worked on a project about interconnecting computers and was one of the original contributors to the ARPAnet. At Bolt, Beranek, and Newman he continued his involvement as the ARPAnet grew into the Internet as well as several other government and commercial packet-switching networks. At Lotus, he was the general manager for the first PIM, Lotus Agenda. Then at Ziff-Davis and later AT&T, he helped lead the formation of Interchange, a ground-breaking online network, which ran headlong into the World Wide Web.

Dedication

Who is John Galt?

Acknowledgments

My family makes this book possible and worthwhile. Thank you again to Stacey, Robin, Rachel, Milo, and Fred.

My name is on the cover, but this book was created by a number of very dedicated people at Que, first among them Holly Allender and Tracy Dunkelberger. Among the many other hard-working people who helped put it together are Dallas Releford, Jeff Durham, Susan Moore, Cynthia Fields, and Benjamin Berg, all of whom worked tirelessly to make this book better than it was when I gave it to them. The mistakes, however, are mine; so send me the email, not them.

Special thanks to my co-author, Mike Kraley, without whom this book would not have been conceivable.

Tell Us What You Think!

As the reader of this book, *you* are our most important critic and commentator. We value your opinion and want to know what we're doing right, what we could do better, what areas you'd like to see us publish in, and any other words of wisdom you're willing to pass our way.

As an associate publisher for Que Corporation, I welcome your comments. You can fax, email, or write me directly to let me know what you did or didn't like about this book—as well as what we can do to make our books stronger.

Please note that I cannot help you with technical problems related to the topic of this book, and that due to the high volume of mail I receive, I might not be able to reply to every message.

When you write, please be sure to include this book's title and author as well as your name and phone or fax number. I will carefully review your comments and share them with the author and editors who worked on the book.

Fax: 317.581.4666

Email: programming@macmillanusa.com

Mail: Associate Publisher
          Que Corporation
          201 West 103rd Street
          Indianapolis, IN 46290 USA

Introduction

This book takes an unusual approach. Rather than teaching you the details of the XML specification, this book, like all the books in the *From Scratch* series, begins by focusing on a real-world problem we want to solve.

We start by analyzing and designing our project, and then we step you through the implementation of our design. Programming skills and XML details are taught in the context of implementing the project; first you understand what you are trying to accomplish, and then you learn the skills needed to get the job done.

What This Book Covers and What I Need to Know

This book will teach you how to use XML and XSL to parse, manipulate, store, and render documents on the Web. Along the way we'll make use of ASP, VB, JavaScript, ADO, and related topics. While our focus will be on XML and XSL, if you are not 100% conversant in these other technologies *don't panic!* I'll explain the tricky parts as I go. If you've never programmed with ASP or WebClasses at all, have never used VB or JavaScript, and don't know what ADO is, you'll want first to read either *WebClasses from Scratch* or *ASP from Scratch*, or another book which introduces all of these topics.

If you want to follow the examples and try out the code, you need to know the following:

- How to set up and administer either Internet Information Server or Personal Web Server
- How to create a virtual directory on your Web server
- How to create and call an ASP page
- How to create and run a project in Visual Basic
- How to set up, administer, and create a database and tables in SQL Server 7

All these skills are covered in my book *WebClasses from Scratch*. If you have read that book, or have comparable knowledge, you will be all set.

If you do *not* have these skills but want to press forward, you will find that the text explains all the code in detail, but you will need help from a knowledgeable friend to get your code up and running on your own machine.

The Key Facts About XML

By the time we're done, you will know

- What XML is
- What XML is used for
- The details of the Document Object Model
- How XSL Style Sheets allow you to manipulate XML documents
- How XML interacts with HTML
- How XML interacts with databases

This book will explain each of these key ideas, in detail, as we go. I'll start with a brief introduction to XML, covering what it is and how it came to be created. I'll provide a number of examples of how XML can be used to solve real-world programming problems, and then I'll describe one such problem and its solution.

Along the way to implementing our project, I'll examine the XML Document Object Model (DOM) in detail, and I'll compare and contrast it with the HTML DOM. I'll show you how to manipulate XML documents with the DOM and also with XSL style sheets, and how to accomplish this using VBScript and JavaScript. You'll see how our XML documents interact with HTML within a Web Application, and you'll see how we store and retrieve data from SQL Server.

Who Should Read This Book?

This book is definitely for you if you are in any way involved in programming Web applications. XML will transform the way you approach programming for the Web, storing documents, or otherwise interacting with content.

Conventions Used in This Book

Some of the unique features in this series include

 Geek Speak—An icon in the margin indicates the use of a new term. New terms will appear in the paragraph in *italics*.

**how tŏŏ
prŏ nouns′ it**

How To Pronounce It—You'll see an icon set in the margin next to a box that contains a technical term and how it should be pronounced. For example, "`cin` is pronounced *see-in*, and `cout` is pronounced *see-out*."

EXCURSIONS

Excursions are short diversions from the main topic being discussed, and they offer an opportunity to flesh out your understanding of a topic.

With a book of this type, a topic might be discussed in multiple places as a result of when and where we add functionality during application development. To help make this all clear, we've included a Concept Web that provides a graphical representation of how all the programming concepts relate to one another. You'll find it on the inside front cover of this book.

Notes offer comments and asides about the topic at hand, as well as full explanations of certain concepts.

Tips provide great shortcuts and hints on how to program in WebClasses more effectively.

Warnings help you avoid the pitfalls of programming, thus preventing you from making mistakes that will make your life miserable.

In addition, you'll find various typographic conventions throughout this book:

- Commands, variables, and other code appear in text in a special `computer font`.
- In this book, I build on existing listings as we examine code further. When I add new sections to existing code, you'll spot it in **`bold computer font`**.

- Commands and such that you type appear in **boldface type**.
- Placeholders in syntax descriptions appear in an *italic computer font* typeface. This indicates that you will replace the placeholder with the actual filename, parameter, or other element that it represents.

Breaking the Code

In some instances, when you look at a code listing, you'll notice that some lines of code have been broken in two and that the line numbers have letters. For example, see lines 10 and 10a:

```
10:      If Len(Session("SomeTextField")) = 0 Then
10a:         Session("SomeTextField") = "Any Value"
```

What has happened here is that I've broken up a single line of code because it was too long to fit on a single line in this book. The rewrite is still legal code, and can be typed in just as you find it (without the line numbers, of course).

The letter *a* is a signal to you that normally I'd combine these two lines into one.

Other times, you'll find that I use the VB line continuation character. In this case, the two lines are broken according to the rules of VB. In this case, I will use normal line numbering as follows:

```
10:      If Len(Session("SomeTextField")) = 0 Then _
11:          Session("SomeTextField") = "Any Value"
```

Finally, in some cases the line does not lend itself to being broken up at all. In this case you'll see the line continuation character, indicating that what you are looking at is one very wide line which can't easily be divided:

```
19:  "<a href=""Javascript:OnChangeRequest('SearchByName')"">
➥<em>A very long prompt might have to go here</em></a>"
```

(Don't worry about the meaning of any of this code, as it is all explained in the text of the book).

Chapter 1

Getting Started with XML

XML is really nothing more than a specification.

 Specification—An agreed-upon protocol for how to create certain kinds of documents.

This makes it tempting for authors of primers on XML to dive right into the structure of the specification, detailing its object model and the syntax of interacting with XML documents. This is much like being taught to conjugate verbs in French, before you have any reason even to want to speak the language!

 Object-oriented languages are created around the concept of an *object model*. The object model describes objects in the language and how they interact with one another.

 A *Document Object Model* describes the objects in a document and how they interact. I'll describe the XML Document Object Model in great detail in this book.

Rather than throwing a great deal of abstract information at you without a meaningful context, I will start by describing a real-world business problem, and then I'll show how XML offers a solution to that problem.

We'll then go ahead and implement that solution, and along the way I'll have the opportunity to explain how XML facilitates our task.

Document Re-Purposing

All across the world, a vast array of businesses are attempting to solve the same problem: document re-purposing. How do we take the documents we already have and make them available on the Web today, and on whatever medium is most useful tomorrow?

Document re-purposing refers to the ability to make documents and other information available in a variety of formats on a variety of media. A typical example includes the ability to publish a directory of information in print both on the Web and to other media such as CD.

For example, a client may have a directory of hospitals and health care facilities currently in print that he would like to publish on the Web, allowing for faster searching, cross referencing, and up-to-date information.

The goal is for the document to look beautiful and appropriate in each medium, and to target and craft the document for each audience.

The brute-force method to re-purposing for the Web is to re-key each document, copying it from whatever form it is in today into an HTML document. Certainly, this is the most straightforward solution, but it is expensive, time-consuming, and error-prone.

An alternative is to create the documents in a word processor such as Microsoft Word, and then use Word's capability to save a document as HTML. This solution brings its own problems: Word does not create the most attractive documents on the Web, and they typically require a great deal of reformatting and tinkering.

Equally important, neither re-keying nor saving as HMTL really solves the problem: The next time we want to use the document in a different way (for example, to display on a PIM or for printing or sending via email) we'll face exactly the same dilemma. Even if we just want to change the look and feel of the document, we face a great deal of re-editing.

Print Versus Online

Beyond the practical consideration of maintaining various renditions of the same document, maintaining Web documents in Word processing files makes no sense. Word processors were created to facilitate the creation of printed documents. They excel at things such as margins, footers, headers, and pagination (counting pages).

The Web is a new world, and new tools are required to make documents look great on the Web.

When moving pictures were first invented, early directors fixed the camera on a tripod, pointed it at the stage, and made movies of plays. This was the medium they knew, so they applied the new technology to their old way of doing business. D.W. Griffith was the first director to take the camera off the tripod and to make what we think of as a modern movie. Web publishing requires that we take the document down off the tripod and change the way we work with documents and how we think about presenting information.

One problem with clicking Save as HTML in your favorite text editor is that you get a Web presentation of a printed document, and it tends to look pretty crummy.

Web documents have elements such as hyperlinks that are undreamed of in print. Web documents are also designed to be displayed onscreen, which makes for a very different use of layout and fonts than does a print medium.

Even within the world of Web documents, we might want a given document displayed in myriad ways, depending on our audience and on our display medium. Some customers want only abstracts or highlights; others will want all the details. Some will view the document at high resolution on a large screen monitor, others through a tiny window in a cellular telephone. Certainly we want to arrange, display, and manipulate the contents of the document differently in each of these cases.

Re-Purposing

We need a better solution than just slapping printed documents onto the Web. Instead, we need to tear the document down to its atomic components, and then mix, match, and manipulate those pieces depending on where we're going to display them.

To do this, we need to disentangle display from content and content from structure. We need, in short, to treat the atomic units of a document as independent components.

Finally, and equally important, we must be able to store our document so that we can reassemble it in various ways as needed. We need to make the component pieces of the document persistent: They must live in a database.

What is the right size for the atomic units we store in a database? Certainly we could save every individual character, but that is absurd at face value.

Characters, words, sentences—even paragraphs—are meaningless by themselves. Articles—small clusters of paragraphs transmitting a coherent idea—are almost certainly the correct atomic unit, though the actual size of such a component will be determined by the specific application. For example, in a newsletter, an individual story will be the atomic unit, but if we're publishing a book to the Web, a chapter, or perhaps a sub-chapter might be the atomic unit.

Real-World Examples

There are any number of examples of companies confronting the problem of how to re-deploy their existing documents. One recent client asked us to help him take all the data from his newsletters and make each article available on the Web. The goal was to use the identical article both on the Web and in print, and then to be able to re-deploy the article quickly to whatever other medium became of interest. We knew, for example, that these same articles would be used again in print to produce annual reviews.

Our customer also needed the ability to search for particular articles based not only on the publication date, author, or title, but also based on words in the content. Each of his articles was written in Word, and all the articles of a particular newsletter were in a single file.

Our task was to break the articles out of the file, save the meta-data (for example, the publication name, author, date and so forth), store it all in a database, and then produce each article in whatever format was appropriate, on demand.

One of Mike's other clients had a vast array of articles about health care. This client provides an interactive Web site, and the articles are supplemental information, served up on demand. He needed to be able to filter and excerpt the appropriate articles based on the context in which they are requested. Furthermore, because different users of the system can choose among various subscription levels, we will need to display differing levels of content based on criteria about the particular user. Once again, we need the articles to be broken down into atomic units that can be mixed and matched and displayed in various formats.

How This Book Came About

It turned out that the solution for our first client was similar to the solution for the second. In fact, as we progressed, we became convinced that this was a classic *design pattern*, along the lines described in the seminal book *Design Patterns: Elements of Reusable Object-Oriented Software* (Addison-Wesley Professional Computing) by Erich Gamma, et al, 1995, ISBN: 0201633612.

When we realized that these solutions were not only similar to one another, but were in fact the pattern for solving hundreds, if not thousands of similar problems faced by Web application developers every day, we decided to write this book. The goal of this book is, in fact, to teach XML and XSL in the context of this design pattern.

The Design Pattern

Design patterns are named, described, and then demonstrated. We'll name our design pattern Canon, because the essential aspect of this pattern is to create a canonical form of the data.

 Canonical Form is the "official" agreed-upon standard form.

Meta-data is information about the data, such as the title, author, date of creation, and so forth.

We need a canonical form: a format and language for storing our documents and maintaining not only the contents, but also the meta-data.

XML is particularly adept at serving in this role because it provides semantic clues, in the form of tags, about the meaning of the data. For example, by storing `<title>Earthquake Rocks Acton</title>`, we know that these three words act as the title of the document.

We will store our XML in a SQL Server 7 database because SQL Server is the best tool for rapid storage and retrieval of Web documents built from XML records. This will allow us to search, filter, and otherwise manage these XML documents using industry-standard SQL commands.

Note   If you are not 100% familiar with SQL *don't panic!* I explain all the SQL used in this book as we go.

So, here's the Canon pattern: Transform the documents into XML, manipulate the documents into articles that can be stored in an SQL database, then publish the articles from XML into the required formats (for example, HTML, PDF, and so forth).

This book will show you how to do it. As you can see, the pattern centers on XML, one of the newest and arguably one of the most powerful technologies of the Web.

What Is XML and Why Do I Care?

A friend of mine, who has been developing Internet applications for nearly a decade, recently said to me, "XML will change the world far more significantly than HTML did." That is quite a statement. If true, it means that XML might be one of the most important technical developments in a generation.

Remember that the Web, and for that matter, the Internet, is a fairly recent development. It was at a computer show in January of 1994 that I saw my first glimpse of the Web, at a booth demonstrating the newly created Mosaic browser. In the six years since Demo 94, the Web has transformed American business. It is now difficult to find a company without a Web site, and all of this development has been facilitated by HTML. HTML literally transformed the way we use computers.

How is it possible that XML will be even more significant? It is because XML will extend the capability of the Web from an interactive information delivery mechanism to an information *exchange* medium. That change means that businesses can go beyond the delivery of information over the Web, to the conduct of mission-critical, enterprise-wide commercial interaction.

In short, XML offers a globally accepted cross-platform mechanism for managing, storing, and communicating information. The XML 1.0 World Wide Web Consortium (W3C) Recommendation is an international standard that has already been endorsed and adopted by Microsoft, Netscape, Sun, IBM, and a plethora of other vendors. XML is here to stay.

XML In Context

In one sense, the hardest thing about XML is understanding quite what it is, and what it is for. To understand this, I'm afraid you need just a bit of the history of how XML came to be created.

It all starts with SGML. SGML stands for Standard Generalized Markup Language. The job of SGML is to describe how a markup language can be built, by specifying the syntax and definitions of the elements and attributes of that language. SGML is a *meta-language*.

A *meta-language* is a language that describes other languages.

The job of SGML is to define the syntax of a markup language. A markup language simply defines how you add meaning to data, typically in a document.

Syntax is the actual characters, punctuation, and order of words in a language.

One of the languages SGML describes is HTML. We say that HTML is an *instance* of an SGML language. Increasingly, the meaning that HTML adds to its document is primarily *presentation* information. For example: `<b>Jesse Liberty</b>`. The `<b>` and `</b>` tags provide additional information to the data "Jesse Liberty"—they tell a browser to present that name in bold.

When programmers talk about an *instance* they mean a concrete example of an abstract idea. Democracy is an idea, the United States is an instance of a democratic country.

One can create any number of languages with SGML, though HTML is by far the most popular SGML-based markup language ever created.

Note that SGML does not define the *structure* of HTML. That task is accomplished by the HTML Document Type Definition (the DTD). The HTML DTD uses the syntax dictated by SGML to define a valid HTML document. The HTML DTD determines the validity of the <br>, <p> and other tags used in HTML; SGML simply provides the syntax.

DTD (Document Type Definition) is the description of the valid syntax of a document.

Finally, neither SGML nor the DTD define the semantics of HTML. The *semantics* are the meaning of each tag; for example, the fact that <b> means bold. This is accomplished by the client code: in this case a browser.

Semantics—The meaning of words and phrases in a language.

Let's review: SGML defines the syntax of HTML. The HTML DTD defines whether a given document is valid. The browser interprets the document and renders the document as instructed by the tags.

XML Simplifies SGML

So where does XML fit in? XML is a subset of SGML. It is, in fact, a simplification of SGML and serves the same purpose as SGML but it is far easier to use. The idea is to maintain the 50% of SGML that is used 90% of the time.

This is not a trivial distinction. SGML was so difficult to use that anyone who was not a specialist could not work with it effectively. This set the price of entry very high: If you wanted to use SGML you needed to invest a lot of time (or money) in achieving the necessary expertise. The effect was that few people used it, and it remained a peripheral technology.

Here's the secret about XML: It isn't difficult. XML is so straightforward, in fact, that after reading one short book on the topic (this one, for example) most developers can put it to work immediately. XML's very simplicity is its strength. A powerful meta-language that is simple to use can transform the way we interact with data; XML is such a meta-language.

XML defines the syntax of languages. You can define HTML in XML, and you can define any number of other languages in XML as well. What is most important about XML is that it was created specifically to be extensible. Unlike HTML, XML does not have a fixed set of tags.

The focus in XML is not on presentation. Typically, XML tags tell you nothing about how to render the data, but they do tell you a great deal about the meaning of the data. It is this capability to provide meaningful tags that gives XML its power, as we'll see.

What Is XML Like?

When you first see an XML document, it looks just like an HTML document except that you quickly notice you've never seen these particular tags before.

The following code is a very short excerpt from an XML file we'll examine later in the book:

```
<book>
<section level="A" id="10000">
<title>Chapter 10</title>
<section level="B" id="10001">
 <title>Leveraging the Standard Template Library</title>
```

Notice that rather than finding tags such as <br> and <div> you see here specialized tags such as <book>, <section>, and <title>. This is the essence of XML, semantically meaningful tags.

One important fact about XML tags is that the author of the XML document is allowed to create tags that are meaningful in his own development context. This means that the same tag will have different meanings within different documents. For example, the <title> tag in my document will refer to the title of the chapter, but in a different document it might refer to a person's title (Mr., Dr., and so forth), and in a third context it might refer to ownership of a house or car.

In the same way, <section> refers to part of a chapter, but in a math book it might mean the profile of something as it would appear if cut through by an intersecting plane, and in a town planning document it might refer to a square mile.

XML Tag Attributes

In XML, tags can also contain meaningful attributes. Just as an HTML Input tag might have the attributes name=action and type=submit, here the Section tag has the attributes level="A" and id="10000".

Again, let's not worry yet about the meaning of these specific tags, but focus instead on the fact that these tags are defined as meaningful in the context of our project. That is, the markup language has been extended to include tags meaningful to our own needs!

Just as the tag must be provided meaning in its context, so too must all the attributes be provided with contextual meaning. The attributes for a book section will, of course, be different from the attributes for a town-planning section.

What Is XSL?

The eXtensible Stylesheet Language is a powerful instance of XML, used to transform and control the display of XML documents.

As you'll see in this book, only one browser currently supports XSL (Internet Explorer 5) and that browser supports only half of XSL: transformations. Fortunately, this is the important half, as the display aspects of XSL can be accomplished, in large measure, by CSS (Cascading Style Sheets), which are supported in IE5. XSL transformations allow you to manipulate the structure and contents of an XML document. We will make extensive use of XSL transformations in this book.

Analysis and Design of Our Project

We begin our project, as all projects, by analyzing the requirements. We'll then design a solution and finally we'll implement that solution. Because this is a rather small demonstration program, the analysis will be briefer than it would be in a real-world project. We are eager to get on to the design and implementation, but let's first ensure that we fully understand the problem we're trying to solve.

BiblioTech

In our fictional scenario, Que Corporation has decided to provide online instruction on a number of topics, based on books in the *From Scratch* series. If this goes well, the idea will be extended to other Que and Macmillan titles. To do this, we'll create a Web site on which readers can ask questions about a variety of subjects. We want to be able to answer those questions by providing excerpts from any of the *From Scratch* books. To accomplish this, we need a tool that can quickly find and render excerpts of the book, or source code, on demand.

Use-Case Analysis

We won't endeavor to create a full and robust use-case analysis of this project because we are going to keep things very simple. (For a full explanation of use-case analysis and object-oriented analysis and design, see the suggested reading list in Appendix A.)

For now, we'll identify the principal *actors* in the system as the author and potentially, eventually, the online students.

In object-oriented analysis and design, an *actor* is any person or system that interacts with the application we're designing.

The principal use cases are these:

1. The author uses BiblioTech to find an appropriate explanation of a concept and can cut and paste that explanation right into a mail message or Web page.
2. The author uses BiblioTech to find a quote from the book on a particular topic, which he will cut and paste into another message.

3. The author uses BiblioTech to review and perhaps eventually to edit the organization of topics.

4. The student uses BiblioTech via the Web to find explanations on particular topics of interest.

There are other use cases one can imagine; however these will give us a good start on understanding the requirements.

Visualization

BiblioTech is a tool that will provide a list of all the topics in a book, either in list form or as a collapsible table of contents. Each topic will be active; clicking on the topic will display the related article. In addition, the user can search for words, either in the title or, ultimately, anywhere in the text.

It is important to get a sense of what this application looks like. This can provide a very powerful insight into how the application will work and how it will be used.

Figure 1.1 illustrates BiblioTech as I envision it.

Figure 1.1

BiblioTech.

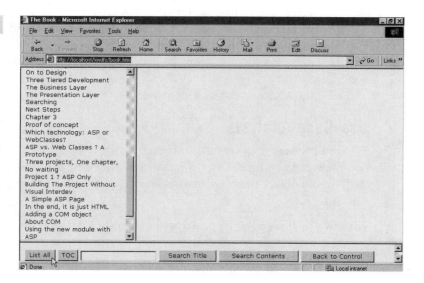

BiblioTech is a fairly straightforward Web application. In the bottom pane are controls that allow a user to list all the topics (as shown in Figure 1.1), or to list a collapsible table of contents, as shown in Figure 1.2.

Figure 1.2

Collapsible TOC.

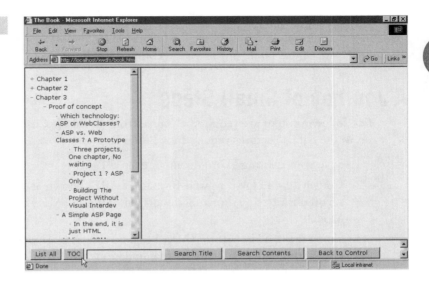

In addition, the user can type a word or phrase into the text entry and search through the titles. An easy extension of this program, left as an exercise to the reader, would be to allow full text searching, as well as filtering and sorting of the contents.

If the user clicks on an article title, it is displayed in the right pane, as shown in Figure 1.3.

Figure 1.3

Article display.

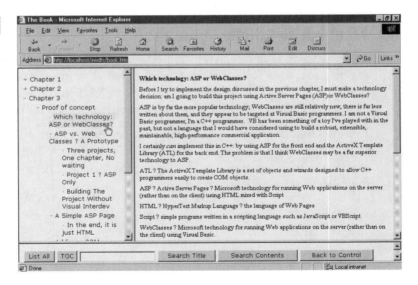

BiblioTech relies, under the covers, on having each section of the book broken out as an article, stored in the database, and available as XML. We'll return to BiblioTech at the end of this book, once we've accomplished these tasks.

A Journey of Small Steps

The following steps are required to move from Word files, each containing a chapter, to the data structures required for BiblioTech:

1. Save your existing Word documents in HTML.
2. Convert the HTML to well-formed HTML (known as XHTML). We'll accomplish this by direct manipulation of the HTML Document Object Model.
3. Convert the XHTML to XML. We'll do this in two steps: first using an XSL style sheet, and then by direct manipulation of the XML Document Object Model (DOM).
4. Split out the stories and save them in a SQL Server database.
5. Build the Table of Contents display.
6. Build the BiblioTech Application.

After we've accomplished these steps, we can embellish the application. In the final chapters we'll then take a look at additional utility applications that will help with understanding and manipulating both XML and XSL.

What I *Won't* Show in the Project

In this project, as in most Web applications, much of the real effort goes into making it look good. I won't do that work here. In fact, I've intentionally kept this application quite sparse. The focus of this book is on XML and XSL; we don't want to be distracted by fancy programming tricks that are not relevant to the task at hand.

Even to build this very sparse application, however, I must make use of the pantheon of Web application technologies, including JavaScript, ASP, ADO, and so forth. I'll explain the tricky parts as I go, but again, the focus will be on XML and XSL, not the related and supporting technologies.

Note The text we'll use in BiblioTech is my earlier book, *WebClasses from Scratch*. Those of you who happened to read that book are no doubt asking, "Why, if you wrote about WebClasses, have you implemented this in ASP?"

The answer is threefold: first, the actual ASP pages are dead-simple, and there was little advantage to WebClasses (which excel in more complicated applications).

Second, for now, ASP is a far more common programming environment, so more readers are likely already to be familiar with it.

Third, ASP pages do not require you to purchase VB, and I wanted to ensure that you could implement all the code in this book without having to purchase a new development environment.

Next Steps

With an overview of the project firmly in hand, let's start by examining the Word documents that hold each chapter of the book. Our goal is to convert these to XML, a goal we will accomplish by saving these documents as HTML, converting them to XML-valid HTML (XHTML), and finally converting them to our canonical format in XML.

Chapter 2

In this chapter

- *Analysis*
- *Converting to HTML*
- *Converting Word To XHTML*
- *Stepping Through the Code*
- *Next Steps*

Moving from HTML to XHTML

In Chapter 1, we discussed the steps necessary to move Word documents into XML. Our goal is to end up with the document in XML, broken into stories (the atomic units) and stored in a database. This will allow us a flexible architecture from which we can restore and re-deploy the articles to any number of formats and uses.

To get there we must make a series of transformations. The first is out of Word's binary, proprietary format and into something we can work with. Along the way, however, we must also interpret the meaning of the document, so we can convert from the existing internal structure to XML and so we don't lose any of the meta-data currently embedded in the Word document. To understand this issue, Listing 2.1 shows an excerpt from the middle of one of the chapters we'll be using for this project: *WebClasses From Scratch* Chapter 2.Doc.

Listing 2.1   Excerpt from Chap2.doc

(c) Analysis

EmployeeNet will manage the human resources needs of middle-sized corporations. The project is being sponsored by Acme Manufacturing, and we'll build it to meet their needs and then generalize for other companies as we go.

Acme employs 2,000 people in the manufacture of high-end consumer products. Their principal products are the Acme Widget and their world-famous Gizmo. They have manufacturing plants in East Podunk and New Boondock and their main offices are in Gotham.

(d) Conceptualization

EmployeeNet will allow the personnel department to track all benefits for employees, and will allow employees to review and edit their own employment records.

continues

Listing 2.1   Continued

(d) Use Cases

There was a time when the typical requirements for a software project were expressed in terms of capabilities and performance. While this ensured that the resulting system met certain specified benchmarks, it did not ensure that anyone could or would want to use it. Typically the user didn't factor into consideration until after the product was out the door.

Object-oriented analysis begins with a thorough understanding of how the product will be *used*. A *use case* is a formal statement of the various ways in which a user will interact with the system, and what he will want to accomplish.

*****BEGIN GEEK SPEAK*****

A *use case* is a formal statement of one way in which the system will be used.

*****END GEEK SPEAK*****

We begin the use case analysis by identifying the principal actors; that is, the users of the system. These include

[lb]   Human resources personnel (entering and updating records)

[lb]   Human resources managers (reviewing the work done in their department and setting policies)

[lb]   Employees (reviewing their own records)

[lb]   Managers (reviewing the employee records of their direct reports)

*****BEGIN GEEK SPEAK*****

An *actor* is a person or other software system that interacts with the system we're creating.

*****END GEEK SPEAK*****

This brief excerpt reveals a number of interesting and relevant facts about this book. The most important is that the Word document is already partially marked-up for publication. When I wrote the book, I marked text as section headings, chapter titles, numbered lists, notes and so forth. I did this in two ways.

First, I used explicit markings in the text. For example, in the text shown above, the Analysis section is a C-level heading. An A-level heading is a chapter number, a

B-level is a chapter title, and a C-level (or level-1 heading) marks a section. A D-level heading is a level-2, that is it is a sub-section for a C-level. There are also E-, F- and G-level headings. This represents the kind of outline structure you will remember from 7th grade English class (or, if you are young enough, from 7th grade Language Arts!)

Having marked Analysis as a C-level heading, I've indicated that it is the name of a major section. As such, the style guidelines dictate that it will be printed in 18 point type, bold, Helvetica Cond B font, and so forth. The D-Level sub-section Conceptualization will be printed in 14 point type, bold, Helvetica Cond B font.

In addition to marking the headings as I've shown, I also set the Word *style* for each. The style is from a set of styles provided by Macmillan and added to my standard Word document template. These styles are meaningful only to Macmillan's production department. Other publishers would use a different style sheet.

For example, Macmillan provides HA, HB, HC, HD, HE, HF, and HG styles for the A-, B-, C-, D-, E-, F- and G- level headings respectively. The C-level heading is prepended with the mark (c) and then set to the Word style HC, as shown in Figure 2.1

Figure 2.1

An example of a c head.

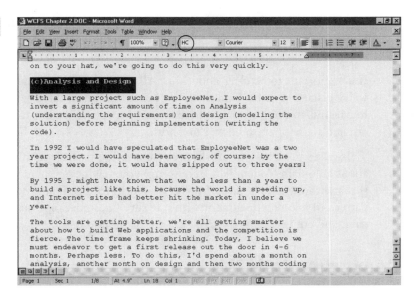

I also flag certain sections for special treatment by the editors. This series includes a special notation called "Geek Speak." These provide definitions of technical terms. When I want to designate a Geek Speak, I enter:

Geek Speak

This is a publishing directive to the editor that the lines between the stars are to be set aside in a Geek Speak, as you see elsewhere in this book. Here's an example:

A *publishing directive* is a markup used as an indication to production that special handling is required.

The Geek Speak is also marked up in one of two special styles: either PD (Publishing Directive) or NO (note). These are used for sidebars, notes, Geek Speak, How to Pronounce It, and so forth.

As another example, when I have a bulleted list, Macmillan asks that I mark each bullet point with [lb]. This will be changed in production to a bullet. In addition, I use two *styles*. Each line is marked with the BL (Bulleted List) style except the last bullet point, which is marked with BX. The BX is a signal to the layout technician that this is the last bullet point and therefore additional leading (vertical space) must be left after this line.

The AU style is used for the author byline or quote credits. The FT style is used for normal text throughout the document.

We'll be particularly interested in source code, which is marked with three styles. A single line of standalone code is indicated with the C1 style. Multiline code is indicated with C2, with the final line indicated with CX. These will become particularly important to us when we transform these documents into our canonical XML format.

It is important to be clear about this: All the styles and special designations that we've discussed so far (and there are many more we've not yet discussed) are specific to Macmillan publications. These are *not* part of XML, but rather are unique to the domain we happen to be working with.

This raises the question of why we're bothering to include this level of specificity about a domain (Macmillan Publishing) you may never again care about. The answer is that although the *details* of this style sheet are specific to Macmillan, the overall pattern of taking a document with one set of designations, markup, styles and metadata, and converting it to XML is a very common task.

Converting to HTML

So, we see that there are two, intertwined issues. One is getting the document out of Word format and into HTML, and the other is understanding and capturing the meta-information currently embedded in Macmillan editorial designations (such as ***Geek Speak***) and also embedded in the use of Word styles.

Ultimately, we do not need to capture the styles. We don't care that a particular line was marked in HA style. We do care, however, about capturing the meta-data currently implied by that style. That is, while we don't care that it was HA style, we do care that it was an A-level heading. What we are doing for Macmillan documents we have done and will continue to do for many other clients; only the details change.

From Word to HTML

Microsoft Word stores its documents in its own cryptic binary format. You can, I suppose, write custom software to read the binary format directly, but that is too painful to contemplate. Alternatively, you can use COM Automation to interact with the Word object model and manipulate the document through the COM interface. That, too, is a painful and difficult task. More important, neither technique is necessary; we can save the document to HTML and then manipulate it easily.

To do so, simply open Word and use the Save As Web Page choice off the File menu, as shown in Figure 2.2

Figure 2.2

Saving the document as a Web page.

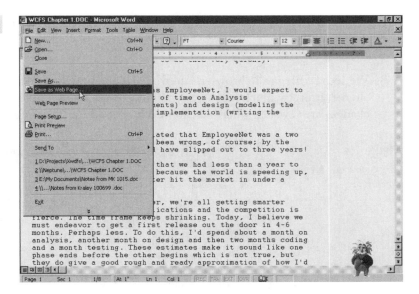

Note

If you don't see Save As Web Page in your File menu from Word, verify first that you have Word 2000 installed (earlier versions of Word won't work for this example), and then try expanding the entire menu, as this choice is often hidden.

If you don't have Word 2000, use the already converted .htm documents which you can download from my Web site: http://www.LibertyAssociates.com.

Let's take a look at the results by choosing File/Web Page Preview, as shown in Figure 2.3.

Figure 2.3

Viewing the new Web page.

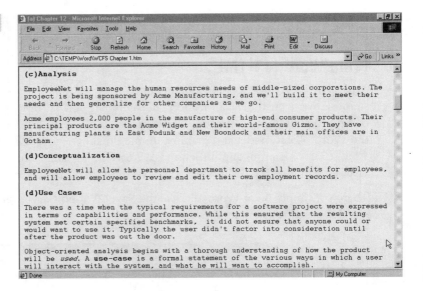

We see the file in the browser, and while some of the detailed styling may be slightly altered, it pretty much looks as we might expect. The significant under-the-covers changes are revealed when we choose View/Source as illustrated in Figure 2.4.

Figure 2.4

View Source has been chosen.

What is all this? This looks nothing like what we'd expect.

For the past few years, Word has offered the capability to save a document as HTML, but this was a very disappointing process. Much of the formatting (for example, columns, initial line indentation, outline numbering, and so forth) was lost in translation. Equally disturbing, saving to HTML was a one-way transformation. There was no easy way to go back to Word; the extra formatting information was irretrievably lost.

In Office 2000, Microsoft has staked itself to using XML as an alternative to its proprietary binary format. The first effect of this shift to XML is that the Web document created by Word now contains all the formatting information, and there is far greater fidelity between the resulting HTML document and the original Word document. Because the meta information is preserved, it is possible to make changes to the HTML document, then save it as a Word document and retrieve all the Word-specific formatting.

Note It is worth noting, however, that although Microsoft is touting its use of XML, the file that results from saving a Word file is not well-formed XML, and the document includes many parts which are not XML at all.

In Figure 2.4 we see an XML Island, which captures the properties of the document (for example, revision history, number of characters, and so forth.) We will skip over this XML Island for now, and scroll down to the beginning of our document, as shown in Figure 2.5.

An *XML Island* is an XML document embedded in an HTML document. This is a Microsoft extension to the HTML specification which makes working with XML easier.

Ahh… much better. Here we see a reasonably traditional set of HTML. Each paragraph is marked with a `<p>` tag, many of which use a CSS class attribute to manage specific styling.

Figure 2.5

*Scroll down in the
source.*

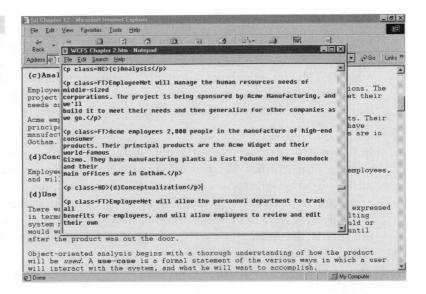

EXCURSION

HTML: The <p> tag indicates a paragraph in HTML. The class attribute is used with Cascading Style Sheets (CSS) to handle styling of the contents of the paragraph.

To follow this, note that the second line above shows

```
<p class=FT>
```

We can see this class defined earlier in the file. Search from the top of the file for .FT (note the period [.]). This will bring you to the following code:

```
p.FT, li.FT, div.FT
    {mso-style-name:FT;
    mso-style-parent:"";
    margin-top:0in;
    margin-right:0in;
    margin-bottom:12.0pt;
    margin-left:0in;
    line-height:12.0pt;
    mso-pagination:widow-orphan;
    font-size:12.0pt;
    mso-bidi-font-size:10.0pt;
    font-family:Courier;
    mso-fareast-font-family:"Times New Roman";
    mso-bidi-font-family:"Times New Roman";}
```

This code is within a style sheet section (not shown). The first line specifies that the class FT, when used within a `<p>`, `<li>`, or `<div>` tag, will be characterized by the style that follows. The defined style corresponds to the mso (Microsoft Office) style named FT and has the characteristics as shown, including a line height of 12.0 points, a font family of Courier, and so forth.

The `class` indication in the `<p>` tag shown in Figure 2.5 directs the browser to apply the indicated style to this paragraph. We'll talk more about CSS styles as we progress.

Well-Formed HTML

The World Wide Web Consortium (W3C) has promulgated a series of recommendations for HTML. These recommendations constitute an international standard for well-formed HTML. This standard is quite flexible. HTML is very forgiving because it was designed for hand-coding (using, for many of us, Notepad!) Thus, for example, many HTML tags do not need to be closed. It is perfectly legal HTML to create a `<p>` tag and never create a `</p>` tag.

XML is just the opposite. XML is designed to be very rigid. Why? Because by making the language rigid, it is easier to create tools: After all, there are fewer exceptions to manage.

Here's why I love Spanish. Once you learn the pronunciation rules, there is no question about how to pronounce just about any word in the language. When you see a new word, say a city name such as Ocho Rios, you do not have to guess. Ocho Rios *must* be pronounced Och-oh (to rhyme with coach-oh) Ree-ose (to rhyme with me-oh with a sibilant s at the end). A rigid language makes life easy.

A flexible language such as English can make you crazy. An Israeli friend once asked me, "Why is it that 'digit' has a soft g and 'dig it' has a hard g?" There probably is a good answer, but for every rule in English, there is at least one exception. In 7th grade we used to ask people, "What does photi spell?" The answer: fish. PH pronounced like in **PH**otograph. O pronounced like in w**O**men. TI pronounced like in mo**TI**on.

The rigidity of XML is its saving grace. It is far easier to build XML tools than HTML tools because XML is more predictable. Unfortunately, this creates a problem for us because saving a document as a Web page from Word creates standard HTML, and converting that to XML will be tricky.

The best way to begin, therefore, is to move our HTML document into XHTML— that is, XML-compliant HTML. Unfortunately, the recommendation for the official XHTML is still in draft, but we don't need to let that stop us. We can simply rewrite our HTML using the rules of well-formed XML. This will still be valid HTML, we'll just ask it to follow XML's more rigid guidelines. That is the essence of XHTML, and we can feel secure that what we produce will be consistent with the final W3C recommendation for XHTML.

The following are key items in making HTML well-formed XML:

- Nested tags must not overlap.
- Tag names must be case sensitive.
- All tags must be closed.
- Attribute values must be quoted.

It turns out that rule number one (nested tags must not overlap) is followed quite well in the Word to HTML conversion. Tag names also appear to be case sensitive. Unfortunately, not all the tags are closed, and not all the attribute values are quoted. But we can fix that.

Fixing Up the HTML

There are a number of approaches we might take to fixing up this HTML. We could, for example, fix it by hand. This, as they say, will not scale well.

An alternative is to use regular expressions and a text parser to fix things up, but that will be a fair amount of work. HTML is not a very strict or regular language and, as in English, there are many exceptions to the rules.

Here's a quote from Mike's early memo to me on this problem:

> *What we really need is an HTML parser that knows all these rules and exceptions and then we can output a well-formed document. We could build our own or we could look around on the Web to see if someone has one to sell or use.*

> *But wait a minute, we have an excellent HTML parser right in our browser. MSHTML, the Microsoft HTML Document Object Model (DOM), is a component that does the heavy lifting of parsing an HTML file and converting it into the DOM tree that we are comfortable manipulating from client-side scripting.*

> *By referencing MSHTML and the Internet Explorer packages in VB, we can easily write a component to do what we want that is guaranteed to handle any HTML file that IE can read. And since we generate the output, we'll ensure that it is well formed.*

Hozzanah! We can use the HTML parser built into IE. Because Microsoft offers this parser as a standalone ActiveX object (MSHTML.DLL) we have full access to its capabilities.

2

The rest of this chapter will discuss how this is done. Before we begin however, let me review one sentence from Mike's memo: MSHTML, the Microsoft HTML Document Object Model (DOM), is a component that does the heavy lifting of parsing an HTML file and converting it into the DOM tree that we are used to manipulating from client-side scripting.

Let's pick this apart. MSHTML is the DLL that we use to access the Microsoft HTML Document Object Model (DOM). It is this DOM which makes DHTML possible. DHTML is, in essence, nothing more than manipulation of the HTML DOM, usually by script code. The script code is typically written in JavaScript, but of course it doesn't have to be: The HTML DOM is language independent.

When working with DHTML, we take the HTML DOM for granted: It represents the HTML document and we manipulate it directly in our script. What Mike is proposing here is that we read the HTML document (saved from Word) up into the HTML DOM provided by MSHTML, and then we will have access to every element of the document through the DOM.

This gives rise to two areas of potential confusion: the difference between the document and the DOM, and the difference between the HTML DOM and the XML DOM.

Documents and DOMs

The HTML Document Object Model is a specification for how HTML documents are structured. When we instantiate the DOM, what we are really doing is creating an abstract model of the HTML document in the computer's memory space.

Until recently, each browser was free to create its own model of the document, and Internet Explorer and Netscape created different models. In the early days (oh, a year or two ago), neither company made their model available to the would-be Web programmer, so it didn't much matter how the model worked; after all, it was proprietary and hidden information.

In an effort to standardize the document object model, a working group at the W3C was charged with creating recommendations for an internationally agreed-upon HTML document model. The goal was for all browsers to support this model and to expose the objects within the model for manipulation through script.

The *objects* in the model are the things that are manipulated in a DHTML application. For example, you might want to manipulate the style or contents of text, change headings, or alter other display details. In addition, you might want to access the contents of text fields or list boxes on a form. The window, form, text fields, and images are all objects within the object model.

DOMs Versus DOMs

The second area of potential confusion is between the HTML Document Object Model and the XML Document Model. MSHTML provides access to the HTML DOM, and thus manipulation of HTML objects, but it knows nothing about XML. We'll see the XML DOM in action in later chapters. For now, the DOM we'll be manipulating will be the HTML DOM.

Converting Word To XHTML

To accomplish the task of converting this Word-created HTML document to XHTML, we'll build an ActiveX object. In VB this is as simple as creating a new project and designating that it will be an ActiveX DLL.

The structure of our overall design is that we will create a single DLL, FromScratch, which will, in turn, have four objects: Word2XHTML, WordXHTML2XML, XSLTransform, and SplitStories. For now, the only one we care about is Word2XHTML. As the name implies, this is the object which will convert our files from Word's HTML to XHTML.

All of this is controlled by `Control.asp`, as shown in Figure 2.6.

Figure 2.6

Control.asp.

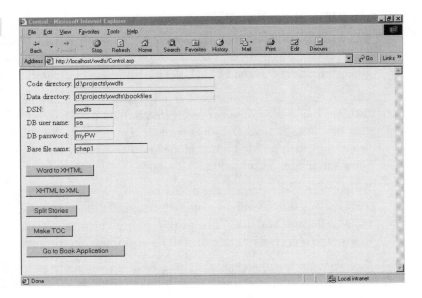

This is the single ASP file we'll use throughout this entire project. Because we want to keep the focus on XML, this ASP file is really a quick hack to gather the information we need (directories, passwords and so forth) and launch our ActiveX objects. We'll examine the ASP as we go, but we won't dwell on it.

Let's take a brief look at it right now to see what is required to launch Word2XHTML, our first component, whose job is to convert the HTML produced by Word to XHTML.

We'll examine how the ASP page works and how it invokes Word2XHTML now, and we'll return to the rest of this ASP file as we progress to see how it interacts with the other components in our application.

 Note   You do *not* need to follow any of this to continue with our work on XML. You can simply use the ASP page as provided on my Web site (http://www.LibertyAssociates.com). Of course, you still must install the Database provided on my Web site and you must set a DSN connection to that database, as explained below.

The start of `control.asp` is shown in Listing 2.2.

Listing 2.2 `Control.asp` **(excerpt)**

```
0:  <%
1:      Option Explicit
2:      Dim DBConn, rs, fso, DSN, DBUser, DBPass,
        ➥codeDir, dataDir, baseName, dataPath
3:
4:      'some of our operations may take a long time
5:      Server.ScriptTimeout = 3000
6:
7:      'if one of our command buttons was pressed,
        ➥store the params as cookie
8:      if Request("Cmd") <> "" then
9:          SetCookieVal "CodeDir"
10:         SetCookieVal "DataDir"
11:         SetCookieVal "DSN"
12:         SetCookieVal "DBUser"
13:         SetCookieVal "DBPass"
14:         SetCookieVal "BaseName"
15:         'expire in a year
16:         response.cookies("XWDFS").Expires = dateadd("yyyy", 1, date)
17:     end if
18:
19:     'retrieve the params from the cookie
20:     codeDir = GetInput("CodeDir")
21:     dataDir = GetInput("DataDir")
22:     DSN = GetInput("DSN")
23:     DBUser = GetInput("DBUser")
24:     DBPass = GetInput("DBPass")
```

continues

Listing 2.2   Continued

```
25:        baseName = GetInput("BaseName")
26:
27:
28:        'we almost always need a database connection
29:        set DBConn = Server.CreateObject("ADODB.Connection")
30:
31:        if DSN <> "" and DBUser <> ""  and codeDir <> ""
        ➥and dataDir <> "" and baseName <> "" then
32:
33:            DBConn.Open DSN, DBUser, DBPass
34:
35:            'and also a File System Object to manipulate directories
36:            set fso = Server.CreateObject("Scripting.FileSystemObject")
37:
38:            dataPath = fso.BuildPath(dataDir, baseName)
39:
40:            'now perform the requested actions
41:
42:            select case Request("Cmd")
43:                case "Word to XHTML"
44:                    Response.Write Word2XHTML()
45:
46:                case "XHTML to XML"
47:                    Response.Write XHTML2XML()
48:
49:                case "Split Stories"
50:                    Response.Write SplitStories()
51:
52:                case "Make TOC"
53:                    Response.Write MakeTOC()
54:
55:                case "Go to Book Application"
56:                    Response.redirect "book.htm"
57:
58:                case "Show Chapter as HTML"
59:                    Response.Write ShowHTML()
60:
61:                case "Show Chapter as XML"
62:                    Response.Write ShowXML()
63:
64:            end select
65:        else
66:            Response.write("Please fill in all required fields
            ➥before proceeding.")
67:        end if
68: %>
69:
70: <HTML>
71: <HEAD>
72: <META HTTP-EQUIV="Content-Type" content="text/html;
    ➥charset=iso-8859-1">
```

```
73:   <TITLE>Control</TITLE>
74:   </HEAD>
75:   <BODY>
76:   <form>
77:   <table>
78:   <tr><td>Code directory:</td><td><input size=40 name=CodeDir
      ➥value="<% =CodeDir   %>"></td></tr>
79:   <tr><td>Data directory:</td><td><input size=40 name=DataDir
      ➥value="<% =DataDir   %>"></td></tr>
80:   <tr><td>DSN:</td><td><input size=10 name=DSN
      ➥value="<% =DSN    %>"></td></tr>
81:   <tr><td>DB user name:</td><td><input size=10 name=DBUser
      ➥value="<% =DBUser   %>"></td></tr>
82:   <tr><td>DB password:</td><td><input size=10 name=DBPass
      ➥value="<% =DBPass   %>"></td></tr>
83:   <tr><td>Base file name:</td><td><input size=20
      ➥name=BaseName value="<% =BaseName   %>"></td></tr>
84:   </table>
85:   <p><input type=submit value="Word to XHTML" name=Cmd>
86:   <p><input type=submit value="XHTML to XML" name=Cmd>
87:   <p><input type=submit value="Split Stories" name=Cmd>
88:   <p><input type=submit value="Make TOC" name=Cmd>
89:   <p><input type=submit value="Show Chapter as XML" name=Cmd>
90:   <p><input type=submit value="Show Chapter as HTML" name=Cmd>
91:   <p><input type=submit value="Go to Book Application" name=Cmd>
92:   </form>
93:   </BODY>
94:   </HTML>
95:   <%
96:       Function GetInput(name)
97:           GetInput = Request.Cookies("XWDFS")(name)
98:       End Function
99:
100:      Sub SetCookieVal(name)
101:          Response.Cookies("XWDFS")(name) = Request(name)
102:      End Sub
103:
104:      Function Word2XHTML()
105:          'convert a Word .htm file to XHTML
106:           dim oW2X, inFile, outFile
107:
108:          set oW2X = Server.CreateObject("FromScratch.Word2XHTML")
109:
110:          'the input file from Word should have a .htm extension
111:          inFile = dataPath & ".htm"
112:
113:          'we'll save the output in a .xhtml file
114:          outFile = dataPath & ".xhtml"
115:
116:          oW2X.ConvertToXHTML inFile, outFile
117:          Word2XHTML = "Converted " & inFile & " to " & outFile
118:      End Function
```

On line 0 of control.asp we open server-side script with the <% symbol, which indicates to the browser that what follows is to be executed on the server.

On line 1, Option Explicit directs the VBScript interpreter to complain if variables are used without first having been declared. This saves us from pesky errors caused by misspelling variable names.

We dimension (declare) a number of variables on line 2; we'll use these throughout the ASP file.

On line 5 we set the timeout variable to 50 minutes, which is an absurdly long time, far longer than even the most time-consuming operation we will undertake. You may want to knock this down to 10 or 15 minutes; enough to ensure you won't time out unless the application is hopelessly stuck.

Much of the rest of the script is devoted to managing the cookies that will store our variables. We need to ask the user to tell us where the HTML documents are, where our code modules are, and how to interact with the database. Once we obtain these values we'll store them in a cookie on the client machine, so that the user does not have to enter them again.

If you are unfamiliar with cookies or ASP, please see the reading list in Appendix A. Frankly, you can skip over this entire excursion if you like, and continue with XML, treating the controlling ASP file as magic for now.

Lines 8–17 deal with setting the cookie, and lines 19–25 deal with obtaining the values from the cookie. The actual user interface for obtaining these values from the user is shown on lines 70 through 94.

If you are unfamiliar with ADO, please see the reading list in Appendix A. You should be able to follow this excursion without much ADO knowledge, and again you can simply skip over this part and use the ASP page as provided on the CD.

On line 29 we create an ADO connection object so that we can interact with the Database. On line 31 we check to make sure we have the necessary values to interact with the database, and if so, on line 33 we open that connection, using the DSN, username, and password provided by the user.

Note

To connect to the Database from VB, you must have a system DSN set up for the XML database. Here's how to do it:

1. Open your control panel and click on ODBC Data Sources.

2. Choose the System DSN tab and click Add.

3. Choose SQL Server from the list of drivers and click Finish.

4. Enter a name—I suggest XML. Enter a description if you'd like (for example, Access the XML Test Database) and choose a server. You should see the server on which you are running SQL Server (or local if you're running SQL Server locally). If not, contact your system administrator. Click Next.

5. Click the With SQL Server authentication using a login ID and password entered by the user radio button. Delete Administrator from the loginID field and enter a valid database login ID and password (many people use sa and an empty password). Click Next.

6. Click in Change the Default Database and scroll down to select the XWDFS database. Click Next.

7. Accept all the defaults on the Create A New Data Source to SQL Server dialog box, then click Finish.

8. Click on Test Data Source. If the test does not complete successfully, you'll need help from your SQL Server administrator, system administrator, or Microsoft. In all likelihood, however, you'll see the magic words TEST COMPLETED SUCCESSFULLY!

Congratulations, you now have a system DSN named XML. Click OK. This will return you to the ODBC Data Source Administrator dialog box, click OK.

With the Database and DSN in place, the open command on line 33 establishes the connection. On line 36 we open a file system object and set its path to the data directory and base name provided by the user. This creates a connection to the directory in which we'll work.

This brings us to line 42. When we click "Word to XHTML," which is our first task, line 44 will invoke the Word2XHTML() method and print to the browser its results.

Control skips down to line 104, where Word2XHTML is implemented. We dimension three local variables: one to hold the ActiveX object we'll be using, a second to hold the input file (our HTML file), and a third to hold the output file (our **X**HTML file).

We set the local variable oW2X to the ActiveX object on line 108 and we create the input and output filenames based on the datapath we established earlier.

Finally, on line 116 we call the ConvertToXHTML method in our ActiveX object, passing in the input file and output file names. When we're done, we return the string (for example) "Converted Chap1.htm to Chap1.xhtml" which is printed to the browser.

In the next section I'll describe the ActiveX object that we just called, in detail.

Inside Word2XHTML

Our goal is to turn the HTML into XHTML; that is, to make sure attributes are double-quoted, tags are not nested and so forth. We could write a Perl script and find all the mistakes and fix them, but that would be a long, arduous effort. Instead, we'll take advantage of the fact that IE5 will happily read in the existing HTML and provide us with a document object model.

After the DOM is created in memory, we can easily walk the DOM, find each element, and output it to our file in proper XML syntax.

To get started, `Control.ASP` invokes ConvertToXHTML (line 116 of Listing 2.2), passing in the input filename (our Word-created HTML file) and the output filename (an XML file), as shown in Listing 2.3.

Listing 2.3 `Word2XHTML.cls`

```
 0:    'Converts a HTML file so that the HTML is also well-formed XML
 1:    'Attribute values must be quoted; tags must be closed and
       ➥not overlap; tags must agree in case
 2:    'The approach is to read the document in to an HTML DOM,
       ➥and then output it in well-formed format
 3:    Public Sub ConvertToXHTML(ByVal inPath As String, ByVal
       ➥outPath As String)
 4:        Dim ie As InternetExplorer, doc As MSHTML.HTMLDocument,
       ➥url As String
 5:
 6:        Set ie = New InternetExplorer
 7:
 8:        'this may not work across machines
 9:        url = "file://" & inPath
10:
11:        'open the HTML document
12:        ie.navigate url
13:
14:        'wait until the file finishes loading
15:        Do Until ie.readyState = READYSTATE_COMPLETE
16:            Sleep 1000
17:        Loop
18:
19:        'get the HTML DOM object
```

```
20:     Set doc = ie.document
21:
22:     'open our output file (overwriting if necessary)
23:     Open outPath For Output As #1
24:
25:     'and begin the recursive walk at the root
26:     OutputElement doc.documentElement, ""
27:
28:     Close #1
29: End Sub
```

Analysis

On line 3 the input file and output file are passed in as parameters. On line 4, a local variable `ie` is declared as type `InternetExplorer(!)`. On line 6, this variable is assigned to a new `InternetExplorer` object.

This `InternetExplorer` object allows us to control an instance of IE through the COM automation interface. While this would be a terribly complex subject in C++, in VB it is almost effortless. You simply instantiate a new `InternetExplorer` object as shown on line 6, and then call properties and methods on that object. For example, on line 20 we can directly access the document property. The `Document` property provides us with access to the HTML DOM.

On line 9 we create a URL for the input file and on line 17 we call the navigate method on the Internet Explorer object, passing in that URL.

This causes the document to be loaded into the instance of IE we've created. The XML DOM exposes the property. If this is `true` then the document will be parsed in its own thread. This is handy for a browser that can carry on with other tasks while the document is parsed. In our case, we always set this to false, allowing the parsing to block our program until parsing is completed.

The HTML DOM does not offer this property; it is *always* asynchronous. We can force the program to block until the document is fully loaded, however, by sleeping until IE signals that its `readyState` is `READYSTATE_COMPLETE`, as shown in lines 15–17.

We return to line 20, which as we saw obtains the HTML DOM, and we assign it to doc, which we've properly declared to be of type `MSHTML.HTMLDocument` (Microsoft's type for HTML DOM objects).

On line 23 we open the outpath file for output. This will hold the new XHTML document we'll be generating. The work of this method is, however, on line 26, in which we call `OutputElement`, passing in the element retrieved from the HTML document we obtained on line 20 as shown in Listing 2.4.

Listing 2.4   `Word2XHTML.cls`

```
0:    'Output the contents of the given element in well-formed XML format
1:    'Then recurse to el's children
2:    Private Sub OutputElement(el As Object, indent As String)
3:        Dim c, i As Integer, s As String, a As Object, n As Object
4:
5:        'open tag - note that MSHTML returns all tag names as
         ➥uppercase, so we don't have to worry about case matching
6:        'but I really like lower case tag names
7:        s = indent & "<" & LCase(el.nodeName)
8:
9:        'append all specified attributes, delimiting by space,
         ➥and quoting the value
10:       'note that the attribute value may contain quotes, so
         ➥replace those with single quotes
11:       For Each a In el.Attributes
12:           'the attribute collection includes all possible attributes
             ➥ - so we only care about those
13:           'that are "specified"
14:           If a.specified Then
15:               s = s & " " & a.nodeName & "="""" &
                 ➥Replace(a.nodeValue, """", "'") & """"
16:           End If
17:       Next
18:
19:       'the style is another common attribute, but it is not include
         ➥ in the attribute collections
20:       'note that the DOM likes to change the case of this as well,
         ➥so we normalize it to lowercase
21:       'also change embedded quotes to single quotes
22:       If el.Style.cssText <> "" Then s = s & " style="""" &
         ➥Replace(LCase(el.Style.cssText), """", "'") & """"
23:
24:       'if we have no children, we can just end the tag here,
         ➥indicating it as an empty element
25:       If el.childNodes.length = 0 Then
26:           s = s & " />"
27:           Out s
28:           Exit Sub
29:       End If
30:
31:       'otherwise just close the start tag
32:       s = s & ">"
33:       Out s
34:
35:       'iterate thru the children
36:       For i = 0 To el.childNodes.length - 1
37:           Set n = el.childNodes(i)
38:
39:           'In HTML, a node will either be an element or a text node
40:           If n.nodeType = 1 Then
```

```
41:                  'an element - recurse
42:                  OutputElement n, indent & "   "
43:              Else
44:                  'text node, just output, but check first for special
                     ➥characters
45:                  'the DOM cleverly converts entities to their reserved
                     ➥characters, so we must convert them back again
46:                  Out ConvertTextNode(n.nodeValue)
47:              End If
48:          Next
49:
50:          'and finish with a close tag
51:          Out indent & "</" & LCase(el.nodeName) & ">"
52:      End Sub
```

Analysis

The method begins on line 2. Note that when we call this method we pass in two parameters, as shown on line 26 of Listing 2.3. The first parameter, el, is an element; the first time through it is the documentElement property of the MSHTML.HTMLDocument object. The second parameter is a string that we'll use to indent each line in the output.

The first time through, el is the documentElement object, which is a reference to the root node of the document. This is just what we want. We'll start at the root node of the input document, and we'll walk the tree, recursing into each element and extracting what we need to create an XHTML DOM, which we can then output as the XHTML file.

On line 7 we begin processing by creating a string (s), which will accumulate the output string. We append an open tag (<) and then we append the element name. We obtain the element name by asking el for its tagName, which we force to lowercase.

We now need to iterate over the attributes in our element. We do this with the construct on line 11.

```
11:     For Each a In el.Attributes
```

The Attributes Property

The Attributes property returns just what you'd expect: a collection of all the attributes of the element. In fact, however, the attributes collection actually has an entry for every possible attribute, so on line 14 we call the specified method of the collection to see if each given attribute is in fact specified for this element.

```
14:         If a.specified Then
```

We continue on line 15. Let's assume an attribute is specified. In the HTML the attribute values may or may not have been quoted. Either way, the parser is smart enough to obtain the attribute for us and present it as a string in the object model. We don't know or care if it originally was quoted; when we output the attribute we simply write it out correctly using double quotes.

The net effect is that we do not have to worry about "correcting" the double quotes in the source, we simply let the parser obtain the value and then we write it out in the correct format. Along the way, we'll replace any double quotes in the value with single quotes and surround the entire value with double quotes. So if we started out with

```
<p class = foo>
```

we end with

```
<p class="foo">
```

Lines 11–17 iterate over all the attributes associated with the element. Interestingly, the style attributes are not in the attributes collection, and so must be handled separately. On line 22 we test to see if we have a style attribute, and if so we render the value in lowercase, fixing the quotes as needed.

On line 25 we look to see if this element has no child tags. If so, we are done, and we can write out the string. We see this on line 26: We test the length property of the `childNodes` collection. If this returns `0`, then the collection is empty; we close the tag on line 26 with a trailing slash, making this an empty tag. We then print the string on line 27 and exit this subroutine.

If the element does have children, we proceed on line 31. Again we finish the opening tag (without a slash this time because we're about to give the tag contents). We output the string, but this time we must iterate through all the children of the current element.

2

Line 36 sets up the iteration with a `For` loop, which counts through each child (remember, the collections are zero based, so if this collection of child notes contains five elements, they will be numbered 0–4).

```
36:      For i = 0 To el.childNodes.length - 1
```

On line 37 the local variable n is set to the first child, and as we iterate, it will be set to each subsequent child.

```
37:          Set n = el.childNodes(i)
```

Remember that n was declared only to be an object; it will hold whatever kind of element we retrieve from the collection of children.

In fact, on line 40 we must test the actual type of node we do retrieve. It will be one of two possible types: an element or a text node. If its `nodeType` is `1`, it is an element. Let's skip over this case for just a moment, and consider the second case, shown beginning on line 44, in which it is text.

On line 46 we consider the case of outputting a text node. Getting its value as text is easy; we use the `nodeValue` property. The problem is that the text may not be quite what we want. There are two related problems.

First, Word has special characters, such as smart quotes, which must be converted to their own tags. In addition, when we read the HTML from the document up into the document object model, the IE5 parser conveniently changed our entity equivalents to text. For example, if the parser saw `&lt;` it rendered it as <. Unfortunately, because we're writing this back out as a document, we need to render these back to HTML acceptable form. This work is accomplished by the `ConvertTextNode` method as shown in Listing 2.5

Listing 2.5 `Word2XHTML.cls`

```
0:    'Perform the necessary transformations on a text node
1:    Private Function ConvertTextNode(s As String) As String
2:        'replace HTML special characters with their entity equivalents
3:        s = HTMLQuote(s)
4:
5:        'we want to do what follows _after_ the above,
          ➥since we really want these as tags
6:        'we'll replace Word "smart" quotes with special tags
7:        s = Replace(s, Chr(146), "<char type=""smartApos""/>")
8:        s = Replace(s, Chr(147), "<char type=""smartLQuote""/>")
9:        s = Replace(s, Chr(148), "<char type=""smartRQuote""/>")
10:
11:       'these are typographical shortcuts this
          ➥publisher happens to use
12:       s = Replace(s, "[em]", "<char type=""emSpace""/>")
```

continues

Listing 2.5   Continued

```
13:        s = Replace(s, "[md]", "<char type=""emDash""/>")
14:        s = Replace(s, "[lb]", "<char type=""bullet""/>")
15:
16:        ConvertTextNode = s
17:  End Function
```

On line 3 we call our utility method HTMLQuote to convert all HTML reserved characters back to entity equivalents. On lines 7–9 we handle special quote characters, and on lines 12–14 we handle special characters used by Macmillan Publishing (such as em-dashes and bullets).

Recursion

Let's refer to line 42 of Listing 2.4. Here we are considering the case that the child we're examining (remember, we extracted it from the current element's collection of children) is in fact another element. What do we want to do with this element? Why, precisely what we've done with the current element: Create a string with the tag and attributes, and then find all the children. This is exactly what the current method (OutputElement) does for a living. We need only call it, again, with the child element.

```
42:            OutputElement n, indent & "  "
```

This, as you may know, is called recursion: when a function calls itself. In fact, however, the function is not calling itself. It is calling a copy of itself, and the two functions, while named the same and accomplishing the same tasks, are working on entirely different sets of data. The first OutputElement method is busy with the current element, the second OutputElement will now work on the child. In fact, the first will wait until the second is done before proceeding.

Writing the Close Tag

Let's back up a minute to line 25. Here is where we checked to see if there were child elements.

If there are no child elements, then this test returns true (the length of the collection of children is zero) and we enter the code on line 26. This closes the tag with the special self-closing tag />. Thus, if the element was <br> and there were no children, then we would write it out (on line 26) as <br/>, which is the proper syntax for XML files. Remember, in XML all tags must be closed. If, on the other hand we do have children, the if fails and on line 32 the tag is closed with a normal closing tag.

Stepping Through the Code

To make all of this a bit more understandable, we need to step through the details together. The best way to do this is in the debugger.

You'll find the Word2XHTML class module on my site (www.libertyassociates.com). If you'd like to follow along, load this class module within the FromScratch project. To get this to work, you'll also want to copy control.asp to a directory on your Web server, and then create the necessary virtual directory.

> **Note** If you are unsure about how to set up an ASP file on your Web server or how to create a project in VB, please see Appendix A for the suggested reading list.

Examining the Input

To understand what the code is working on, let's take a look at the first 20 lines of the source Chap2.htm, as shown in Listing 2.6.

Listing 2.6 `Chap2.htm`

```
 0:  <html xmlns:o="urn:schemas-microsoft-com:office:office"
 1:  xmlns:w="urn:schemas-microsoft-com:office:word"
 2:  xmlns="http://www.w3.org/TR/REC-html40">
 3:
 4:  <head>
 5:  <meta http-equiv=Content-Type content="text/html;
      ➥charset=windows-1252">
 6:  <meta name=ProgId content=Word.Document>
 7:  <meta name=Generator content="Microsoft Word 9">
 8:  <meta name=Originator content="Microsoft Word 9">
 9:  <link rel=File-List href="./Chap2_files/filelist.xml">
10:  <title>(a) Chapter 12</title>
11:  <!--[if gte mso 9]><xml>
12:   <o:DocumentProperties>
13:    <o:Author>Jesse Liberty</o:Author>
14:    <o:Template>mcpglobl.dot</o:Template>
15:    <o:LastAuthor>Jesse Liberty</o:LastAuthor>
16:    <o:Revision>2</o:Revision>
17:    <o:TotalTime>1</o:TotalTime>
18:    <o:LastPrinted>1999-07-12T22:11:00Z</o:LastPrinted>
19:    <o:Created>1999-10-27T11:16:00Z</o:Created>
```

Much of this looks like Microsoft Office gibberish, but we don't need to understand what this is doing to watch the code work its way through.

I'll set a break point on the first meaningful line in `ConvertToXHTML`, as shown in Figure 2.7.

Figure 2.7

Breaking in
`ConvertToXHTML`.

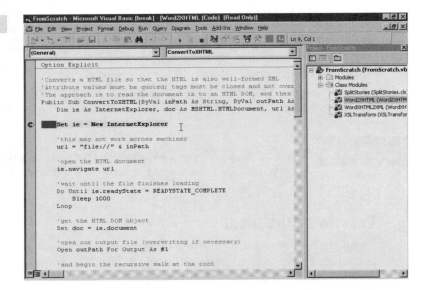

We begin by instantiating the `InternetExplorer` object, as discussed earlier. We can quickly step through this code until we enter the `OutputElement` method.

 **Note**

In Visual Basic, F9 will create a break point and F8 will step into the code. Shift+F8 steps over a method call.

Stopping after we assign the `nodeName` to our string, `s` reveals that our assumptions were correct, as shown in Figure 2.8. The Immediate window, shown on the bottom of the screen, displays the current value of `s`: `<html`, and the Watches window, shown in the upper right of the screen, shows the value of `el.nodeName` `"HTML"`.

This is consistent with the earlier description, so let's proceed. Because most of the attributes will be unspecified, the quickest way to get to line 11 of Listing 2.4 is to put a break point on it (F9). Be sure to put a break point after the `For` loop as well, in the event that this HTML tag does not have attributes. Go (F5) to the first break point.

We find ourselves on line 22 of Listing 2.4, having skipped over all the attributes, as shown in Figure 2.9.

Figure 2.8

Examining the string.

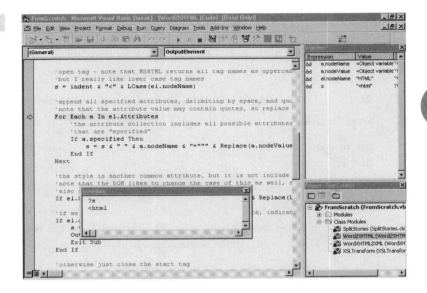

Figure 2.9

Line 22 is displayed.

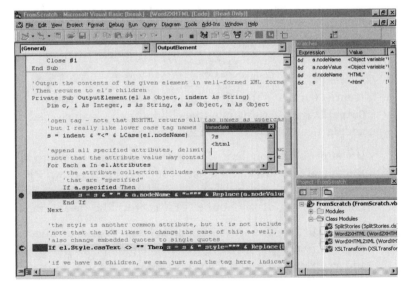

As you can see, we've skipped over the attributes, and our string s has only `<html>`. Looking back at Listing 2.6, we see that the HTML tag looks like this:

```
0:    <html xmlns:o="urn:schemas-microsoft-com:office:office"
1:    xmlns:w="urn:schemas-microsoft-com:office:word"
2:    xmlns="http://www.w3.org/TR/REC-html40">
```

The HTML DOM does not recognize any of these attributes; nor should it—none of them is HTML. Therefore, the HTML DOM does not recognize any specified attributes, and we're on to the next line of code: looking for styles.

Stepping through the code, we skip over the If statement on line 22 of Listing 2.4

```
22:        If el.Style.cssText <> "" Then s = s & " style="""" &
➥Replace(LCase(el.Style.cssText), """", "'") & """"
```

because we have no style tags in this element, and we skip over the If statement on line 25

```
25:        If el.childNodes.length = 0 Then
```

because el.childNodes.length is not zero, nor would we expect it to be. Remember that el is in this case the root node (HTML), childNodes is the collection of children of HTML, and length is the count of nodes in that collection.

We continue with lines 36–42 of Listing 2.4.

```
36:        For i = 0 To el.childNodes.length - 1
37:            Set n = el.childNodes(i)
38:
39:            'In HTML, a node will either be an element or a text node
40:            If n.nodeType = 1 Then
41:                'an element - recurse
42:                OutputElement n, indent & "  "
```

It turns out that n (the first child of <HTML>) is an element, so we will call OutputElement passing in n (the child we just obtained) and our indent string but adding a pair of spaces to the indent string.

If you press F8 from line 42, you will appear to go back to the start of OuputElement. But you are not back at the start, you are recursed down a level. That is, the function you were working in has been suspended. Back in that earlier function el is <HTML>. Here, however, el will not be HTML, it will be <head>, the first child of HTML.

Once again, neither attributes nor styles are found, and once again, there are children. In fact, this time there are seven children. Again, we assign n to the first child and again we recurse into OutputElement. This time el is <head>'s first child: <title>. This element, <title>, has no children, however, so we enter the If statement on line 25.

```
25:        If el.childNodes.length = 0 Then
26:            s = s & " />"
27:            Out s
28:            Exit Sub
29:        End If
```

We close off the tag and exit from the subroutine. Where do we exit to? We "pop" up out of one level of recursion to the `OutputElement` method, which called us: That is the one in which `<head>` is `el`. This returns us to line 37, that is the iteration through the children. We've iterated through the first child of `<head>`, which was `<title>`. Because `<title>` had no children, we're ready to iterate to the second child of `<head>`: `<meta>`.

Note that we are still in the first child of `<HTML>`, which was `<head>`, but we're up to `<head>`'s second child, `<meta>`. If we return to the source document, shown in Listing 2.6, we're now on line 5.

```
5:  <meta http-equiv=Content-Type content="text/html;
    ➥charset=windows-1252">
```

The DOM decided that `<title>` (line 10) was the first child, and `<meta>` (line 5) is the second. Let that be a warning to you: The order is not guaranteed.

We continue to step through the code, and this time the parser finds an attribute has been specified, stopping on lines 14–16 to pick it up:

```
14:         If a.specified Then
15:             s = s & " " & a.nodeName & "=""" &
                ➥Replace(a.nodeValue, """", "'") & """"
16:         End If
```

We loop through all the attributes, formatting them properly as illustrated in the immediate window at the bottom of Figure 2.10.

Figure 2.10

After picking up the attributes.

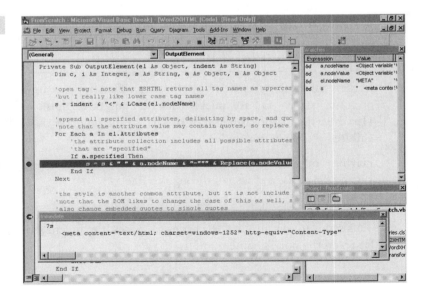

`<meta>` has no children, so we're on to the next of the seven children of `<head>`, which is also a `<meta>` tag. There are in fact a few `<meta>` tags to churn through before we come to a `<link>` tag, representing line 9 from our source document:

```
9:    <link rel=File-List href="./WCFS%20Chapter%201_files/filelist.xml">
```

We next pick up a `<style>` child of `<head>`, from line 56 of the source code as shown in Listing 2.7

Listing 2.7   `Chap2.htm`

```
56:  <style>
57:  <!--
58:   /* Font Definitions */
59:  @font-face
60:      {font-family:Courier;
61:      panose-1:0 0 0 0 0 0 0 0;
62:      mso-font-charset:0;
63:      mso-generic-font-family:modern;
64:      mso-font-format:other;
65:      mso-font-pitch:fixed;
66:      mso-font-signature:3 0 0 0 1 0;}
67:   /* Style Definitions */
68:  p.MsoNormal, li.MsoNormal, div.MsoNormal
69:      {mso-style-parent:"";
70:      margin:0in;
71:      margin-bottom:.0001pt;
72:      line-height:12.0pt;
73:      mso-pagination:widow-orphan;
74:      font-size:12.0pt;
75:      mso-bidi-font-size:10.0pt;
76:      font-family:Courier;
77:      mso-fareast-font-family:"Times New Roman";
78:      mso-bidi-font-family:"Times New Roman";}
```

Because all these styles are in a comment, we do not pick up any attributes or children for `<style>` and are quickly back iterating through the children of `<head>`. However, that is the last child of `<head>`, so the function that is iterating over the children of `<head>` concludes.

Having worked through all its children, the For loop that runs from lines 35–48 of Listing 2.4 ends, and we fall through to line 51:

```
51:      Out indent & "</" & LCase(el.nodeName) & ">"
```

This sends to our output file a series of spaces (the indent string), plus a close tag, based on the node's name.

Having closed the tag, our method returns. To where? Back up a level to the function which is iterating over the two children of <HTML>. We are, in short, now ready for the second child of <HTML>: <body>, found on line 1,538 of our source document:

```
1538:   <body lang=EN-US style='tab-interval:.5in'>
```

Habeas Corpus

The <body> tag represents the text to be displayed in an HTML document. The <head> tag, you'll remember, contained meta-information; it is in the <body> tag where the heavy lifting is done.

It is with this tag that we see the first use of style. The only change made to the original code is that we force the style attribute to be surrounded by double quotes.

From the <body> tag we get the children, and find a <div> tag; from the <div> tag, the children bring us to a <p> tag.

While examining the <p> tag, press Control+L to bring up the Call Stack window, as shown in Figure 2.11

Figure 2.11

The Call Stack.

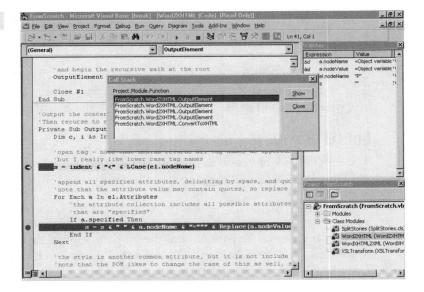

Here we see the recursion at work. The function calls are in reverse order (most recent first). Thus, ConvertToXHTML called OutputElement, which called OutputElement, which called OutputElement, which in turn called OutputElement.

If we look in the Watch window, we can see that the el.nodeName is P. By clicking on one function call back in the list, we can see that the earlier function call's el.NodeName is Div, as shown in Figure 2.12.

Figure 2.12

The Watch window.

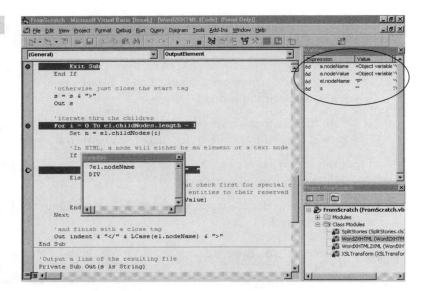

Clicking back one more level of recursion, we see that el.NodeName is Body, and one level higher we see that el.NodeName is HTML, as we'd expect. So we are in a child of Div, which is a child of Body, which is in turn a child of HTML.

Let 'Er Rip

The program continues on in this fashion; picking up each tag and all its children, recursing into itself until the entire tree has been read and re-created as our output document.

There is no output to the user along the way (again, left as an exercise for the reader), so you must be patient until the program reports that it has completed the conversion. This can take up to a few minutes, depending on the size of the input file.

When that is finished, however, you can examine the resulting XHTML file. Listing 2.8 illustrates the first 12 lines.

Listing 2.8   `Chap2.xhtml`

```
0:   <html>
1:     <head>
2:       <title />
3:       <meta content="text/html; charset=windows-1252"
      ➥http-equiv="Content-Type" />
4:       <meta content="Word.Document" name="ProgId" />
5:       <meta content="Microsoft Word 9" name="Generator" />
6:       <meta content="Microsoft Word 9" name="Originator" />
7:       <link href="./Chap2_files/filelist.xml" rel="File-List" />
8:       <style />
9:     </head>
10:    <body lang="EN-US" style="tab-interval: .5in">
11:      <div class="Section1">
12:        <p class="FT">
```

The structure of the tags is graphically represented by indentation. The first (root) tag is <html>, the <head> and <body> tags are represented one level in. Under <body> is <div> and under <div> is <p>, just as we saw in stepping through the code.

Note that all the attributes are now quoted, and all the tags are nested properly. You see self-closing tags on lines 2 and 8.

Next Steps

We now have a valid XHTML file to work with. Our next task is to convert this file to XML.

Chapter 3

Validating the Document with the Document Type Definition

The result of the work in Chapter 2 is that we now have at least one chapter from *WebClasses from Scratch* in XHTML. In fact, you have three files. The first file is the original Word file. The second is the .htm file that Word created when you asked it to save the document as a Web page. The third file is the XHTML file we created. It is time to transform the contents of the XHTML file into our canonical storage format.

From XHTML to XML

The XHTML document is both valid HTML and also valid XML. That is to say, it meets both specifications. As such, it is an XML document already. Why then do we need to convert it? Why not keep it and store it the way it is?

As it stands, the document is filled with HTML presentation tags. This is appropriate for an HTML document, and were we only going to use this document on the Web, it would be just fine to store it as is.

Our goal, however, is to have far greater flexibility. We may want to publish this document in different formats using different layouts. Storing the document in HTML makes this difficult, storing it in XML makes it easy. We may want to select which sections to display and how we display them based on dynamic information (such as a subscriber's profile.) Again, XML will make this simple. More challenging to HTML, but playing to XML's strength, is the requirement that we be able to publish this document not only to the Web, but also to print, to email, and on other devices such as PIMs (Personal Information Managers) and so forth.

To meet these specifications, we need to disentangle the presentation-specific markup from the semantic and structural details. We'll save only the contents and meta-data describing the contents and its structure.

Making the Structure Explicit

One significant motivation for transforming our XHTML document to our canonical form is that the XHTML document (like the HTML and Word documents, which are its ancestors) does not provide explicit information about the structure of the document. That is, the XHTML document does not show C-level headings enclosing D-level headings, they are just in sequence, one after the other. The fact that d-level headings are contained within C-level is *implicit*—it is understood by the editor but it is not explicit in the document structure. That implied structure, however, is intrinsic to the meaning of the document and we want to make it explicit in our canonical form.

We impose that structure on the printed document by following typesetting conventions. The editor knows, by mutual agreement, that sections are marked with C-heads and subsections with D-heads. With this knowledge, she is able to produce a Table of Contents which reflects the intrinsic structure. This is not explicit in the XHTML, it is implicit; picked up by a human who knows the rules.

We would like to codify these rules in our XML document and make the structure explicit. This will allow us to automate processes that currently require human intervention.

Let's be clear: The canonical form is canonical only to us. The XHTML document is already valid XML. There is nothing magical about the canonical form; it is specific to this application. Other applications will have their own canonical form.

We'll capture the grammar of our Canonical form in a Document Type Definition (DTD).

Grammar—The syntax and structure of a document.

Document Type Definition (DTD)—A document that defines the valid grammar of an XML document.

By observing and understanding this DTD, you will find it easy to create your own DTD for your own Canonical storage format.

Ensuring the Validity of XML Documents

There are a number of ways in which the DTD defines the structure of an XML document, and thus defines the grammar of our canonical form. For example, the DTD defines the tag names used in the document. If a tag name does not appear in the DTD, then it may not appear in our XML document. If such an unknown tag *does* appear, then we say the XML document is "not valid." That is, it has violated the constraints of its DTD.

Valid—An XML document is valid if it meets the requirements and constraints of its DTD.

Well-formed—An XML document is well-formed if it meets the XML specification. Among these requirements are that nested tags must not overlap, tag names must be case sensitive, all tags must be closed, and attributes must be quoted. A document can be well-formed even if it is not valid.

Updating The DTD

If we want to add a new tag, therefore, we must update our DTD. This makes the new tag valid, and adding it to the document will leave the document valid.

The DTD also defines the structural relationships among the tags—that is which tags contain other tags, as well as which tags are required or optional. It is even possible to define the order in which tags will appear. The DTD also describes the optional or required attributes for each element.

Once again, if these constraints are broken, then the document will no longer be valid (though it may be well-formed!)

A document does not require an explicit DTD, but if one is provided, then the parser will be able to report not only on whether the XML is well-formed (that is, it meets the XML standard) but also on whether the document is valid, that is whether it meets the requirements of the DTD.

> There are a number of parsers available on the Web and from the W3C. The parser we'll be using for this book is MSXML. MSXML is Microsoft's XML parser, and it is included as an ActiveX object with IE5 as MSXML.DLL. If you install IE5, you'll find MSXML.DLL in `WinNT\system32`.

A parser that can validate a document against its DTD is called a *validating parser*. A parser that ignores the DTD is called a *non-validating parser*. MSXML (and thus IE5) is a validating parser.

Validating Parser

Validating parsers are much more complex than non-validating parsers, but they provide you with additional tools to use while creating your documents. A validating parser will raise an error if it encounters anything in your document that violates the constraints of the DTD.

This is a desirable trait in a parser because it makes validating, debugging, and repairing your document quicker and easier. It is the same argument in favor of using strongly typed languages (such as C++), or turning option explicit on in Visual Basic, or using Declared Referential Integrity in SQL. What all these have in common is that they enlist the software in helping you protect the integrity of your source code; they help you find bugs *before* you ship the product to your customer.

> It is worth noting that even if you don't provide an explicit DTD, you certainly have an *implicit* one, stored perhaps only in your brain. After all, you know which tags you are using and what they mean; a DTD simply writes down these rules so that the browser can validate your document against your own set of constraints.

A DTD can also be valuable when more than one person (or group) is working on a set of documents or tools. The DTD tells each group what tags are valid and how they must be nested. You can see how this would be tremendously valuable in keeping everyone in sync. If a new tag is to be added, it is put first in the DTD, so that everyone knows its syntax and its meaning.

A DTD can also be a good design tool. By building the DTD before you start coding, you can design the structure of your XML document rather than simply letting it form itself haphazardly as you program.

The degree to which you build your DTD *before* you write any code is both a matter of personal style and a function of the size of the project. In a large project, especially one with many developers, an explicit DTD is a necessity.

Goals of the Transformation

The DTD defines a valid BiblioTech XML document. In order to create a DTD we must know what tags we want to allow and what the overall structure of the document should be. The DTD simply specifies these rules.

This is an essential point. By analogy, it would be a mistake to think that the United States Constitution created our freedoms. It wasn't as if the authors of the

Constitution wrote it all down and thus discovered the freedoms; their understanding of freedom came first. When they were clear in their thinking, then they could write a document that could be used to enforce those freedoms.

Similarly, until we know what rules we want to enforce, we are ill-equipped to write a DTD. Once we know what we're trying to accomplish, however, then the difficulty in writing a DTD is just getting the syntax right.

The Constraints We Want to Enforce

In examining the XHTML document, we find that it is too focused on display and presentation issues. We want to ensure that our canonical form is data- and structure-centric. We will make six types of changes to move from XHTML to our Canonical XML:

1. Remove all HTML we don't care about, such as `<meta>` and `<style>` tags, or which don't apply, such as `<html>`.
2. Mark all code lines so that we can manage them separately.
3. Store space runs and tabs more efficiently.
4. Mark all Geek Speak, How To Pronounce It, Notes, and other sidebars so that we can manage them separately.
5. Break out sections, and build the nested hierarchy, identifying each section uniquely.
6. Pass along all meaningful HTML

Let's examine these goals in more detail.

Removing HTML We Don't Need

There are many HTML tags in the XHTML document that we simply don't need. Let's take a look at the first 29 lines of the XHTML file, as shown in Listing 3.1.

Listing 3.1   `Chap3.xhtml`

```
0:   <html>
1:     <head>
2:       <title />
3:       <meta content="text/html; charset=windows-1252"
         ↪http-equiv="Content-Type" />
4:       <meta content="Word.Document" name="ProgId" />
5:       <meta content="Microsoft Word 9" name="Generator" />
6:       <meta content="Microsoft Word 9" name="Originator" />
7:       <link href="./Chap3_files/filelist.xml" rel="File-List" />
8:       <style />
9:     </head>
10:    <body lang="EN-US" style="tab-interval: .5in">
```

continues

Listing 3.1   continued

```
11:        <div class="Section1">
12:          <p class="HA">
13:  (a)3
14:          </p>
15:          <p class="HB">
16:  (b)Proof of concept
17:          </p>
18:          <p class="FT">
19:  Enough theory! Before we go any further in thinking through how
     ➥we'll implement EmployeeNet, we need to take a look at the
     ➥implementation technology and get something working.
20:          </p>
21:          <p class="FT">
22:  While I believe in analysis and design, my number one rule
     ➥of programming is this:
23:          </p>
24:          <p class="FT">
25:            <b style="mso-bidi-font-weight: normal">
26:              <i style="mso-bidi-font-style: normal">
27:  Get something working right away, and keep it
     ➥working until it&apos;s done
28:              </i>
```

Analysis

We see that there are a number of tags that are HTML-specific. For example, we can get rid of the <meta> tag on lines 3, 4, 5, and 6 as they are meaningless in our XML document, and provide no information about the content of the document.

To be specific and crystal clear: The <meta> tag is required in an HTML document, but it is not required in our XML document and does not appear in our DTD. Thus, it must be removed. Similarly, we'll throw away the <head> tag as it is not meaningful in our XML document.

When and if we publish this document to the Web, we'll create a new HTML document, and a new <head> tag. None of the information in the current document's <head> tag or <meta> tags will be needed, so there is no penalty in not storing them.

While we're at it, we'll transform the <p> tags to <div> tags. I'll point out the other tags we don't need as we go, but the philosophy is to focus on content and structure, and to ignore information about specific HTML display characteristics.

Marking Code Lines

The second transformation we wish to accomplish is to create code blocks and blocks of notes. If you examine the printed version of this book, as shown in Figure 3.1, on pages 60 and 61, you'll see that the human eye naturally creates a code block or a Note block based on type, shading, spacing, and other print conventions.

There is currently nothing intrinsic in our XHTML document to create these blocks. The XHTML simply provides the styles and cues to the publisher, but the structure is entirely implicit. We'd like to make it *explicit*. To do so, we'll aggregate contiguous blocks of code between semantically meaningful tags. We'll do the same with Notes, Geek Speak and the other blocks that represent departures from the normal flow of the book.

If we examine the XHTML, we find that the code is marked with a listing identification, and that each line of code is set with the style C2, except for the last line which is CX. Single lines of code are marked with the style C1. For example, Chapter 3 in *WebClasses from Scratch* has code like that shown in Listing 3.2.

Listing 3.2

```
1: Function GetTheData() As Recordset
2:     Dim rs As ADODB.Recordset
3:     Set rs = New Recordset
4:     Call rs.Open("select * from publishers",
    ➥"dsn=pubs", UID=sa; PWD=;")
5:     Set GetTheData = rs
6: End Function
```

When Word writes this out to HTML, these style indications are preserved as shown in Listing 3.3

Listing 3.3   Chap3.HTM

```
2149:   <p class=C2>1: Function GetTheData() As Recordset</p>
2150:
2151:   <p class=C2>2:<span style="mso-spacerun: yes">      </span>Dim rs As
2152:   ADODB.Recordset</p>
2153:
2154:   <p class=C2>3:<span style="mso-spacerun: yes">
    ➥</span>Set rs = New
2155:   Recordset</p>
2156:
2157:   <p class=C2>4:<span style="mso-spacerun: yes">      </span>Call
2158:   rs.Open(&quot;select * from publishers&quot;,
    ➥&quot;dsn=pubs&quot;,<span
2159:   style="mso-spacerun: yes">  </span>UID=sa; PWD=;&quot;)</p>
2160:
2161:   <p class=C2>5:<span style="mso-spacerun: yes">
    ➥</span>Set GetTheData = rs</p>
2162:
2163:   <p class=CX>6: End Function</p>
```

Figure 3.1

Blocks of Code and Notes.

Listing 3.4

```
0:  Option Explicit
1:  Option Compare Text
2:
3:  Private Sub Publishers_ProcessTag_
4:  (ByVal TagName As String, TagContents As String,_
5:   SendTags As Boolean)
6:
7:      Select Case TagName
8:
9:      Case "WC@Publishers"
10:         Dim rs As Recordset
11:         Dim bizObj As New PubsGetData
12:         Set rs = bizObj.GetTheData
13:
14:         TagContents = _
15:         "<TABLE WIDTH=75% BORDER=1 " _
16:         & "CELLSPACING=1 CELLPADDING=1>"
17:         TagContents = TagContents & vbCrLf & vbCrLf
18:         While Not rs.EOF
19:             TagContents = TagContents _
20:             & Chr(9) & "<TR>" & vbCrLf
21:             TagContents = TagContents _
22:             & Chr(9) & Chr(9) & "<TD>" & rs("pub_id") _
23:             & "</TD>" & vbCrLf
24:             TagContents = TagContents _
25:             & Chr(9) & Chr(9) & "<TD>" _
26:             & rs("pub_name") & "</TD>" & vbCrLf
27:             TagContents = TagContents _
28:             & Chr(9) & Chr(9) & "<TD>" _
29:             & rs("city") & "</TD>" & vbCrLf
30:             TagContents = TagContents _
31:             & Chr(9) & "</TR>" _
32:             & vbCrLf & vbCrLf
33:             rs.MoveNext
34:         Wend
35:      End Select
36:
37:      TagContents = TagContents & "</table>"
38:
39:  End Sub
40:
41:  Private Sub Publishers_Respond()
42:      Publishers.WriteTemplate
43:  End Sub
44:
45:  Private Sub WebClass_Start()
46:      Set NextItem = Publishers
47:  End Sub
```

Figure 3.1

Blocks of Code and Notes.

> There is quite a bit of advanced VB in this code. If this is new to you, *don't panic!* I provide quite a bit of detail about VB in the Visual Basic excursions in future chapters. For now, follow the logic of what we're doing;the details can come later.

Whenever NextItem is set, the Respond method is called. In this case, it is Publishers_Respond. This code appears on line 41, and we invoke the WriteTemplate method on line 42. This tells VB to write the template file to the browser and call ProcessTag.

In ProcessTag, we respond to the tags in the template with code. Whatever we put into TagContents is injected into the HTML stream in place of the tag. In other words, our template is streamed to the client line by line, and each time a tag is found ProcessTag is called, giving us an opportunity to read the tag and respond appropriately.

Let's examine ProcessTag in some detail. On line 10, we declare a recordset object; on line 11, we create a new business object from the PubsGetData object we created in the previous exercise. On line 12, we call its GetTheData method and assign the resulting recordset to the rs variable we created on line 10.

> I added some VB code to create indentation and new lines in the HTML output. This will make explicit that the HTML sent from the WebClass is identical to the HTML sent from ASP.

We then start spitting out HTML. Note on line 14 that we assign to TagContents the string `"<TABLE WIDTH=75% BORDER=1 CELLSPACING=1 CELLPADDING=1>"`. We then add in HTML for the rows, interspersing the strings returned from the recordset. When we're done, TagContents is one long string of HTML. We can set a break point on line 17, as shown in Figure 3.24, and use the *Immediate* window to examine the contents of TagContents.

You can see what is in TagContents by opening the Immediate window (Ctrl-G), as shown in Figure 3.25.

Note, however, that this is produced within a loop. The next time through we *add* to the TagContents string, building up the table as we go. By the time the loop is finished and we hit the final line (where we add the closing tag for the table), we have built up a complete HTML string for output to the browser.

The styles used in Word are preserved in the HTML file as attributes of the <p> tag, for example, <p class=c2>. Class is a Cascading Style Sheet designation for a style, defined at the top of the Web page. Again, we see here presentation rather than structural information, though the structure is implicit.

The transformation from HTML to XHTML was responsible for turning the HMTL into XML-Compliant HTML, as shown in Chapter 2. This transformation did not eliminate any tags, it just ensured that they are XML-compliant, that is that they don't overlap, and that they are properly quoted. The styles captured in the HTML survive into the XHTML as shown in Listing 3.4

Listing 3.4   `Chap3.xhtml`

```
1167:  1: Function GetTheData() As Recordset
1168:        </p>
1169:        <p class="C2">
1170:  2:
1171:          <span style="mso-spacerun: yes">
1172:
1173:          </span>
1174:  Dim rs As ADODB.Recordset
1175:        </p>
1176:        <p class="C2">
1177:  3:
1178:          <span style="mso-spacerun: yes">
1179:
1180:          </span>
1181:  Set rs = New Recordset
1182:        </p>
1183:        <p class="C2">
1184:  4:
1185:          <span style="mso-spacerun: yes">
1186:
1187:          </span>
1188:  Call rs.Open(&quot;select * from publishers&quot;,
        ➥ &quot;dsn=pubs&quot;,
1189:          <span style="mso-spacerun: yes">
1190:
1191:          </span>
1192:  UID=sa; PWD=;&quot;)
1193:        </p>
1194:        <p class="C2">
1195:  5:
1196:          <span style="mso-spacerun: yes">
1197:
1198:          </span>
1199:  Set GetTheData = rs
1200:        </p>
1201:        <p class="CX">
1202:  6: End Function
```

Analysis

We see no change to the <p> tags; they still maintain the styles, and there is still no explicit structural information tying the code together as a block of code.

We actually want to make a few different transformations here. First, we don't want to keep the style codes; we want instead to tag each line as a line of code.

Second, we don't care about distinguishing the final line from any other line of code; after all, we don't know how we'll want to display this code, and the last line may or may not be displayed differently from any other line.

Third, we want to mark the entire block of code, making the structure of the listing explicit.

When we're done, this section will look like the code in Listing 3.5.

Listing 3.5　`Chap3.xml`

```
946:     <code><codeline>
947: 1: Function GetTheData() As Recordset
948:        </codeline>
949:           <codeline>
950: 2:
951:        <spacerun len="4"/>
952:
953: Dim rs As ADODB.Recordset
954:        </codeline>
955:           <codeline>
956: 3:
957:          <spacerun len="4"/>
958:
959: Set rs = New Recordset
960:        </codeline>
961:           <codeline>
962: 4:
963:          <spacerun len="4"/>
964:
965: Call rs.Open("select * from publishers", "dsn=pubs",
966:          <spacerun len="1"/>
967:
968: UID=sa; PWD=;")
969:        </codeline>
970:           <codeline>
971: 5:
972:          <spacerun len="4"/>
973:
974: Set GetTheData = rs
```

continues

Listing 3.5   continued

```
975:          </codeline>
976:              <codeline>
977:  6: End Function
978:          </codeline>
979:        </code>
```

The entire code listing is surrounded by <code> tags, and each line is marked with <codeline> tags.

Spaceruns and Tabs

You no doubt noticed that in the original listing of code, shown in Listing 3.2, many of the lines are indented. Here are the first two lines:

```
1: Function GetTheData() As Recordset
2:     Dim rs As ADODB.Recordset
```

Indentation presents a challenge to Word when it translates the document to HTML. The convention in HTML is to collapse all spaces into a single space. Word resolves that issue by creating a <span> as shown in this excerpt from Listing 3.3.

```
2156:  <p class=C2>2:<span style="mso-spacerun: yes">        </span>
```

Word creates a span, with the attribute style, whose value is mso (Microsoft Office) spaceRun: yes. Word then puts in a single space followed by a series of non-breaking space characters ( ), and then ends the span.

The span statement survives the translation to XHTML. While this approach works, XSL will not render it properly and it is a kludge that is not needed in XML. After all, in XML we can make our own tags, and give them meaningful attributes. We will encode indentation in a way that can be preserved through future transformations.

We will translate these spans into our own spacerun tag, with an attribute that details how many spaces are captured:

```
<spacerun len="4"/>
```

This tag indicates a space run with a length of 4. It is cleaner than the Microsoft HTML span, and XSL will have no trouble with it as it is standard XML.

Note   As previously mentioned, because this tag does not have a value, rather than writing <spacerun len="4"></spacerun> we can compress the start and end tags into a single tag by including the trailing slash <spacerun len="4"/>.

Marking Sidebars and Notes

We have solved the problem of aggregating code into a meaningful structure; we face the same problem with Notes, Geek Speak, How To Pronounce It, and the other sidebars.

 Note

For simplicity, we'll treat all these sidebars as Notes, though you may want to take on the exercise of breaking them out each into its own tag.

Our approach to Notes will be the same as was our approach to Code. We don't need to preserve the styling, but we do want to make the structure, which is implicit in the Word document and the XHTML, explicit in our XML document.

The following Note is from Chapter 3 of *WebClasses from Scratch*.

BEGIN NOTE

Here are the steps for Visual InterDev. As explained in the previous chapter, the exact details may be different on your computer or network, or if you are using different Internet-enabling technology.

END NOTE

Listing 3.6 shows how that listing appears in the XHTML file:

Listing 3.6 `Chap3.xhtml`

```
191:        <p class="PD">
192: ***Begin Note***
193:        </p>
194:        <p class="NO">
195:  Here are the steps for Visual InterDev. As explained in the
     ➥previous chapter, the exact details may be different on your
     ➥computer or network, or if you are using different
     ➥Internet enabling technology.
196:        </p>
197:        <p class="PD">
198: ***End Note***
199:        </p>
```

Listing 3.7 shows what this will look like in the final XML file:

Listing 3.7 `Chap3.xml`

```
155:    <note><noteline>
156: Here are the steps for Visual InterDev. As explained in the
     ➡previous chapter, the exact details may be different on your
     ➡computer or network, or if you are using different
     ➡Internet enabling technology.
157:      </noteline>
158:    </note>
```

Each paragraph in the note is marked with a `<noteline>` tag, and the entire note is surrounded by `<note>` tags.

Breaking Out Sections

The Word document as submitted by the author does not have an explicit outline structure, though one is implied. For example, Chapter 2 of *WebClasses From Scratch* might be submitted as shown in Listing 3.8 (I've cut a number of lines of text to make this listing shorter):

Listing 3.8

```
0:  (a)2
1:  (b)Analysis and Design
2:  (c)Analysis and Design
3:  (c)Analysis
4:  (d)Conceptualization
5:  (d)Use Cases
6:  (d)Domain Analysis
7:  (c)On to Design
8:  (d)Three Tiered Development
```

Within this document is an implied structure. By convention, the editor and author agree that (D) level heads are "below" and "contained by" (C) level heads. This becomes a more traditional outline, as shown in Figure 3.2.

Figure 3.2

Traditional Outline.

Chapter 2
Analysis and Design
Analysis
Conceptualization
Use Cases
Domain Analysis
On To Design
Three Tiered Development

We want the XML document to reflect this containment structure. In fact, however, we see an even deeper structure. The nesting in the traditional outline actually reflects a concept of containment, as shown in Figure 3.3.

Figure 3.3

Containment.

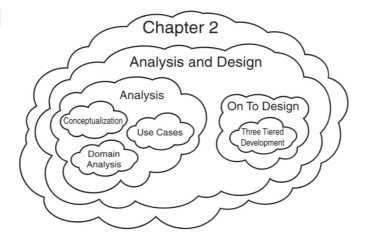

This is closer to the way we think about the data. XML is quite good at capturing this concept of containment, though it does so in what looks like a hierarchical tree, as shown in Figure 3.4.

Figure 3.4

Containment shown as a hierarchy.

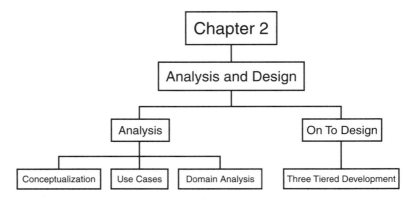

There is an isomorphic mapping between the clouds in Figure 3.3 and the tree in Figure 3.4.

isomorphic—one for one. An *isomorphic* relationship means that for every object in one, there is exactly one corresponding object in the other.

XML allows us to create the hierarchy in Figure 3.4 by explicitly defining new elements to be children of other existing elements. Thus, we can create the (C) level element, and then the (D) level element, and explicitly define the (D) level element to be a child element of the (C) level element. In fact, we can control and make explicit the order of the children, so that (D) level elements will be in explicit ordered sibling relationships with one another. This will become very important when we create our collapsible Table of Contents.

Passing Through the Remaining HTML

The final task in our transformations is to ensure that we pass through all the remaining meaningful tags and text to the final XML file. We need to be explicit about what tags are to be passed through, as we want to distinguish between tags we recognize and intend to pass along to the final document on the one hand, and tags we simply missed or don't recognize on the other. We must capture these latter unanticipated and unknown tags, so that we can extend our DTD to accommodate them.

Creating the DTD

Now that we know what we're trying to accomplish, we can see the path to getting there:

1. Create a DTD that captures the constraints on our XML documents.
2. Transform the XHTML document to a valid XML document.

Let's start by creating and examining the DTD. We'll look at how we transform the XHTML document using XSL in the next chapter. Listing 3.9 shows the complete DTD. We'll take a look at it line by line.

Listing 3.9 `Canon.dtd`

```
 0:      <!-- DTD for XWDFS documents -->
 1:
 2:      <!--
 3:          This is a "macro" that defines normal body text, which
 4:          might contain miscellaneous markup. We define it as an
 5:          entity because we need to reference it from many places
 6:          in the DTD. This mandates that this DTD be referenced
 7:          externally
 8:        -->
 9:      <!ENTITY % text "#PCDATA ¦ b ¦ i ¦ u ¦
         ➥sub ¦ sup ¦ tab ¦ spacerun ¦ char">
10:
11:      <!-- The root element. Books are made up of one or
         ➥more sections -->
```

3

```
12:      <!ELEMENT book (section+)>
13:
14:      <!-- Sections have level and id attributes
         ➥and begin with a title.
15:      Sections may contain other sections -->
16:      <!ELEMENT section (title, (section ¦ div ¦ note ¦ code)*)>
17:      <!ATTLIST section
18:         level CDATA #REQUIRED
19:         id CDATA #REQUIRED>
20:
21:      <!-- Titles are just text, which may contain styling markup -->
22:      <!ELEMENT title (%text;)*>
23:
24:      <!--
25:         Div elements are our main body content and corresponds
26:         to paragraphs. Each contains a class attribute, which
27:         is a copy of the original Word style name
28:      -->
29:      <!ELEMENT div (%text;)*>
30:      <!ATTLIST div
31:         class CDATA #REQUIRED>
32:
33:      <!--
34:         Notes and code blocks are our collections of
35:         non-ordinary text. Each has a encompassing element
36:         (note, code) and an element for each line/paragraph
37:         contained in the block (noteline, codeline)
38:        -->
39:      <!ELEMENT note (noteline+)>
40:      <!ELEMENT code (codeline+)>
41:      <!ELEMENT noteline (%text;)*>
42:      <!ELEMENT codeline (%text;)*>
43:
44:      <!-- The char tag is for special characters -->
45:      <!ELEMENT char EMPTY>
46:      <!ATTLIST char
47:         type CDATA #REQUIRED>
48:
49:      <!-- special formatting elements to deal with white space -->
50:      <!ELEMENT tab EMPTY>
51:      <!ELEMENT spacerun EMPTY>
52:      <!ATTLIST spacerun
53:         len CDATA #REQUIRED>
54:
55:      <!-- inline formatting elements,
56:      derived from the familiar HTML tags -->
57:      <!ELEMENT b (%text;)*>
58:      <!ELEMENT i (%text;)*>
59:      <!ELEMENT u (%text;)*>
60:      <!ELEMENT sub (%text;)*>
61:      <!ELEMENT sup (%text;)*>
```

Analysis

The first lines are comments, and you'll note that the DTD uses the normal HTML comment syntax `<!-- comment here -->`.

To get started, let's skip down to line 12. We'll come back to line 9 in just a moment.

Line 12 declares our outermost element, `book`. In the XML document that uses this DTD, we will expect to find a DOCTYPE instruction that will reference this DTD and will also specify the root element: `book`.

Each declaration in the DTD begins with `<!` followed by either one or many keywords. In our DTD we use only ELEMENT or ATTRIBUTE. We use the former to declare all the elements in the Document Type Definition, and we use the latter to declare the attributes for each element type we declare.

Line 12 declares `book` to be an element. It is, in fact, the root element of our canonical form. XML documents are always hierarchical. Every element must be contained within the declaration of its parent element, and element tags may not overlap. The topmost element, in our case `<book>`, serves as the root for the entire document. If we return to our earlier drawing, in Figure 3.3, the outermost cloud is `<book>`, as shown in Figure 3.5.

Figure 3.5

The outermost cloud has changed.

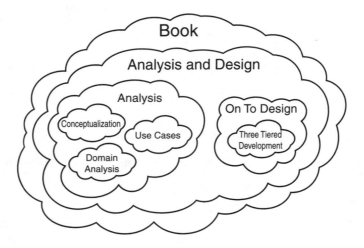

Line 12 goes on to define the contents of a `<book>` element. It will consist of one or more section elements. The plus sign indicates 1 or more. Thus, we know that for a BiblioTech document to be *valid* it must consist of a book element that contains at least one section element.

The section element itself is defined on line 16.

```
16:     <!ELEMENT section (title, (section ¦ div ¦ note ¦ code)*)>
```

Once again we see an Element declaration, this time for section. A section, according to this line in our DTD, will consist of a title and zero or more elements of type section *or* div *or* note *or* code. The asterisk (*) denotes zero or more. The vertical lines between section, div, note, and code indicate the logical or relationship.

> **Note**
>
> The comma in the section declaration implies ordering. Therefore, the title must come first, followed by zero or more of the other elements listed.

Since there is no cardinality (+ or *) for title, the DTD signals exactly 1. Note that the question mark (?) can also be used in this context, to signal zero or 1.

Thus, a section will always have one title, and it can have zero or more of each of the other four elements. Note also that one of these four elements is a section, so we know that sections can contain other sections.

Line 17 begins the attribute list for the element section. The first attribute is level, and it is of type CDATA. CDATA is *unparsed* text: That is, the XML document will accept any text and will not try to parse that text as XML. This allows you to put in otherwise restricted characters such as < or >. Finally, the level attribute is marked #REQUIRED, which indicates that every section *must* have a level attribute to be valid.

#REQUIRED is an attribute modifier. The other modifiers are #IMPLIED and #FIXED. The modifier #IMPLIED indicates that the attribute is optional and that there is no default value provided. #FIXED indicates that only a specific value will be allowed for that attribute.

The second attribute, id, is also of type CDATA and is also required.

Parameter Entities

On line 22 we declare the title ELEMENT. It turns out that the title ELEMENT contains zero or more of the following element types: b or i or u or sub or sup or tab or spacerun or char. It can also contain text characters, which can be parsed. This text is marked #PCDATA, which stands for Parsed Character DATA. The declaration for title should be

```
<!ELEMENT title (#PCDATA ¦ b ¦ i ¦ u ¦ sub ¦ sup ¦ tab ¦ spacerun ¦ char")*>
```

This would indicate that title will have zero or more of any of these nine element types. It turns out that there are other elements that also are of these types. In fact, we think of all of these types as *text*, and so it would be handy to create a quick macro or shorthand for this long string.

The DTD syntax allows for creating such a macro. You may create an *entity* for text substitution. If you want that text to be substituted in the actual XML file you use a simple entity declaration like this:

```
<!ENTITY LA "Liberty Associates, Inc."
```

This would allow me to use an entity reference &LA; in my document, and the parser would substitute Liberty Associates, Inc. This is directly analogous to using &gt, which the browser turns into >.

In our case, however, we don't want the substitution to take place in the XML document, we want it to take place in the DTD itself. For that we use a *parameter entity*.

Entity Reference—A text substitution for use in an XML document.

Parameter Entity—A text substitution for use in a DTD document.

The syntax for a parameter entity is to declare the entity with a percent symbol (%). Thus

```
<!ENTITY % LA "Liberty Associates, Inc.">
```

would declare a parameter entity for use in the DTD. When I wanted to make the substitution, I'd simply enter %LA; and the text Liberty Associates, Inc. would be inserted into the DTD.

On line 9 we declare just such a Parameter Entity. The name of the entity is text, and if we write %text; anywhere in the DTD, the string #PCDATA ¦ b ¦ i ¦ u ¦ sub ¦ sup ¦ tab ¦ spacerun ¦ char will be inserted.

Line 22 uses this parameter entity, and so line 22 is written

```
22:     <!ELEMENT title (%text;)*>
```

but the net effect is exactly as if we had written

```
22:        <!ELEMENT title (#PCDATA ¦ b ¦ i ¦ u ¦ sub ¦ sup
        ➥¦ tab ¦ spacerun ¦ char)*>
```

On line 29 we declare a new element, div, which is also defined to consist of zero or more text elements (that is, of zero or more of the elements #PCDATA ¦ b ¦ i ¦ u ¦ sub ¦ sup ¦ tab ¦ spacerun ¦ char). The div element also has one required attribute, which is class. Class itself is declared to be of type CDATA.

On line 40 we declare the note element, and it consists of one or more notelines, which in turn are declared on line 41 to consist of zero or more text elements. Similarly, on line 40, code is declared to consist of one or more codelines, which are declared on line 42 to consist of zero or more text elements.

This is a very formal and terse, yet easily understood way of detailing what we know about notelines and codelines. To translate just lines 39 and 41 into English, we would say "A note consists of one or more lines of text, where text is zero or more parsed characters and/or the tags for bold, italics, underline, sub- or superscript, tabs, spaceruns, or special characters."

The only potentially confusing aspect of that definition is the char element. This is a tag created specifically for special characters. It is declared on lines 45–47.

The element itself is declared on line 45 with the keyword EMPTY. The EMPTY keyword indicates that the element has no content. In our case, that is because the actual value of the special character will be in the attribute.

The attributes for char are declared on line 46 and 47. This indicates that char has an attribute named type which is of type CDATA and which is required.

You would thus expect to find a char element that looks like this:

```
<char type="#018" />
```

On line 50 we declare the tab element, and we indicate that it will always be empty. Thus, we may have

```
<tab/>
```

or

```
<tab></tab>
```

but we may not have

```
<tab>4</tab>
```

if we are going to have a *valid* document. Remember, the very concept of validity is defined by this DTD. When we say "this document is valid" we mean that it conforms to the constraints of its DTD.

On lines 51–53 we declare the spacerun element, which is also empty and which has an attribute len, which is of type CDTA and which is required.

Finally, on lines 57–61 we declare the elements b, i, u, sub, and sup, and we declare that each contains zero or more elements of type #PCDATA or b or i or u or sub or sup or tab or spacerun or char.

What the DTD Has Told Us

The DTD has laid out the structure of our Canonical form. Every canonical document will have at its root a `<book>` tag, which will contain at least one section.

The section in turn will consist of a title and then zero or more sections, div (paragraphs), notes, or code blocks.

The title will consist of zero or more of the various text types (`PCDATA`, `b`, `i`, `u`, `sub`, `sup`, `tab`, `spacerun` or `char`). The `b`, `i`, `u`, `sub` and `sup` themselves also consist of zero or more of the various text types.

The `div` also consists of zero or more of these text types, but it has an attribute, `class`, which is required and is of type `CDATA`.

Notes consist of one or more notelines, which are in turn text types. Code consists of zero or more codelines, which again are text types.

We have a special char type, which is one of the text types, which is an empty tag with a required `CDATA` attribute.

The text types also include `tab`, which is an empty element, and `spacerun`, which is also empty but which has a required attribute `len`.

Next Steps

Now that we know, in detail, what our canonical form is, we are ready to transform the XHTML document into an XML document that conforms to our DTD. We will do this in two steps: first using XSL and then manipulating the XML Document Model. We begin with the XSL in Chapter 4, "Using XSL to Create an XML Document."

Chapter 4

Transformation with XSL— eXtensible Stylesheet Language

With the DTD in hand, we can see the transformations required to move from our existing XHTML document to an XML document, which is valid for our DTD.

We will accomplish the transformations in two stages. In the first stage we will work with XSL, in the second, with the XML Document Object Model.

The XSL was created with two goals in mind: displaying XML and transforming XML. The first, displaying XML is very similar to the role of CSS (Cascading Style Sheets) in HTML. The second role for XSL—transformations—is completely different. Transformation rules allow you to take an input XML file and produce a somewhat different output XML file.

It turns out that IE5 supports the transformation aspect of XSL, but not the styling. That is good news for us, as our focus is on transformation.

We will use the transformation capabilities of XSL first to transform our XHTML document to our canonical form. Later, we may want to use XSL again to transform from our canonical form to a display format, perhaps even back to HTML. It is probably true that today, for most companies, XSL is used primarily to transform XML to HTML for rendering on the Web. We'll see that done later in the book.

Inputs and Outputs

XSL pages are written in XML, though they have an internal syntax all their own. You work with XSL by providing the stylesheet Processor (in our case MSXML) the following three XML documents:

1. The original XML document (in our case, the XHTML document)
2. A well-formed XSL Style Sheet (which, you'll remember *is* an XML document)
3. Optionally, an output XML document

The essential step is calling the method `transformNodeToObject` on the input DOM. This method takes two parameters: the DOM for the XSL stylesheet, and an output XML DOM.

We'll start by creating a small component XSLTransform, which will serve as a convenience wrapper around `transformNodeToObject`. It will be the job of XSLTransform to create and prepare the three DOMs, so that we can specify the input document by URL, filename, or by passing in an object or by passing in the XML string itself.

Our steps will be as follows:

1. Instantiate the utility `XSLTransform`.
2. Specify the filename using the `InputFile` property of `XSLTransform` and pass in the input filename. This causes `XSLTransform` to read that file in and create its Document Object Model.
3. Specify the filename using the `XSLFile` property of `XSLTransform` and pass in the `XSL` filename. This causes `XSLTransform` to read in the XSL file and create its Document Object Model.
4. Call the `Transform` method on `XSLTransform`, which creates an empty output DOM, and calls `transformNodeToObject` on the input DOM, passing in as parameters the XSL DOM we just created and the new Output DOM.

Invoking the Methods

To get started, we return to the `control.asp` file considered in Chapter 2. This time through, we'll consider what happens when you click the button XHTML to XML.

You will recall from Chapter 2 that a number of state variables are preserved in cookies. These include the directories for both the programs and the files, as well as the DSN and password for accessing the database.

When the user clicks a button, the page is submitted to itself, and the script switches on the specific button clicked as shown in Listing 4.1.

Listing 4.1　`Control.asp`

```
42:          select case Request("Cmd")
43:              case "Word to XHTML"
44:                  Response.Write Word2XHTML()
45:
46:              case "XHTML to XML"
47:                  Response.Write XHTML2XML()
```

As shown in the bold print above, in this case we will invoke the function
`XHTML2XML()`, illustrated in Listing 4.2.

Listing 4.2　`Control.asp`

```
120:     Function XHTML2XML()
121:         'convert XHTML file to our canonical XML form
122:         dim oXSL, oH2X, xmlFN, fn0, dtdFN
123:
124:         set oXSL = Server.CreateObject("FromScratch.XSLTransform")
125:
126:         'convert xhtml to xml via a stylesheet
127:         oXSL.InputFile = dataPath & ".xhtml"
128:         oXSL.XSLFile = fso.BuildPath(codeDir, "WordXHTML2XML.xsl")
129:
130:         oXSL.Transform
131:
132:         'save output as .xml0
133:         xmlFN = dataPath & ".xml"
134:         fn0 = xmlFN & "0"
135:         oXSL.SaveOutputAsFile fn0
136:
137:         'we assume that the dtd is in the same directory as the data
138:         dtdFN = "canon.dtd"
139:
140:         'now pipe the .xml0 to the VB component to do the rest of
             ➥the transformation
141:         set oH2X = Server.CreateObject("FromScratch.WordXHTML2XML")
142:         oH2X.Convert fn0, xmlFN, dtdFN
143:
144:         'and we no longer need the intermediate file
145:         fso.DeleteFile fn0
146:
147:         XHTML2XML = "Converted " & dataPath & ".xhtml" &
             ➥" to " & xmlFN
148:     End Function
```

On line 124, we create the FromScratch library's `XSLTransform` object, and assign it
to the variable `oXLS`.

Our next step is to create the Document Object Model for the input file. On line
127 we set the property `myInputFile` in our object with the string that contains the
input file's name as shown in Listing 4.3.

Listing 4.3 `XSLTransform.cls`

```
 0:  Property Let InputFile(ByVal newValue As String)
 1:      Dim fso As New Scripting.FileSystemObject,
         ➥f As TextStream, xml As String
 2:
 3:      'read the contents of the file
 4:      'should we do this via DOM.load()?
 5:
 6:      myInputFile = newValue
 7:      Set f = fso.OpenTextFile(myInputFile)
 8:      xml = f.ReadAll
 9:      f.Close
10:
11:      Set myInputDOM = ParseIntoDOM(xml, False, "Input from File")
12:  End Property
```

We pass in the filename as a string.

> **Note**
>
> If we had, instead, a URL for the input file, we would call `InputURL`. The point of this component, `XSLTransform`, is only to make it easy to instantiate the various Document Object Models needed for the transformation.

On line 7 we open the file with the name provided as a parameter, and on line 8 we read in the contents of that file into a string we've named `xml`. We then close the file and pass `xml` to our helper method `ParseIntoDOM`, shown in Listing 4.4.

Listing 4.4 `XSLTransform.cls`

```
 0:  'worker function to read an input source into a new DOM
 1:  'if isURL is true, then data is the text of a URL;
     ➥else data is an XML string
 2:  Private Function ParseIntoDOM(data As String, isURL As Boolean,
     ➥src As String) As DOMDocument
 3:      Dim dom As New DOMDocument, result As Boolean
 4:      dom.async = False
 5:      If isURL Then
 6:          result = dom.Load(data)
 7:      Else
 8:          result = dom.loadXML(data)
 9:      End If
10:      If Not result Then
11:          ReportParseError src, dom
12:      End If
13:      Set ParseIntoDOM = dom
14:  End Function
```

`ParseIntoDom` receives three parameters: the string with the document, the value `false` indicating that we're not sending in a URL, and the string `Input from File`, which we will use to report an error, if necessary.

Because we have not passed in a URL, the `if` statement on line 5 fails and the `else` statement is invoked on line 8. We call `loadXML`, and pass in the string of the entire document, which we read in earlier.

This loads the DOM, in memory, building up the object model from the string we created by reading the document from the disk. When we're done, we have a DOM of the input file.

Loading the XSL

Returning to Listing 4.2 we see that the next action in our ASP file, on line 128, is to call the `XSLFile` method, this time passing in the path to the XSL document.

```
128:    oXSL.XSLFile = fso.BuildPath(codeDir, "WordXHTML2XML.xsl")
```

This invokes `XSLFile` as shown in Listing 4.5.

Listing 4.5 `XSLTransform.cls`

```
0:  Property Let XSLFile(ByVal newValue As String)
1:      Dim fso As New Scripting.FileSystemObject, f As TextStream,
        ➥xml As String
2:
3:      myXSLFile = newValue
4:      Set f = fso.OpenTextFile(myXSLFile)
5:      xml = f.ReadAll
6:      f.Close
7:
8:      Set myXSLDOM = ParseIntoDOM(xml, False, "XSL from file")
9:  End Property
```

Once again, we invoke `ParseIntoDom`, and the result is the creation in memory of the XSL DOM.

At this point, we're ready to start the transformation. We don't have an output DOM yet, but we'll take care of that in a moment. Line 122 of Listing 3.10 shows the following invocation:

```
8:      oXSL.Transform
```

This calls the `Transform` method of our object, shown in Listing 4.6.

Listing 4.6 `XSLTransform.cls`

```
0:  'the function that does the work - actually transforms input
    ➡via XSL to output
1:  Public Sub Transform()
2:      Set myOutputDOM = New DOMDocument
3:      myInputDOM.transformNodeToObject myXSLDOM, myOutputDOM
4:      If myOutputDOM.parseError.errorCode <> 0 Then _
4a:         ReportParseError "Output", myOutputDOM
5:  End Sub
```

As promised, on line 2 the outputDOM is created with a call to new DOMDocument. On line 3, we then call the `transformNodeToObject` method on the inputDom. This method takes two parameters: an XSL DOM and an `outputDOM`, and that is exactly what we provide.

The net result is that there are now three Document Object Models in existence: input, XSL, and output. The call to `transformNodeToObject` will do the work of reading the XSL and transforming the input DOM accordingly, placing the results in the output DOM.

Note that on line 4 we check for a parseError, and report it if one is found. An errorCode of 0 indicates no error.

The purpose of the `XSLTransform` module is just to create the necessary DOMs and invoke the correct method (`transformNodeToObject`) passing in the correct parameters. At this point, however, the XSL parser takes over, and the work is automagic.

If the XSL document is well-formed and valid, and the rules and commands within it are correct, you will need to take no further action; the parser will output the correct XML with all the transformations accomplished. Otherwise the component will report the error.

Note   MSXML itself does a good job of reporting the error, but unlike a compiler, only the first error is reported, and all errors are fatal.

XSL In Detail

We've set up our input and output files, and read the XSL into memory. Once we call `transformNodeToObject`, we just sit back and let XSL do the work.

Listing 4.7 shows the entire XSL document. We'll go through it step by step for the remainder of this chapter.

Listing 4.7 `WordXHTML2XML.xsl`

```
0:   <?xml version="1.0"?>
1:   <xsl:stylesheet
2:       xmlns:xsl="http://www.w3.org/TR/WD-xsl"
3:       xmlns="http://www/w3/org/TR/REC-xml"
4:       result-ns="">
5:
6:       <!-- default rules -->
7:       <xsl:template match="text()"><xsl:value-of/>
     ➥</xsl:template>
8:
9:       <xsl:template match="/">
10:          <xsl:pi name="xml">version="1.0"</xsl:pi>
11:          <xsl:apply-templates />
12:      </xsl:template>
13:
14:      <!-- catch any unknown tags -->
15:      <xsl:template match="*">
16:          <unknown><xsl:attribute name="tag"><xsl:node-name/>
         ➥</xsl:attribute>
17:              <xsl:apply-templates />
18:          </unknown>
19:      </xsl:template>
20:
21:          <!-- our top level tag -->
22:      <xsl:template match="html">
23:          <html>
24:              <xsl:apply-templates/>
25:          </html>
26:      </xsl:template>
27:
28:      <!-- tags we can ignore -->
29:      <xsl:template match="head|title|style|body|script|
     ➥a|meta|link|div"><xsl:apply-
     ➥templates/></xsl:template>
30:
31:      <!-- p contain the bulk of the content. we'll map them to
     ➥div and include their class attribute -->
32:      <xsl:template match="p">
33:          <div><xsl:attribute name="class"><xsl:value-of
         ➥select="@class"/></xsl:attribute>
34:          <xsl:apply-templates/>
35:          </div>
36:      </xsl:template>
37:
38:      <!-- convert all code elements to one tagname -->
39:      <xsl:template match="p[@class='C1'] | p[@class='C2'] |
     ➥p[@class='CX']">
40:          <codeline><xsl:apply-templates/></codeline>
41:      </xsl:template>
42:
```

continues

Listing 4.7   Continued

```
43:     <!-- special tag for all paras that are part of
        ➥notes or sidebars -->
44:     <xsl:template match="p[@class='NO'] ¦ p[@class='SB']">
45:         <noteline><xsl:apply-templates/></noteline>
46:     </xsl:template>
47:
48:     <!-- just pass special chars along - include all
        ➥their attributes-->
49:     <xsl:template match="char">
50:         <char><xsl:attribute name="type"><xsl:value-of select=
            ➥"@type"/></xsl:attribute></char>
51:     </xsl:template>
52:
53:     <!-- handle vanilla HTML-like tags - just map them to the same
        ➥ thing, ignoring any attributes which may be present -->
54:     <xsl:template match="b¦i¦sub¦sup¦u¦br">
55:         <xsl:element><xsl:apply-templates/></xsl:element>
56:     </xsl:template>
57:
58:     <!-- Word puts in a bunch of <o:p> tags (with no content)
        ➥inside the "real" <p> tags. These tend to mess up the
59:         HTML rendering, so we'll take them out. This looks
            ➥for any p nested inside another p and
            ➥ignores it.  -->
60:     <xsl:template match="p//p">
61:     </xsl:template>
62:
63:     <!-- Word outputs span tags for a bunch of different
        ➥purposes. Here we handle all the subcases
64:             that have a style attribute -->
65:     <xsl:template match="span[@style]">
66:         <xsl:choose>
67:             <!-- Word's way of outputting a tab - we'll
                ➥convert to a special tag -->
68:             <xsl:when expr="getStyleName(this) == 'mso-tab-count'">
69:                 <tab />
70:             </xsl:when>
71:
72:             <!-- How Word encodes consecutive spaces - since
                ➥ HTML would swallow them up
73:                 we change to a tag that denotes the number of spaces -->
74:             <xsl:when expr="getStyleName(this) == 'mso-spacerun'">
75:                 <spacerun><xsl:attribute name="len"><xsl:eval>
                    ➥CountOccurrences(this.firstChild.nodeValue, '\xa0'
                    ➥ )</xsl:eval></xsl:attribute></spacerun>
76:             </xsl:when>
77:
78:             <!-- we ignore these -->
79:             <xsl:when expr="getStyleName(this) == 'mso-bookmark'">
80:                 <xsl:apply-templates />
81:             </xsl:when>
82:
```

```
83:                    <!-- we'll also ignore local font changes -->
84:                    <xsl:when expr="getStyleName(this) == 'font-family'">
85:                        <xsl:apply-templates />
86:                    </xsl:when>
87:
88:                    <xsl:when expr="getStyleName(this) == 'font-style'">
89:                        <xsl:apply-templates />
90:                    </xsl:when>
91:
92:                    <!-- can't even figure out what this is,
                     ➥so we'll ignore it -->
93:                    <xsl:when expr="getStyleName(this) ==
                     ➥'layout-grid-mode'">
94:                        <xsl:apply-templates />
95:                    </xsl:when>
96:
97:                    <!-- flag any other cases, recording their tagname and
                     ➥ style so we can debug our stylesheet -->
98:                    <xsl:otherwise>
99:                        <unknown>
100:                           <xsl:attribute name="tag">span</xsl:attribute>
101:                           <xsl:attribute name="val"><xsl:eval>
                     ➥getStyleName(this)</xsl:eval></xsl:attribute>
102:                           <xsl:apply-templates />
103:                        </unknown>
104:                    </xsl:otherwise>
105:              </xsl:choose>
106:        </xsl:template>
107:
108: <xsl:script>
109: <![CDATA[
110:     // return number of c characters in the string s
111:     function CountOccurrences(s, c)
112:     {
113:         var n = 0;
114:         for(var i = 0; i < s.length; i++)
115:         {
116:             if (s.charAt(i) == c) n++;
117:         }
118:         return n;
119:     }
120:
121:     // return the part of the style attribute's value
         ➥before the colon
122:     function getStyleName(me)
123:     {
124:         var styleArg = me.getAttribute("style");
125:         var p = styleArg.indexOf(':');
126:         return styleArg.substr(0, p);
127:     }
128: ]]>
129: </xsl:script>
130: </xsl:stylesheet>
```

Namespace

The very first line in Listing 4.7 declares that this stylesheet is written to conform to XML version 1. Remember that an XSL page is written in well-formed XML.

Line 1 declares the style sheet, and as part of that declaration establishes three *namespaces*. The concept of namespaces is not unique to XML; you will find namespaces in C++ and a variety of other languages.

The idea of a namespace is to allow you to create meaningful tag names without worrying that the tag name you choose will conflict with a tag name from some other organization. The W3C has declared a number of reserved namespaces, including namespaces for HTML, XSL, and XML.

This turns out to be very helpful while reading through the style sheet. The namespace helps us distinguish between those tags that are specific to XSL and those that are XML.

On line 2 we declare that we will be using the Namespace XSL (the syntax is `xmlns:xsl`), which we set to the specification found at the URL `http://www.w3.org/TR/WD-xsl`. Note that this URL may or may not point to a meaningful document. What is essential is that the URL is guaranteed to be unique. In effect, the URL serves as a globally unique identifier.

We want to declare the XML namespace to be the one found at the URL `http://www/w3/org/TR/REC-xml`. Notice however, that the syntax on line 3 is different. Here we declare an *unnamed* namespace. This indicates that if we do not specifically name a namespace in a tag, then we can assume the XML namespace.

Finally, on line 4, we set the `result-ns` attribute. This is a standard attribute of the `xsl-stylesheet` element and it is used to indicate the output of the XSL processor. In our case, we've set it to the empty string, indicating the unnamed namespace: in this case XML. It turns out that in IE5 all output is XML, and this attribute is ignored!

The style sheet element open tag spans four lines and finishes on line 4. The close tag for the style sheet is on line 130.

Templates, Filters, and Patterns

Our goal for the rest of the XSL style sheet is to search for and locate elements in our source document (the XHTML document) and manipulate them and output them to the target document (the new XML document).

The difficulty with XSL for most programmers is that it is a declarative rather than a procedural language. That is, in an XSL document you declare all the elements you want to find (using pattern matching) and the action to take upon those elements. This can take a bit of getting used to. It is much easier to understand this in the context of an example.

To get started, let's skip down to line 9 to examine a reasonably straightforward example of matching an element and taking an action. What we want to accomplish here is to direct the XSL processor to process all of the elements from the root node on down. Here's how we do it:

```
 9:       <xsl:template match="/">
10:           <xsl:pi name="xml">version="1.0"</xsl:pi>
11:           <xsl:apply-templates />
12:       </xsl:template>
```

On line 9, we see the template tag in the `xsl` namespace. The `xsl:` indicates the XSL namespace, and so, based on the namespace declaration at the top of the file, we know this element `template` is an XSL element.

A template is an XSL element that specifies a pattern to be matched in the input Document Object Model.

The target pattern is specified in this case in the match attribute. In this case, the pattern is "/", which turns out to be a special pattern that matches the root node.

The root node is an implied element in every XML document: It is the topmost starting point for the document.

The value of the template appears, as with all tags, between the open and close tag. In this case the value of the template is on lines 10 and 11. When an element in the input document matches the template, the value of the template will be placed in the output.

On line 10 we create an XML Processing Instruction (PI) whose name is `xml` and whose value is `version="1.0"`. You see this PI at the top of every XML file, and we'll add it to ours as well.

On line 11 we find the XSL element `apply-templates`, which causes the XSL parser to recurse into the current node. The current node is the node which matched the pattern in the `xsl:template` element on line 9.

In the case we're examining, the current node is the root node. This call to `apply-templates` has not specified any children (which it would otherwise do with a `select` attribute). When there are no specified children, the processor will attempt to find matching templates for *all* the children of the current node.

On line 12 the xsl:template node is closed, as all XML elements must be closed. The effect of lines 9–12 is to cause the parser to search for matches of every node in the input document.

Let's back up now to line 7:

```
7:      <xsl:template match="text()"><xsl:value-of/></xsl:template>
```

Here we see another template. This time the attribute match is set to "text()". This will match any text node. The value of the template tag is dictated by the xsl:value-of element, which returns the value of the matched node as a string. The effect is to copy the text of the matching node to the output document. Note that the template tag is closed, as all XML tags must be.

Thus, any text nodes in the source document (the XHTML) will be copied unmolested into the output document. This is the default behavior for XSL, but we have created a rule for it, as IE5 does not do so automatically.

We've now examined the first 13 lines of the XSL page. All the rest follow this fundamental approach of matching elements in the source document and then taking the appropriate action.

Template Matching

One way to think of the XSL document is to envision a coin sorter, as shown in Figure 4.1.

The coins enter the sorter and roll down a ramp until they find an opening through which they can fit. When they pass over a large enough slot, they fall into the right tube. If you are creating such a coin sorter, you must pay attention to the order of the slots. If you put the quarter slot before the penny slot, then pennies would fall through into the quarter tube, which is undesirable. Therefore, the slots must be ordered smallest to largest, so that dimes come first, followed by pennies, then nickels, and finally quarters. The order is not decided by their relative value, but by their relative size.

Similarly, the contents of our source document "roll down" a sorting ramp, where we must check the most specific cases before checking the more general. After all, if we have a slot marked "any element" then all elements will fall through that slot and never make it to the more specific matching pattern.

The ramp in this case runs from the bottom of the document towards the top. That is, IE5 checks the bottommost pattern in the document before checking the one above, and it works its way *up* the XSL document until it finds a good match.

Figure 4.1

Coin Sorter.

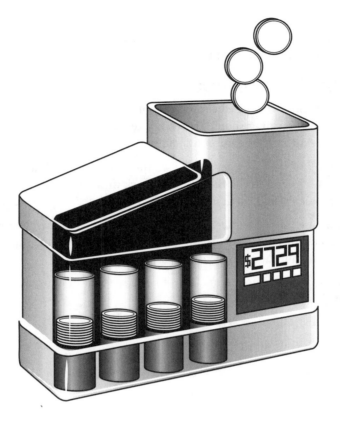

EXCURSION

Sorting bottom to top is a Microsoft-specific convention. The W3C recommendation states that when there are multiple matches, "…all matching template rules that are less important than the most important matching template rule or rules are eliminated from consideration."

That is, the specification says that if there is more than one matching template, the match is only to the most important.

Importance is measured by the location of the template. It is possible to import style sheets into your "main" style sheet, but templates in these imported style sheets are less important than those in the main style sheet.

It is also possible for the developer to set a priority for a given template rule. This priority can be expressed as a negative or positive integer. The default value is 0. By setting the priorities, the developer is free to determine which rules are most important.

IE5 does not support the concept of importance, nor does it support importing style sheets.

Because IE5 will evaluate the matches from the bottom of the file up to the top, we will put our most general matches near the top. This ensures that we'll catch any elements that were otherwise unmatched.

Finding Unknown Tags

We want the XSL style sheet to account for every tag in our source (the XHTML document). Each tag should be recognized, and processed in some way, if only to be passed on intact to the output document.

As part of our debugging process, we therefore need to find any tags that we didn't anticipate finding in the file. We will mark these spurious tags as "unknown" so that we can quickly find them in the output file and decide what to do with them.

For example, suppose there is a tag <xyz> in the XHTML. Further suppose that we have no idea what this tag is, and so have not handled it in the style sheet. We want to have the output include <unknown tag = "xyz"/>.

If the <xyz> tag has contents, we'd like to see that in our output as well. Thus, if the source has

```
<xyz>Cogito Ergo Sum</xyz>
```

we want the output to include

```
<unknown tag="xyz">Cogito Ergo Sum</unknown>
```

Here's how we do this. To start, at the top of the file we create a "match every element rule":

```
15:      <xsl:template match="*">
```

The * indicates "every element." Remember, if it is at the top of the file it will only be matched if all the other matches fail.

 **Note** * matches only elements, and thus it also does not match the root node, text nodes, comments, processing instructions, or other nodes that are not elements.

When we get such a match, we'll create an <unknown> tag, and we'll assign an attribute tag to that <unknown> tag. We accomplish this with the xsl:attribute element, which takes as *its* attribute the name of the attribute to assign to the current element.

That sentence is a bit hard to digest, so let's break it down with an example. If we create the <unknown> tag we can give it the attribute tag by writing

```
<xsl:attribute name="tag">
```

This says "assign to the current tag (`<unknown>`) an attribute whose name is `tag`."

The body of the `attribute` tag becomes the value of that attribute in `<unknown>`. Thus we could write

```
<unknown><xsl:attribute name="tag">"xyz"</xsl:attribute>
```

This says "assign to the current tag an attribute whose name is tag and whose value is xyz." The result would be

```
<unknown tag="xyz"/>
```

This would work fine if we knew that the tag we were working with was xyz. Unfortunately, we can't know what tag we'll run into, so we must ask the source document what the unknown tag's name is. We do that with `xsl:node-name`.

```
16:        <unknown><xsl:attribute name="tag"><xsl:node-name/></xsl:attribute>
```

You read this "create a tag `<unknown>` and give it an attribute whose name is `tag` and whose value is whatever is in `<xsl:node-name>`." The result in this case is the following:

```
<unknown tag="xyz"/>
```

Having created the `<unknown>` tag, we must pick up all its children. We do this by recursively calling `xsl:apply-templates`, which will cause the parser to examine the contents of the `<xyz>` tag. In the case shown above

```
<xyz>Cogito Ergo Sum</xyz>
```

This recursion will match the pattern we examined on line 7

```
7:     <xsl:template match="text()"><xsl:value-of/></xsl:template>
```

The result will be that the text will be set as a child-node of the `<unknown>` tag, just as we hoped. The result is

```
<unknown tag="xyz">Cogito Ergo Sum</unknown>
```

Note

Note that we do not have a rule for iterating through the attributes of this node, so we would not pick up any attributes in our unknown tag. We simply throw them away. Thus, if our original node were

```
<xyz size="3">Cogito Ergo Sum</xyz>
```

our output would not include the size attribute, and would still be

```
<unknown tag="xyz">Cogito Ergo Sum</unknown>
```

Lines 14–19 show this entire sequence.

```
14:        <!-- catch any unknown tags -->
15:         <xsl:template match="*">
16:             <unknown><xsl:attribute name="tag"><xsl:node-name/>
            ↪</xsl:attribute>
17:                 <xsl:apply-templates />
18:             </unknown>
19:         </xsl:template>
```

Assume again that we've come across an `<xyz>` tag in our source document. We'll not match that `<xyz>` tag on any line below line 15 as we were not expecting this tag. We will match it on line 15, as * matches anything.

We generate an `<unknown>` tag and give it an attribute "tag=xyz" as shown on line 16. We then call apply-templates to this xyz tag to ensure that if it has any children, they too will be processed. Finally, on line 18 we close off the unknown tag and on line 19 we close off the template.

Building the DOM

Here's an interesting question to consider before we go on. If the source file had the following:

```
<xyz value="foo">
```

what would the output document contain? The answer is

```
<unknown tag="xyz" />
```

As stated above, we throw away the attribute foo, but how did we get the self-closing tag? After all, our source shows a closing `</unknown>`. Shouldn't we get the following output?

```
<unknown tag="xyz"></unknown>
```

To understand this, you must remember what is really going on. We have read the source document up into a Document Object Model. We have also read the XSL document into a Document Object Model, and our output is in its own DOM. When we create the `<unknown>` tag, we do so not in a file, but in the DOM itself. This output DOM now contains a tag Unknown that has an attribute tag, which has the value xyz. If there are no child objects (because there was not text) then when we write the output DOM to a text file (for example, Chap2.xml) the parser will create the self-closing tag:

```
<unknown tag="xyz" />
```

In the case where the source document had

```
<xyz>Cogito Ergo Sum</xyz>
```

the output DOM has an `<unknown>` tag with an attribute `tag` whose value is `xyz`, but it also has a child tag of type `text` whose value is `Cogito Ergo Sum`. Thus, when this is written to the output document, it is written as

```
<unknown tag="xyz">Cogito Ergo Sum</unknown>
```

All of this is an automatic result of writing out the contents of the output DOM.

Parsing the XSL

We've worked our way down through line 18 of our XSL document. The next template statement is fairly straightforward:

```
22:     <xsl:template match="html">
23:         <html>
24:             <xsl:apply-templates/>
25:         </html>
26:     </xsl:template>
```

We match any element where the tag is `html`. There will normally be only one such element. We could eliminate the HTML tag at this point; after all our output XML document won't be an HTML document and thus won't need the HTML tag.

Because we are accomplishing the transformation to our canonical form in two steps, we will be building a temporary XML file. That file needs a root node, and for now it is simpler to leave it as HMTL, so we simply copy the HTML tag in place. During the second stage of the transition we'll replace the HTML tag with our new root element: `<book>`.

Tags We Can Ignore

Line 29 finds all the tags we don't care about in the source document, and it tosses them on the floor.

```
29:     <xsl:template match="head¦title¦style¦body¦script¦
        ➥a¦meta¦link¦div"><xsl:apply-templates/></xsl:template>
```

The syntax here is that this template matches on `head` *or* `title` *or* `style` and so forth, through this entire list. The action is to call `apply-templates`, which ensures that if any of these elements has children, we'll pick up the children. We take no other action, including copying the tag into our output document, and so the tag is effectively thrown away.

Handling `<p>` Tags

Examination of the source document shows that the bulk of the content is held in `<p>` tags. This is not surprising; most of the book is the text of the book, and the text is stored by Word as paragraphs marked by `<p>` tags when Word exports to HTML.

The <p> tag has evolved since early HTML, and it is now considered to be a hybrid of a structural and a presentation element. This makes the behavior of <p> tags somewhat less reliable. We've decided to map these paragraphs to <div>.

```
32:       <xsl:template match="p">
 33:          <div><xsl:attribute name="class"><xsl:value-of
              ➥select="@class"/></xsl:attribute>
 34:          <xsl:apply-templates/>
 35:          </div>
 36:       </xsl:template>
```

On line 32 we match all P elements. Let's break line 33 into its four parts:

```
33a:          <div>
33b:       <xsl:attribute name="class">
33c:       <xsl:value-of select="@class"/>
33d:        </xsl:attribute>
```

In part (a), we write a <div> statement to the output. Thus, each time we have a <p> we'll replace it with a <div>.

In part (b) we assign an attribute to the div, named "class". Thus our div will be <div class=

In part (c) we pick up the value of the <p>, selecting only the class attribute. The @ sign indicates attribute. The net is that we pick up the class attribute from <p>. If we started with <p class="FT") we will end with <div class="FT">

Finally, in part (d) we close off the attribute element we began in part (b).

Aggregating the Code Lines and Notes

You will remember from the earlier discussion that we want to aggregate all the code lines. We will do so in two steps. The first step is to pick up all the lines with the style "C1," "C2," or "C3" and mark them with the tag <codeline>. In the next chapter we'll see how these are aggregated into <code> blocks. The conversion to <codeline> is shown in lines 38–41:

```
38:       <!-- convert all code elements to one tagname -->
39:       <xsl:template match="p[@class='C1'] ¦ p[@class='C2'] ¦
          ➥p[@class='CX']">
40:          <codeline><xsl:apply-templates/></codeline>
41:       </xsl:template>
```

Here our match is against a pattern. We are looking for p elements that have the attribute class='c1' *or* that have the attribute class = 'c2' *or* class='c3'. If we match *any* of these, we write the <codeline> tag, and then call apply-templates to get their children (in this case, to get the text). We then close off with the </codeline> endtag, and on line 41 we close with the </xsl:template> endtag.

When we create the input DOM, we may come across the following lines in the XHTML from Chapter 3:

```
1166:      <p class="C2">
1167: 1: Function GetTheData() As Recordset
1168:      </p>
```

This creates a p element in the Document Object Model. The p element will have an attribute (class='c2') and it will have a single child: a text node whose value is 1: Function GetTheData() As Recordset.

Our style sheet will transform the P element into a code line element in the output file. The call to apply-templates will then recurse into the P element, finding the text() node. This will match the earlier pattern:

```
7:      <xsl:template match="text()"><xsl:value-of/></xsl:template>
```

which will cause the output DOM to create a text node with the same text (1: Function GetTheData() As Recordset) and assign that text node to the new code line element. When this is written out to the output document, the result will be:

```
<codeline>
   1: Function GetTheData() As Recordset
</codeline>
```

The exact same design pattern is applied to notes on lines 44–46.

```
44:      <xsl:template match="p[@class='NO'] ¦ p[@class='SB']">
45:          <noteline><xsl:apply-templates/></noteline>
46:      </xsl:template>
```

The only difference between this code and the code just considered is that here we are picking up code marked with either the "NO" class or the "SB" class. SB stands for sidebar and occasionally the editors format certain sidebars with that style rather than with NO.

Special Characters

Lines 49–51 handle the presence of special characters in the XHTML. You will remember from the previous chapter that we had special processing for certain characters. There are two types of characters of interest. One is smart quotes, which we tagged as char with this code:

```
s = Replace(s, Chr(146), "<char type=""smartApos""/>")
s = Replace(s, Chr(147), "<char type=""smartLQuote""/>")
s = Replace(s, Chr(148), "<char type=""smartRQuote""/>")
```

The other was Macmillan characters, such as the em-dash, which we tagged with this code:

```
s = Replace(s, "[em]", "<char type=""emSpace""/>")
s = Replace(s, "[md]", "<char type=""emDash""/>")
s = Replace(s, "[lb]", "<char type=""bullet""/>")
```

The XHTML file now has a number of char elements with an attribute of type, whose value tells us what kind of character they are. We'll just pass these along for now. To do so, we must create a `<char>` type in the output document and then assign to it the attribute found in the source document:

```
49:        <xsl:template match="char">
50:            <char><xsl:attribute name="type"><xsl:value-of
               ➡select="@type"/></xsl:attribute></char>
51:        </xsl:template>
```

Line 49 matches on these char elements. Let's break line 50 into four parts:

```
50a:           <char>
50b:       <xsl:attribute name="type">
50c:       <xsl:value-of select="@type"/>
50d:        </xsl:attribute></char>
```

In part (a) we write the `<char>` element to the output DOM. In part (b) we assign to that `<char>` element an attribute whose name is type. In (c) we give that new attribute a value, specifically the value obtained by calling value-of and selecting for the attribute type in the source element. Finally, in part (d) we close off the attribute we created in 50(b) and we close the new char element we created in 50a. On line 51, we close the template we began on line 49.

The next three lines pass along certain html elements (b, i, sub, sup, u, and br) but ignore any attributes they might have.

```
54:        <xsl:template match="b¦i¦sub¦sup¦u¦br">
55:            <xsl:element><xsl:apply-templates/></xsl:element>
56:        </xsl:template>
```

The logic is nearly identical, but the syntax is somewhat different. Because we can't know which element we're creating (it can be any of the six that match), we use xsl:element. This constructs an output element that by default is named with the tagname of the current element. Thus if we have matched a `<b>` tag, then xsl:element will construct a `<b>` tag in the output document.

We then call apply-templates to pick up any children of these nodes. If the source has

```
<b>This text in bold</b>
```

then the child of this b element is a text node with the text This text in bold.

Cleaning Up Nested Paragraph Markings

As indicated in the comments, when Word outputs to a Web page it scatters a series of <o:p> tags, which have no content. Nested <p> tags are very unusual and we have empirical evidence that this creates problems with rendering the output document (that is, we tried it and it looked goofy). So we take the nested <p> tags out with the code on lines 60 and 61.

```
60:        <xsl:template match="p//p">
61:        </xsl:template>
```

The double slash is a special XSL symbol meaning "any descendents." Thus you read this match, "find any descendents of p which are also p"—that is, find any nested p elements.

The action taken? None at all. We just close off the template. The net effect is that these are removed from the document.

XSL Script

It turns out that when Word outputs the file to HTML, Word creates a number of different span tags. A quick check of our Chapter 3 XHTML file reveals a few:

```
14:        <span style="mso-tab-count: 1">
49:        <span style="mso-spacerun: yes">
```

We'll also find lines with style="mso-bookmark" and style="font-family" or style="font-style" as well as the obscure style="layout-grid-mode". We want to take different actions on each of these, and the easiest way to do so is to parse out which style we're seeing within the span tags, and switch on that style.

On line 64 we match any element of type span with a style attribute:

```
65:        <xsl:template match="span[@style]">
```

The pattern matching only goes so far. To narrow down to the exact style we want to match, we resort to script.

In C++ or Java we would create a switch statement; in Visual Basic we would create a Select Case statement. In XSL we write xsl:choose:

```
66:        <xsl:choose>
```

Just as a C++ or Java `switch` statement is followed by `case` statements, and a VB `Select` statement is followed by `Case` statements, so an XSL `choose` statement is followed by a series of `xsl:when` statements. The first condition we'll work with is when the style is a tab.

```
68:                    <xsl:when expr="getStyleName(this) == 'mso-tab-count'">
69:                        <tab />
70:                    </xsl:when>
```

On line 68 the `when` will execute when the expression evaluates `true`. The expression is `"getStyleName(this) == 'mso-tab-count'"`.

`expr` is a boolean test for the `xsl:when` statement. If the test returns `true`, then the contents of the `when` (in this case shown on line 69) are put in the output. The result of `expr` proving `true` in this case is that a tab will be output. Note that the tab uses the self-closing endtag.

`GetStyleName` is not a standard XSL test. It is a function we've written in xsl:script. We pass in the current element as a parameter. `this` is a reserved word in XSL that is used to represent the current element.

Unlike HTML, XML has no capability to add script, but XSL does. You begin XSL script with the `xsl:script` tag, as shown on line 108. You then follow by declaring a CDATA section. CDATA is text that is not to be parsed by the XSL parser. We do this because it is possible that the script will include symbols such as `<` or `>`, which are reserved in XSL. By putting the script within a CDATA section, the parser will not try to translate these symbols.

CDATA sections begin with the character sequence `<![CDATA[` (as shown on line 109) and end with the sequence `]]>` (as shown on line 128).

The `GetStyleName` method is shown on lines 122–127:

```
122:    function getStyleName(me)
123:    {
124:        var styleArg = me.getAttribute("style");
125:        var p = styleArg.indexOf(':');
126:        return styleArg.substr(0, p);
127:    }
```

The element is passed in as a parameter. On line 124 we retrieve the attribute from the element by calling `getAttribute`, a method that can be called on any XML DOM element; passing in the name of the attribute we want to retrieve. We stash that in a local variable `styleArg`. We then find the colon in the attribute, and return everything before the colon. In the case that we've matched on

```
<span style="mso-tab-count: 1">
```

this will return `mso-tab-count`. We compare this returned value on line 68. In the event that we do have `mso-tab-count`, the expr will evaluate `true`, and the tab will be written to the output file. We close the `xsl:when` tag that we opened on line 68 with a closing tag on line 70.

On lines 74–76 we consider the case where we match `mso-spacerun`. The logic for matching the style is identical, but the action we take is somewhat different.

If the spacerun is matched on line 74, we output a `<spacerun>` tag on line 75. We then assign that spacerun tag an attribute using `<xsl:attribute name="len">`. As discussed earlier, this creates a tag in the output

```
<spacerun len=
```

We now need to fill in a value for that attribute `len`. As you'll remember, `xsl:attribute` will fill in as the value of the new attribute, whatever is between the `xsl:attribute` tag and its closing tag. In this case, what we find between these tags is

```
<xsl:eval>CountOccurrences(this.firstChild.nodeValue, '\xa0')</xsl:eval>
```

The `xsl:eval` tag will evaluate and return the value of whatever is between its opening and closing tags. In this case, what is between these tags is a call to our script function `CountOccurrences`, to which we pass two parameters: `this.firstChild.nodeValue` and `'\xa0'`.

The first parameter is the node value of the firstChild of the current element. Remember that the current element in this case is a span. The first child will be the text element, whose nodeValue will be the actual text. Thus, we've retrieved whatever is held in the span. It turns out that when Word creates these spans representing white space, it puts in a single space character and then a series of `a0` hexadecimal characters: one for each white space it is reserving. We simply want to count these `a0` characters.

`CountOccurences` is shown on lines 111–113.

```
111:    function CountOccurrences(s, c)
112:    {
113:        var n = 0;
114:        for(var i = 0; i < s.length; i++)
115:        {
116:            if (s.charAt(i) == c) n++;
117:        }
118:        return n;
119:    }
```

The string is represented by the parameter s; the character by the parameter c. The `for` loop increments n once for each occurrence of c found in the string s, and returns that value.

The net effect of the call to xsl:eval on line 75 is to assign that value, the number of occurences of a0 to the len attribute of the new spacerun tag. The rest of line 75 simply closes the eval, attributes, and spacerun tags.

In lines 79–81 we match mso-bookmark tags, and we ignore them. We do call apply-templates so that if there are elements within the bookmark (or text) we'll pick them up with our other match patterns.

```
79:                    <xsl:when expr="getStyleName(this) == 'mso-bookmark'">
80:                        <xsl:apply-templates />
81:                    </xsl:when>
```

The same logic is applied to font-family, font-style, and layout-grid-mode: All are ignored, as shown on lines 83–95.

```
83:                    <!-- we'll also ignore local font changes -->
84:                    <xsl:when expr="getStyleName(this) == 'font-family'">
85:                        <xsl:apply-templates />
86:                    </xsl:when>
87:
88:                    <xsl:when expr="getStyleName(this) == 'font-style'">
89:                        <xsl:apply-templates />
90:                    </xsl:when>
91:
92:                    <!-- can't even figure out what this is,
                       ➥so we'll ignore it -->
93:                    <xsl:when expr="getStyleName(this) ==
                       ➥ 'layout-grid-mode'">
94:                        <xsl:apply-templates />
95:                    </xsl:when>
```

Finally, we must ensure that there are no span styles that are slipping by without being noticed, so we create a catch for them similar to the catch we created for unknown HTML tag names.

On line 98 we invoke the xsl:otherwise. Just as C++ and Java have a default: case in their switch statements, and VB has an else: statement in its select case, XSL has otherwise. If we do not match any other mso- pattern, the otherwise will match. In that case, on line 99 we create an <unknown> tag with the attribute tag, whose value is span. We then assign a *second* attribute to our unknown tag, style, whose value is the mso- style.

```
98:                <xsl:otherwise>
99:                    <unknown>
100:                        <xsl:attribute name="tag">span</xsl:attribute>
101:                        <xsl:attribute name="val"> <xsl:eval>
                           ➥getStyleName(this) </xsl:eval> </xsl:attribute>
102:                        <xsl:apply-templates />
103:            </unknown>
```

Finally, on lines 104 and 105 we close off the `otherwise` and `choose` statements, and then close the `template` statement on line 106.

```
104:                </xsl:otherwise>
105:              </xsl:choose>
106:          </xsl:template>
```

Running XHTML to XML

We followed `control.asp` as far as line 130, where we invoked `transform`. That led us into our exploration of the transformation and the XSL style sheet. When the transformation is complete, we return to `control.asp`, as shown in Listing 4.8.

Listing 4.8   `Control.asp`

```
120:     Function XHTML2XML()
121:         'convert XHTML file to our canonical XML form
122:         dim oXSL, oH2X, xmlFN, fn0, dtdFN
123:
124:         set oXSL = Server.CreateObject("FromScratch.XSLTransform")
125:
126:         'convert xhtml to xml via a stylesheet
127:         oXSL.InputFile = dataPath & ".xhtml"
128:         oXSL.XSLFile = fso.BuildPath(codeDir, "WordXHTML2XML.xsl")
129:
130:         oXSL.Transform
131:
132:         'save output as .xml0
133:         xmlFN = dataPath & ".xml"
134:         fn0 = xmlFN & "0"
135:         oXSL.SaveOutputAsFile fn0
136:
137:         'we assume that the dtd is in the same
                ➥directory as the data
138:         dtdFN = "canon.dtd"
139:
140:         'now pipe the .xml0 to the VB component to
                ➥do the rest of the transformation
141:         set oH2X = Server.CreateObject("FromScratch.WordXHTML2XML")
142:         oH2X.Convert fn0, xmlFN, dtdFN
143:
144:         'and we no longer need the intermediate file
145:         fso.DeleteFile fn0
146:
147:         XHTML2XML = "Converted " & dataPath & ".xhtml" & " to " & xmlFN
148:     End Function
```

The output of the XSL transformation is stored in an XML file with the number 0 appended. Thus, if we were transforming Chap2, the interim output file would be `Chap2.xml0`.

This file, Chap2.xml0, serves as the input to the next phase of transformation, considered in the next chapter. At the completion of the second phase, the interim file is deleted, as shown on line 145.

The program does not pause between phases I and II. The phases follow on automatically; by the time the program reports its completion (which actually happens quite quickly) the interim file has been erased. If you'd like to examine the interim file, however, you may do so by commenting out line 145 so that it is not deleted:

```
145:          ' fso.DeleteFile fn0
```

Comparing the interim file with the final XML file can help you disentangle what work is done by the XSL transformation, and what work is done by the XML DOM manipulation considered next.

Next Steps

In the next chapter we'll examine the final steps of the transformation to our canonical form. To complete this transformation we'll manipulate the XML Document Object Model directly.

Chapter 5

Manipulating the Document Object Model

The result of the transformations shown in Chapter 4 is an intermediate file, on the way to our final canonical XML file. So far we've used XSL to transform the tags; what remains is to aggregate the sections into a hierarchy, and to aggregate the code listings and notes.

We will accomplish these tasks in two ways. First we will create the hierarchy of sections by walking the existing XML Document Object Model (DOM) and creating a new DOM for output. The new DOM will reflect the hierarchy of sections.

Second, we will manipulate that new DOM in place to aggregate the code and notes listings. By "in place," I mean that we'll manipulate the elements within the DOM itself rather than writing out the changed structure to a new output DOM.

If you want to reorganize your bookshelf there are two ways you can do so. In the first way, you build a new bookshelf, and then take books from the old and place them where you want them in the new. The alternative is to take books out off the shelf and then reinsert them back into the same shelf, but in a different arrangement.

Examining the Intermediate File

The intermediate files produced by XSLTransform are named chap?.xml0. For example, the intermediate file for Chapter 3 is Chap3.xml0. Let's take a look at an excerpt from that file, and get an idea of why it needs further work, as shown in Listing 5.1.

Listing 5.1   `Chapt3.xml0`

```
  0:  <?xml version="1.0"?>
  1:  <html>
  2:      <div class="HA">
  3:  (a)3
  4:          </div>
  5:      <div class="HB">
  6:  (b)Proof of concept
  7:          </div>
  8:      <div class="FT">
  9:  Enough theory! Before we go any further in thinking through
     ➥how we'll implement EmployeeNet, we need to take
     ➥a look at the implementation technology and get something working.
 10:          </div>170:      <div class="PD">
171:  ***Begin Note***
172:          </div>
173:      <noteline>
174:  Here are the steps for Visual InterDev. As explained in the
     ➥previous chapter, the exact details may be  different
     ➥on your computer or network, or if you are using different
     ➥Internet enabling technology.
175:      </noteline>
176:      <div class="PD">
177:  ***End Note***
982:  Listing 3.2
983:          </div>
984:      <codeline>
985:  1: Function GetTheData() As Recordset
986:          </codeline>
987:      <codeline>
988:  2:
989:          <spacerun len="4"/>
990:
991:  Dim rs As ADODB.Recordset
992:          </codeline>
993:      <codeline>
994:  3:
995:          <spacerun len="4"/>
996:
997:  Set rs = New Recordset
998:          </codeline>
999:      <codeline>
1000:  4:
1001:          <spacerun len="4"/>
1002:
1003:  Call rs.Open("select * from publishers", "dsn=pubs",
1004:          <spacerun len="1"/>
1005:
1006:  UID=sa; PWD=;")
1007:          </codeline>
1008:      <codeline>
1009:  5:
```

```
1010:            <spacerun len="4"/>
1011:
1012:  Set GetTheData = rs
1013:         </codeline>
1014:        <codeline>
1015:  6: End Function
1016:         </codeline>
1017:        <div class="FT">
1018:  Your screen should look like Figure 3.11, with the project
       ➥listed in the project window on the right, and the code
       ➥shown in the GetTheData method on the left.
1019:         </div>
```

I've cut out much of this listing to save space, and focused on three significant areas of concern. While this file is closer to our canonical form than was the XHTML file, it still does not match the requirements expressed in our DTD, and would not be valid in our application.

Analysis

On line 1 we see the xml element stating that this file is XML version 1. Remember that while this file is not valid (that is, it does not match our DTD) it is still well-formed (that is, it is still XML).

Line 2 shows that the root element is <html>, but it should be <book> as codified in our DTD. We'll fix that in our next transformation.

Note also that our DTD is not referenced in the intermediate file. The final XML file will have the following line:

```
1:  <!DOCTYPE book SYSTEM "canon.dtd">
```

When we make the transformation from the intermediate to the final document, we'll need to add this line.

The DOCTYPE element is optional in any XML document. If it does appear, it can only appear once, and it defines the DTD for that page. The DOCTYPE element is followed by the name of the document (in our case book) and then either the keyword PUBLIC or SYSTEM.

The PUBLIC keyword is followed by an identifier, which will be used by the parser to fetch the DTD from an internal or external repository. This is typically followed by a URL, so that if the parser cannot otherwise find the DTD using the identifier, it can use the URL.

In our case we use the keyword SYSTEM, which instructs the parser to go directly to the URL provided. We also provide the name of a file, which will be located in the same directory as the source document.

Examining the Intermediate File in Detail

Lines 3–7 of Listing 5.1 show that we have changed our A-level heading to a `<div>`, which is all for the good, but an examination of the DTD shows that we have decided that these headings must be placed within a `<section>`, which we've not yet accomplished.

Continuing with the intermediate file, on line 6 we see the B-level heading declared in a div. Again, no relationship yet exists in this XML file between the sections; they continue to reflect the linear format of the original document. Our goal for the next transformation is to establish a hierarchical set of relationships among the various sections.

Lines 173–175 show the noteline tag we created in the XSL transformation, but careful examination of the DTD reveals that these are to be contained within `<note>` `</note>` tags. Similarly, lines 984–1016 show a series of codeline tags, but again the DTD requires that these be bound by `<code></code>` tags. We'll fix all these problems in this round of transformations.

Creating Sections

Our task is to move the A-, B-, C-, and D-level headings into a hierarchical relationship within sections. If you were to read the existing intermediate file up into a DOMDocument it would be very flat. All of the A–D level headings would be immediately under the root element, as illustrated schematically in Figure 5.1.

Figure 5.1

The intermediate document is flat.

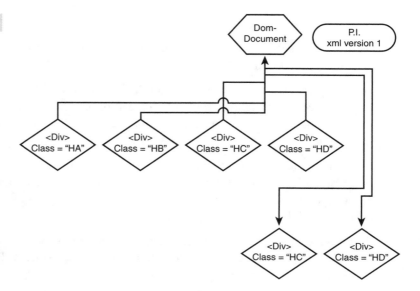

What we want, instead, is to transform these into sections which are hierarchically arranged, as illustrated in the schematic in Figure 5.2.

Figure 5.2

Hierarchical arrangement.

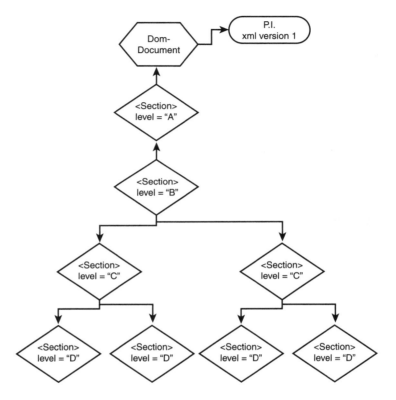

As you can see, this new DOMDocument will reflect the relationships among the sections as we naturally think about them: C sections containing D sections and being in turn contained by the B section.

The Definition of a Section

Take a look at the DTD definition of a section. Listing 5.2 is an excerpt from the DTD as it appeared in Listing 3.9 in Chapter 3:

Listing 5.2   `Canon.dtd`

```
14:      <!-- Sections have level and id attributes
         ↪and begin with a title.
15:      Sections may contain other sections -->
16:      <!ELEMENT section (title, (section ¦ div ¦ note ¦ code)*)>
17:      <!ATTLIST section
18:          level CDATA #REQUIRED
19:          id CDATA #REQUIRED>
```

We decided that every section would have exactly one title (that is, it must have a title and only one title). It also may have zero or more other sections, div, note, or code blocks within it. In addition, we see that sections *require* two attributes: a level and an ID, both of which are CDATA—that is unparsed text.

EXCURSION

PCData is parsed text: That is, it is simple text that the XML parser will examine for tags so that it might be modified appropriately. CDATA is unparsed text: We use this whenever we might have special symbols such as the less than (<) or greater than (>) symbol, which would confuse the parser.

Listing 5.3 illustrates how the A- and B-level headings will look in our final XML file, as well as how the <note> tags will be added.

Listing 5.3

```
<section level="A" id="3000">
<title>Chapter 3</title>
<section level="B" id="3001">
<title>Proof of concept</title>

<note>
    <noteline>
        Here are the steps for Visual InterDev. As explained in the
        ➥previous chapter, the exact details may be different on your computer
        ➥or network, or if you are using different Internet enabling
        ➥technology.
    </noteline>
</note>
```

XHTML to XML Transformation—Second Step

You will remember that our control.asp file created the html0 (intermediate) file. It will also launch the second stage in our transformation. Listing 5.4 shows the relevant excerpt from Control.asp.

Listing 5.4   Control.asp

```
120:      Function XHTML2XML()
121:          'convert XHTML file to our canonical XML form
122:          dim oXSL, oH2X, xmlFN, fn0, dtdFN
123:
124:          set oXSL = Server.CreateObject("FromScratch.XSLTransform")
125:
126:          'convert xhtml to xml via a stylesheet
```

```
127:          oXSL.InputFile = dataPath & ".xhtml"
128:          oXSL.XSLFile = fso.BuildPath(codeDir, "WordXHTML2XML.xsl")
129:
130:          oXSL.Transform
131:
132:          'save output as .xml0
133:          xmlFN = dataPath & ".xml"
134:          fn0 = xmlFN & "0"
135:          oXSL.SaveOutputAsFile fn0
136:
137:          'we assume that the dtd is in the same directory as the data
138:          dtdFN = "canon.dtd"
139:
140:          'now pipe the .xml0 to the VB component to do the rest of
              ➥the transformation
141:          set oH2X = Server.CreateObject("FromScratch.WordXHTML2XML")
142:          oH2X.Convert fn0, xmlFN, dtdFN
143:
144:          'and we no longer need the intermediate file
145:          fso.DeleteFile fn0
146:
147:          XHTML2XML = "Converted " & dataPath & ".xhtml" &
              ➥" to " & xmlFN
148:    End Function
```

Analysis

Lines 120–135 initiate the work that was shown in Chapter 4. The output file (in this case Chap3.xml0) is saved on line 135.

On line 138 the local variable dtdFN is set to canon.dtd—our Data Type Definition.

 Note

> To keep this code simple, we assume that canon.dtd is in the same directory with the data files. You can make this more flexible by using a URL to point to your DTD. If you want to use it as shown, be sure to copy the canon.dtd file (available on the CD) into the data directory (the directory with chap3.xml0 in it).

On line 141 we instantiate the ActiveX object WordXHTML2XML and on line 142 we call the Convert method on that object, passing in the intermediate filename (Chap3.xml0), the output filename (chap3.xml) and the dtd filename (canon.dtd).

We wrote this module in Visual Basic, as shown in Listing 5.5.

Listing 5.5   `WordXHTML2XML.cls`

```
0:  'Takes the result of the first phase of XHTML to XML conversion
    ➥(performed by the
1:  'stylesheet) and then continues the conversion process, doing
    ➥the "bundling"
2:  'of elements.
3:  Public Sub Convert(ByVal inPath As String, ByVal outPath As String,
    ➥Optional ByVal dtdPath As String = "")
4:      Dim inDom As New DOMDocument, outDom As DOMDocument,
        ➥outStr As String, dtdStr As String
5:
6:      'load the XML from the file into a DOM
7:      inDom.async = False
8:      inDom.Load inPath
9:
10:     'the first operation is collecting the A,B,C,... level sections
11:     Set outDom = CollectSections(inDom)
12:
13:     'next we collect all the contiguous <codeline> lines
        ➥into a <code> tag
14:     CollectContig outDom, "code"
15:
16:     'ditto for note lines
17:     CollectContig outDom, "note"
18:
19:     'get the results into a string
20:     outStr = outDom.xml
21:
22:     'if a DTD has been specified, insert the doctype and
        ➥external reference
23:     'seems like there should be a way to do it via the DOM,
        ➥but I can't figure it out
24:     If dtdPath <> "" Then
25:         dtdStr = "<!DOCTYPE book SYSTEM """ &
            ➥dtdPath & """>" & vbCrLf
26:         'we want to insert it right after the xml pi
27:         outStr = Replace(outStr, "?>" & vbCrLf, "?>" &
            ➥vbCrLf & dtdStr, , 1)
28:     End If
29:
30:     'and now we save the results into a file
31:     Open outPath For Output As #1
32:     Print #1, outStr
33:     Close #1
34: End Sub
```

Analysis

On line 3 we see the parameters passed in from the controlling asp file. On line 4 we create four local variables. The first two are DOMDocument objects.

The only XML object that you create directly is Dom Document. All other objects, such as elements, are created via methods of DOMDocument, as we'll see shortly.

On line 7 we set the async property of our input DOM to false. Doing so means that when we load this document, our program will wait for it to be fully loaded into memory before proceeding. Asynchronous loading is convenient when your program might be busy with other tasks, but in this case we're happy to wait.

On line 8 we load in the document, passing in the name of the file to load. The relationship between this file (Chap3.xml0) and the DOM in memory is more subtle than first appears.

The Object-Oriented Perspective

Every programmer understands the difference between a file on disk and a representation of that file in memory, but we still get tripped up in the subtleties of interacting with the DOM. Here's why: We're actually dealing with four entities, not two.

> Entity 1: The physical document on disk: A series of bytes stored by the operating system on permanent storage.
>
> Entity 2: The logical document as we might view it in an editor or a browser.
>
> Entity 3: The physical DOM—bytes in memory.
>
> Entity 4: The logical DOM—the elements and nodes in a hierarchy as described by the W3C recommendation.

Let's be clear, for the rest of the book I'm never talking about the physical bytes, either on disk or in memory. I'm concerned only with the logical entities.

Yes, of course the document and the DOM must ultimately come down to bytes, but why stop there? Bytes are really just epiphenomenona arising out of the momentary state of electrical circuits. In fact, electrical circuits are just a metaphor for the quantum state of indeterminate particles. What we care about is always the logical abstraction; the bytes are just an implementation mechanism.

The Document and the DOM

The relationship between the document and the DOM is complex and interesting. The Document Object Model is an object-oriented representation of the document. Every element in the document is represented by an object in the DOM. The relationship is reciprocal: The document is a linear representation of the DOM.

When we create a DOMDocument we can either populate it by adding elements as we need them, or by calling the new DOMDocument's load method and passing in an XML Document. In this latter case, the DOM springs forth fully formed like Athena from the head of Zeus; a direct object representation of the XML Document passed in. This is how we create our input DOMDocument, as shown on line 8.

```
8:      inDom.Load inPath
```

On line 9 we call `CollectSections`, passing in the new, fully loaded input DOM. The return value from this method call will be yet another new DOMDocument, which we'll assign to `outDom`.

Collecting Sections: Strategy

You will recall that in Figure 5.1 we showed a flat tree, with the A-, B-, C-, and D-level headers all connected to the root. Our strategy will be to walk through this tree, creating a new tree with the newly created sections in the correct position.

Remember that there are many other elements in the original tree as well. In fact, our schematic for Figure 5.1 would be more accurate (but still simplified) if it included elements for text, notes, code, and so forth.

Our strategy will be to walk the source DOM (created from the intermediate file), and examine each element. If it is a `<DIV>` element with a class = "H?", we'll create a new `<section>` element in the destination DOM (which we'll later save as our `.xml` file).

We'll use a local variable called `curParent`, which will initially point to the root element. We'll add our first section as a child of `curParent` (root), and then point `curParent` to that section.

We'll continue to walk the source DOMDocument, adding each element we find as a child of `curParent` (our first Section) until we hit a `<DIV>` element with a class = "H?". At that point we'll create a new section, make it a child of `curParent` and then change `curParent` to point to the new Section just added.

Once again we'll walk the source tree, now making every element we find a child of the current `curParent` (our second child).

We repeat this process until we've migrated every element in the source DOM to the destination DOM.

Collecting Sections: Implementation

We implement this strategy with the `CollectSections` method as shown in Listing 5.6.

Listing 5.6   `WordXHTML2XML.cls`

```
0:  'in Word, we just know when a section begins. What we want is
    ➥ the entire contents of
1:  'a given section (including all descendants) to be enclosed in
    ➥a <section> tag
2:
3:  'the approach is to walk thru all the elements, looking
    ➥for section headers
4:  'we create a new node to serve as the section element
5:  'as we encounter each new section head, we push or pop
    ➥ the current section element
6:  'based on the "level" of the section
7:
8:  'note that here we walk thru all the input and build up
    ➥a new output tree (vs. below)
9:  Private Function CollectSections(inDom As DOMDocument) As DOMDocument
10:     Dim i As Long, outDom As DOMDocument, children As IXMLDOMNodeList
11:     Dim c As IXMLDOMElement, className As String, curParent
    ➥As IXMLDOMElement
12:     Dim newC As IXMLDOMElement, omit As Boolean,
    ➥title As IXMLDOMElement, s As String
13:     Dim sectionId As Long, pi As IXMLDOMProcessingInstruction
14:
15:     'we're going to give each section a unique id,
    ➥but we need to know where to start
16:     'for these documents, the A head in each chapter is a chapter number,
    ➥so we'll multiply that by 1000
17:     'and use the result as the starting id
18:     Set c = inDom.selectSingleNode("//div[@class='HA']")
19:     sectionId = CLng(StripParenLetter(c.Text) & "000")
20:
21:     'create a new DOM for the output
22:     Set outDom = New DOMDocument
23:
24:     'add the XML processing instruction
25:     Set pi = outDom.createProcessingInstruction
    ➥("xml", "version='1.0'")
26:     outDom.appendChild pi
27:
28:     'and give it a top level element - which will also be where we
    ➥begin inserting the output
29:     Set curParent = outDom.createElement("book")
30:     curParent.setAttribute "level", "0"    'temp
31:     outDom.appendChild curParent
32:
```

continues

Listing 5.6 continued

```
33:     'we want to enumerate all the immediate children of the top-level
        ➥element (<html>) of the input
34:     Set children = inDom.documentElement.childNodes
35:
36:     For i = 0 To children.length - 1
37:         omit = False
38:         If children(i).nodeType = NODE_ELEMENT Then
39:             Set c = children(i)
40:             If c.nodeName = "div" Then
41:                 className = c.getAttribute("class")
42:                 If Left(className, 1) = "H" Then
43:                     'we have a new header - create an element to
                        ➥hold its sub-tree
44:                     Set newC = outDom.createElement("section")
45:                     newC.setAttribute "level", Right(className, 1)
46:                     newC.setAttribute "id", sectionId
47:                     sectionId = sectionId + 1
48:
49:                     'the current contents of this element will become
                        ➥the title of the section
50:                     Set title = outDom.createElement("title")
51:                     s = Trim(c.Text)
52:
53:                     'most of the headers contain "(x)" at the beginning -
                        ➥we can strip that
54:                     s = StripParenLetter(s)
55:
56:                     'A levels just give the chapter number -
                        ➥let's flesh that out
57:                     If className = "HA" Then s = "Chapter " & s
58:
59:                     'now insert the title element as a child of
                        ➥the section
60:                     title.Text = s
61:                     newC.appendChild title
62:
63:                     'what we do depends on the relative level to our
                        ➥current parent
64:                     If newC.getAttribute("level") > curParent.
                        ➥getAttribute("level") Then
65:                         'higher level, ie. at a greater depth in the
                            ➥tree, create and push a new level
66:                         curParent.appendChild newC
67:                     ElseIf newC.getAttribute("level") = curParent.
                        ➥getAttribute("level") Then
68:                         'this is a peer to the current parent
69:                         curParent.parentNode.appendChild newC
70:                     Else
71:                         'we are popping the tree
72:                         Do
73:                             Set curParent = curParent.parentNode
```

```
74:                                      'go until we find a peer
75:                                      If curParent.getAttribute("level") =
                                      ➥newC.getAttribute("level") Then Exit Do
76:                                  Loop
77:                                  'and we can insert the new element under
                                  ➥our parent
78:                                  curParent.parentNode.appendChild newC
79:                              End If
80:                              'now we want all new addtions to be children
                              ➥of newC
81:                              Set curParent = newC
82:                              'and we don't need to insert ourself
83:                              omit = True
84:                          End If
85:                      End If
86:              End If
87:
88:              'add this node to the output
89:              If Not omit Then curParent.appendChild c.cloneNode(True)
90:          Next
91:
92:          outDom.documentElement.removeAttribute "level"  'don't need it
          ➥any more
93:
94:          'return the newly constructed dom
95:          Set CollectSections = outDom
96:   End Function
```

Analysis

On line 9 we see the input DOMDocument passed in as a parameter, and we also see the declaration that the output of this function will be a DOMDocument. That output document is created on line 22.

Let's back up to line 18. Here the local variable c, which is declared on line 12 to be an IXMLDOMElement, is assigned the result of calling selectSingleNode on the input DOM. The method selectSingleNode takes a parameter: a pattern matching string. selectSingleNode returns a single node, which matches the pattern.

The pattern is "//div[@class='HA']" This pattern breaks down into four parts:

Part 1: //

Part 2: div

Part 3: [@class=]

Part 4: 'HA'

There are two ways to indicate searching for descendents. A single slash (/) indicates "the immediate children of the current node," and a double slash (//) indicates "all descendents of the current node." In the case we're considering, we are looking for all descendents of the current (root) node.

Part 2 is the element type to look for, in our case div. Thus we will look for all div elements in the entire document.

Part 3 indicates that we want to match only those div elements which have a specific attribute (the at sign [@] indicates attribute), and Part 4 tells us that the attribute we're looking for is 'HA'.

The net result is that we match any <div> tag where the attribute is class='HA' and assign it to the variable c. Examination of the input document will find only one such element.

Here is what that element looks like in the input document, Chap3.xml0:

```
 8:      <div class="HA">
 9:   (a)3
10:    </div>
```

As a result of this work, c is an element <div> with an attribute class whose value is HA. C also has a child text element whose value is (a)3.

Note selectSingleNode returns a node. We implicitly down-cast this to an element by assigning it to c, which is defined not as a Node but as an Element (specifically an IXMLDOMElement). Nodes are more general than elements; to a C++ or Java programmer an element is a "derived" type of node, that is, it is a special kind of Node. Only elements can have attributes, other nodes cannot.

Creating the Section ID

We continue with line 19, which is also somewhat complex.

```
19:      sectionId = CLng(StripParenLetter(c.Text) & "000")
```

Here we extract the Text property from our element, that is (a)3 and pass it to StripParenLetter, shown in Listing 5.7

Listing 5.7 WordXHTML2XML.cls

```
0:  Private Function StripParenLetter(ByVal s As String) As String
1:      'remove leading "(x)"
2:      If Left(s, 1) = "(" And Mid(s, 3, 1) = ")" Then s = Mid(s, 4)
3:      StripParenLetter = s
4:  End Function
```

The result is to return the string "3", the Chapter number. We append the string "000" to the "3" and then pass that to CLng, which turns it into the number 3000. This value is assigned to sectionID.

Each chapter will be numbered accordingly. Thus, Chapter 4 will have sections numbered in the range 4,000 to 4,999. We take it as given that no chapter will have more than 999 sections (in fact, no chapter will have more than 100 sections). Crude, but effective.

Creating a Processing Instruction

We now come back to line 22 where the output DOMDocument is created. This output document will be in XML, and every XML document requires a processing instruction at the very top of the file, such as the following:

```
<?xml version="1.0"?>
```

Our first task is to create that processing instruction, which we do on line 25. Note the declaration of pi on line 13; it is an IXMLDomProcessingInstruction.

Processing Instructions are created by calling createProcessingInstruction() on the DOMDocument object, passing in two parameters: the target and the data. The target becomes the nodename (xml) for the PI and the data becomes the nodevalue ("version=1.0").

Now that we have a processing instruction, we append it to the output DOMDocument on line 26. This adds the processing instruction to the DOMDocument's childNodes collection. DOMDocument, like every element, has a collection of child nodes; its first such child will now be this processing instruction.

Creating the Hierarchy

We are now ready to make the implicit relationship among the sections in the input document into explicit relationships in the output document. We'll do this by creating a B-level section as a child element of the A-level tag, and then creating a C-level section as children of the B-level. Finally, we'll create d-level sections as children of the C-level sections.

To accomplish all of this, we must keep track of where we are in the document. When we come across a D-level section we must decide where it fits in the new hierarchy. If the current element is a C-level section, then the new D-level will be its child. If the current element is a D-level, however, then the new D-level will be a sibling and must be inserted as a child of the current element's parent. (Your sister is your parent's child.)

Finally, if the current element is an E-level section, then the new D-level section will be its aunt and must be inserted as a child of the current element's grandparent!

Creating the Top Level Element

According to our DTD, the top level element in our document will be <book>. We start by creating that element on line 29, by calling createElement on the output DOMDocument.

```
29:     Set curParent = outDom.createElement("book")
```

createElement takes one parameter (the element name) and returns the newly created element. We pass in the name for the element (book) and assign the resulting element to curParent.

To keep track of the relationships, we'll assign each element an attribute for its "level". The root element (book) will not need a level-designation when we are done, but while we are creating the tree it is convenient for it to have the level 0, indicating top-most. On line 30 we give it the attribute level, with a value 0. On line 31 we append the root element to our new output DOMDocument. Our DOMDocument now looks like Figure 5.3.

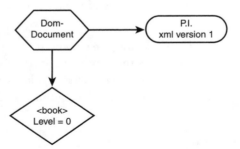

We are now ready to walk the input DOMDocument (which represents Chap3.xml0), creating new elements in the output DOMDocument as we go.

Every DOMDocument has a property documentElement, which is the root node in the document. On line 34 we access that node, which in the case of the input DOM is HTML.

```
34:     Set children = inDom.documentElement.childNodes
```

We then access the childNodes property of that root node, which returns a collection of all the immediate children of HTML. It turns out that in the input document, *all* the sections are immediate children of HTML. Remember, the input document has no hierarchical structure; that is exactly what we're creating now.

The net effect is that the collection `children` has all the elements and text nodes from the input document. The number of such elements is returned by the `length` property. We use that number in our `for` loop on line 36, which will allow us to iterate through each element in the collection.

```
36:      For i = 0 To children.length - 1
```

On line 37 we initialize the local variable `omit` to false. We'll return to the meaning of this variable in just a moment.

The `childNodes` collection will contain two types of nodes: elements and text. On line 38 we test the current child's nodeType to see if it is an element. If so, we enter the code on line 39, where we assign that node to `c`, which you'll remember we declared to be an `IXMLDOMElement`. Once again, we've implicitly downcast this node to an element.

```
38:          If children(i).nodeType = NODE_ELEMENT Then
39:              Set c = children(i)
```

On line 40 we test to see if the element we have is a `<div>`. All of the sections are marked as divs, so they are the only elements we care about.

If we do have a `div` element, on line 41 we get its class attribute, and assign the value to the local string variable `className`. On line 42 we check to see if the first letter of the `className` attribute is "H", indicating that we do have a header. If so, we're finally ready to do some work, as we now know we have a section header.

```
40:              If c.nodeName = "div" Then
41:                  className = c.getAttribute("class")
42:                  If Left(className, 1) = "H" Then
```

On line 44 we create a new element of type `section`. On line 45 we assign to that new element an attribute, `level`, whose value is whatever came after the H in the original `<div>` element. Thus, if the current input element is `HC` then we have now created a `section` element with the attribute level = "C". We also add a second attribute, `id`, which we give the value of `sectionID`, which you'll remember we initialized to 3000 for Chapter 3. On line 47 we increment the value of `sectionID`.

```
44:                      Set newC = outDom.createElement("section")
45:                      newC.setAttribute "level", Right(className, 1)
46:                      newC.setAttribute "id", sectionId
47:                      sectionId = sectionId + 1
```

Every section must have a title, according to our DTD. We create a new element of type `title` and assign it to the local `IXMLDOMElement` variable `title`.

Our next task is to assign a value to the new title we just created. We'll base the new title on the input document's title, but with a few modifications. If the input title is, for example, `(C) Which Technology`, we'll strip off the `(c)` and render the new title `Which Technology`.

The one exception to this is the (A) level header, which in the input file has nothing but the chapter number, for example, (A)3. We'll take the opportunity to spell this out in our output document, stripping off the (A) and adding the word "Chapter" to produce Chapter 3.

On line 51 we trim the input title, removing all extra leading and trailing white space. On line 54 we pass the string to StripParenLetter, which removes the (A). On line 57 we flesh out the chapter title, and on line 60 we set the new title's text to the string we've now built.

```
50:                    Set title = outDom.createElement("title")
51:                    s = Trim(c.Text)
52:
53:                    'most of the headers contain "(x)" at the
                       ➥beginning - we can strip that
54:                    s = StripParenLetter(s)
55:
56:                    'A levels just give the chapter number -
                       ➥let's flesh that out
57:                    If className = "HA" Then s = "Chapter " & s
58:
59:                    'now insert the title element as a child of
                       ➥the section
60:                    title.Text = s
```

The title is now ready to go and we append it to newC. We now have a <section>, all ready to be added to the output DOMDocument. In this first case, the new section looks like Figure 5.4.

Figure 5.4

The new section.

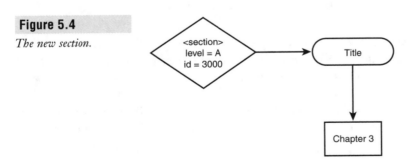

But where do we insert it? On line 64 we get the level attribute from our new section and we compare it with the level in the current parent.

```
64:                    If newC.getAttribute("level") >
                       ➥curParent.getAttribute("level") Then
```

You see here why we provided a (temporary) level to the root node <book>. We compare the new element's level (A) with the root element's level (0) and discover that this new element should be a child of the root. The `if` statement on line 64 thus evaluates `true` and we append the `newChild` to the current parent (the root).

Our tree now looks like Figure 5.5.

Figure 5.5

After appending the `newChild`.

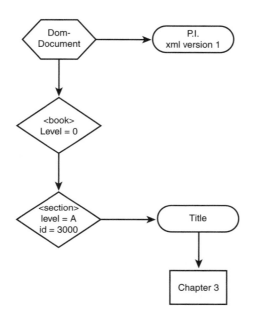

With the new element added, we drop down to line 81, and set the local variable `curParent` to point to the new element (the one we just added). We then set the flag `omit` to `true` so that this element won't be added again. This causes us to fall through to the `Next` statement on line 90, popping us up to the top of the `for` loop on line 36.

After five sections have been added, the output DOMDocument looks like the tree shown in Figure 5.6.

Here we are beginning to see a containment hierarchy. The relationship among the classes is expressed well with a tree drawing, but a containment drawing as shown in Figure 5.7 really drives the point home.

Section D is now a child of and *contained by* Section C. This is exactly the relationship we were striving for. A diagram of boxes within boxes becomes unwieldy, and it is more convenient to think in terms of a tree, and so Figure 5.6 is a more common way of picturing these relationships. The problem with a tree, however, is that it is easy to lose sight of the containment implicit in the hierarchy.

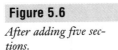

Figure 5.6

After adding five sections.

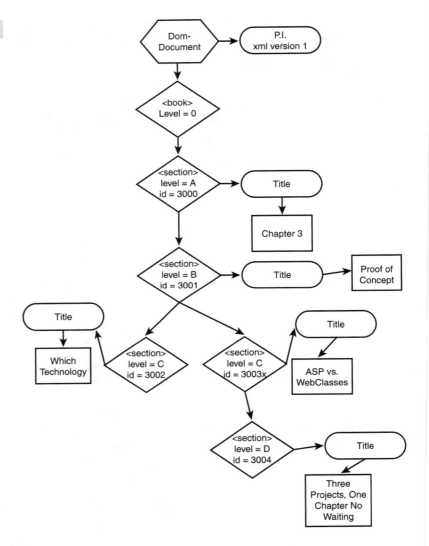

Locating Elements

Every element in our output DOM Document can be neatly and precisely identified in terms of its relationship to other documents. Just as I am the second son of the fourth child of my grandfather, so the element "Three Projects, One Chapter, No Waiting" is the first child of the second child of the B-level heading "Chapter 3".

When this tree is complete, it will directly and explicitly reflect the relationships among the "articles" or sections of the book. From this diagram we can (and will!) easily build a table of contents, and we'll be able to navigate among the sections in a logically consistent and intuitive manner.

Figure 5.7

Containment.

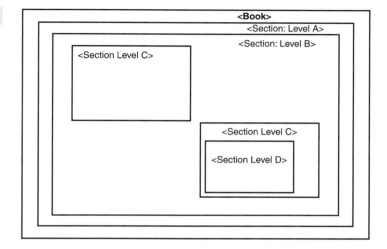

Siblings and Aunts

We considered the case of inserting a C-level element under a B-Level element on line 64. How did we mange to insert the sibling C-level element shown in the diagram? In this case the new element's level would be exactly equal to the "curParent's" level. That is, after we inserted the first C-level element it became the current parent. When the second C-level element came along the `if` statement on line 67 would evaluate true.

```
67:    ElseIf newC.getAttribute("level") =
       ➥curParent.getAttribute("level") Then
```

In this case, on line 69 we retrieve the parent node to the `curParent` element (that is, we get the B-level element) and we append the new element (our second C-level) to it, adding a second child to its collection of children.

```
69:                    curParent.parentNode.appendChild newC
```

When we add the D-level to that second C-level we're back in the first condition shown on line 64. That new D-level element becomes the `curParent`. What happens when we then come across a C-level? Now it is time to pop our way up the tree, from D all the way back up to B so that we can add the C-level. This code is shown on lines 72–76.

```
72:    Do
73:       Set curParent = curParent.parentNode
74:       'go until we find a peer
75:       If curParent.getAttribute("level") =
          ➥newC.getAttribute("level") Then Exit Do
76:    Loop
```

We continue to compare the `curParent` to the new element. If the new element is of a higher level then we set the `curParent` to the parent of the `curParent`. That is, if we're pointing to a D and the new element is, say a C, we set `curParent` to the parent of the D (the C element which is its parent). We continue to do this until we're sufficiently high in the tree to be able to add the new node.

You will remember that the very first `if` statement, on line 38, checks to see if we are working with an element. If that fails, we fall through to line 89. Omit was set to `false` initially, and it is only set to `true` within the `if` statements, so again, if the current node is not an element, here we are on line 89 and omit is `false`. In that case, we want to create a copy of the current node from the input document and append it to the current element in the output document. The Boolean `true` creates a "deep" copy, copying the element and all its children and descendents.

```
89:          If Not omit Then curParent.appendChild c.cloneNode(True)
```

When the loop ends and we fall to line 92 we've added all the elements to the new output DOMDocument. We can now remove the attribute "level" from our root node. We are done with aggregating the sections, and we can return the output DOMDocument to the ASP page that called. This returns us to line 11 of Listing 5.5:

```
11:          Set outDom = CollectSections(inDom)
```

The next command in the `Convert` method is on line 14:

```
14:          CollectContig outDom, "code"
```

This launches the second half of our effort, to aggregate the contiguous `<codeline>` entries into `<code></code>` blocks.

Code Blocks

The XSL transformation marked all of the code lines with the `<codeline></codeline>` tag, as shown in Listing 5.1. Our task now is to distinguish the blocks of code and mark them with `<code></code>` tags. Our goal is to be able to cut, copy, paste, mail, display, and otherwise manipulate these blocks of code.

Before examining the code in detail, let's review the overall approach. We start with each codeline as an individual element, as illustrated schematically in Figure 5.8.

Here is an interesting fact about these elements that we can take advantage of: Each element knows its parent and its previous sibling. Thus, the codeline A3 knows that its parent is Section ID 3002, and that its previous sibling is Codeline A2. Similarly, Codeline A5 knows that its previous sibling is a Text element.

Figure 5.8

Each codeline as an element.

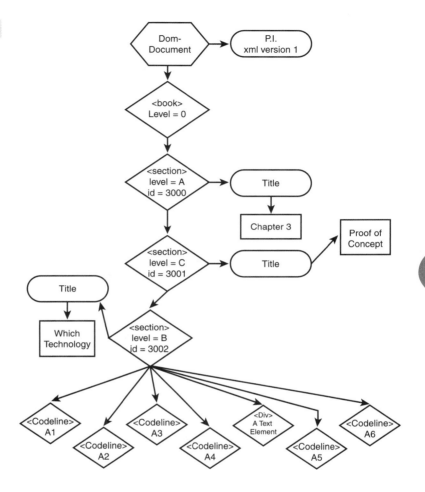

We can thus state that a new block of code begins with a codeline whose previous sibling is *not* a codeline element. For example, Codeline A5 begins a new block, as does Codeline A1.

Our goal, when we are done with the next transformation, is to create a structure that looks more like Figure 5.9.

The obvious, straightforward way to accomplish this would be to insert a code element into the structure, and then simply move all the codelines under it. Unfortunately, this won't work. If we move Codeline A1 under our new code element, then when we ask Codeline A2 for its previous sibling we'll get the wrong answer (Codeline A1 will no longer be there!).

Figure 5.9

Our target structure.

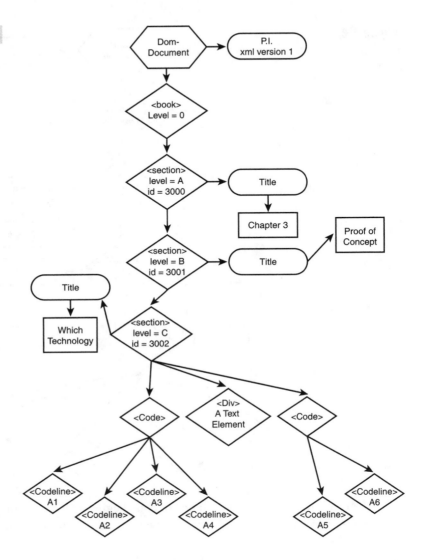

What we must do then is to *copy* Codeline A1 under the new Code element, then ask A2 for its previous sibling (which will still be A1). Now that we know A2 is part of the same code block, we can delete the original A1, so that it appears *only* as a child of the new code element.

To accomplish this, we'll start by creating a collection of every node tagged as a `codeline`.

We can now work our way through that collection looking for codeline elements whose previous sibling is not a codeline. We'll then create a code element and then copy the codeline elements to be children of that new code element, deleting them as we move along to later siblings.

Listing 5.8 shows the CollectContig method.

Listing 5.8   WordXHTML2XML.cls

```
 0:  'Combine all the contiguous elements into one parent element
 1:  'we do this for a few different kinds of things,
     ➥so we make the code generic
 2:  'the tag name for the individual elements is, e.g. <codeline>
     ➥while the parent element is <code>
 3:  'in this case we pass "code" as elName
 4:
 5:  'here we manipulate the tree in place (vs. above)
 6:  Private Sub CollectContig(ByRef inDom As DOMDocument,
     ➥elName As String)
 7:      Dim baseElems As IXMLDOMNodeList, c As IXMLDOMNode
 8:      Dim prevEl As IXMLDOMElement, lastIndex As Long,
         ➥curParent As IXMLDOMElement
 9:
10:      'get a collection of all xxxline elements
11:      Set baseElems = inDom.getElementsByTagName(elName & "line")
12:      For Each c In baseElems
13:          'is this element the next sibling of the previous one?
14:          If Not c.previousSibling Is prevEl Then
15:              'not contiguous - create new parent
16:              Set curParent = inDom.createElement(elName)
17:              'and insert it as a sibling of the element we are
                 ➥looking at
18:              'that puts it in the right place - and it is inserted
                 ➥before, so we don't interfere
19:              'with the later siblings
20:              c.parentNode.insertBefore curParent, c
21:          End If
22:
23:          'put a copy of the current element as a child of the
             ➥current parent
24:          'it has to be a copy, since we still have to check to
             ➥see if the next element
25:          'is a next sibling
26:          curParent.appendChild c.cloneNode(True)
27:
28:          'we're now done with the previous element, so delete it
29:          If Not prevEl Is Nothing Then prevEl.parentNode.removeChild
             ➥prevEl
30:
31:          'and keep a pointer to the current element for checking
             ➥the next one
```

continues

Listing 5.8   continued

```
32:          Set prevEl = c
33:      Next
34:
35:      'delete the last prevEl, if any
36:      If Not prevEl Is Nothing Then prevEl.parentNode.removeChild
         ➥prevEl
37:
38:  End Sub
```

Two parameters are passed into the `CollectContig` method. The first is the DOMDocument. It is important to note that the DOMDocument passed in here is the *output* DOMDocument created by `CollectSections`.

While the previous method, `CollectSections`, worked by creating a new output DOMDocument, this method, `collectContig`, works by manipulating the elements of the DOMDocument *in place*. To return to our earlier analogy, here we are shuffling the books within the shelves of a bookcase, rather than moving them to a new bookcase.

Because we are going to do nearly the same work to the note sections, we've made this code polymorphic: That is, we'll use the same function for both. We'll distinguish which we're working on by the parameter. Thus, the second parameter passed in to this method is the element name, in this case "code." (The second time through, we'll pass in "note.")

On line 11, we append the string "line" to this parameter, creating "Codeline" (or "Noteline".) This new string is passed as a parameter to `getElementsByTagName`, which will return a list of Nodes with the name "codeLine".

That collection is stored in `baseElems`. The local variable c acts as an iterator on this collection; each time through the `for` loop on line 12 c is assigned to the next node in the `baseElems` collection.

On line 14 we compare the previous sibling of the current element with a local variable `prevEl`. This `if` statement says, "compare the current node's `previousSibling` with the element we just finished with. Are they the same? If not, this is a new block of codelines."

If this *is* a new block, then we create a `<code>` element on line 16 and assign it to the variable `curParent`.

Let's pretend that the first time through this loop, c refers to codeline A1 from Figure 5.6. `PrevEl` is empty, so we know A1 begins a new Code block.

We will insert this new code element into the hierarchy as a sibling to the codeline elements. We will then do the work to move the codeline elements down a level, to be children of this new code element.

Inserting the New Element

We want to insert this new code element at the same position in our hierarchy as the code line currently resides. To do this, we'll make the new code element a child of A1's parent. We do so on line 20. We tell the parent of c to insert a new child curParent (which is the new code element) before the child c.

At this point we have inserted the new code element (curParent) as a sibling of c; we now need to move c (and all the subsequent code lines) to be children of the new code element, curParent.

To accomplish this we *clone* c and append the new copy as a child of curParent. We now have c as a child and also as a sibling of curParent, as shown in Figure 5.10.

Figure 5.10

c is now a child and a sibling of curParent.

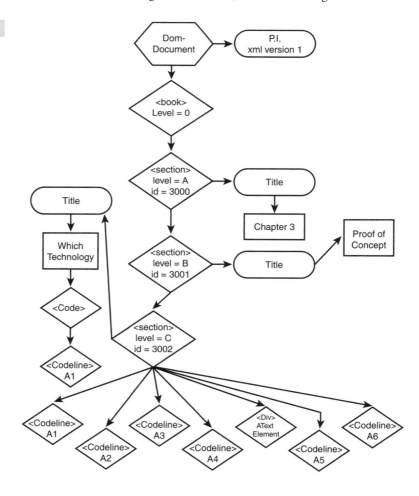

At this point `prevEl` has no value, so the `then` clause on line 29 is skipped. Now that A1 is both a child and a sibling of `curParent`, we can set `prevEl` to `c` (A1), as shown on line 32.

We are ready to iterate through the loop a second time. This time `c` is set to A2. The `if` statement on line 14 fails. A2's previous sibling is A1. Since `prevEl` is also A1 (we set it on line 32 in the previous iteration) these values are equal and so the `if` statement is skipped.

We thus skip down to line 26 and make a clone of A2 and add it as a child of the `<code>` element. Now the code element has two children, both of whom are also siblings of the code element.

On line 29 we examine `prevEl`, which has codeline A1. We tell its parentNode to remove Child `prevEl`. That removes A1 from its original position and now it exists in the DOM *only* as a child of the new Code element. The structure now looks like Figure 5.11.

We'll add A3 and A4 in the same way. Each time we add a new child to `<code>` we eliminate the previous sibling node. Thus when we added A2 we were able to eliminate the original A2. When we add A3 as a child of the code element, we will be ready to eliminate the old A2.

When we come to A5 we *will* have a new code element to add; `prevEl` will be the Text element and that will *not* be A5's previous Sibling (A4).

A5 and A6 will be added as children of the second new `Code` element. The tree will be almost right, except that A6 will still be attached to its old parent. We clean that up on line 36.

When we are done, each of the codeline elements has migrated to its new position, under a code element as shown in Figure 5.7 (repeated for emphasis).

Figure 5.11

A1 as a child of the new element.

5

Figure 5.7

Containment.

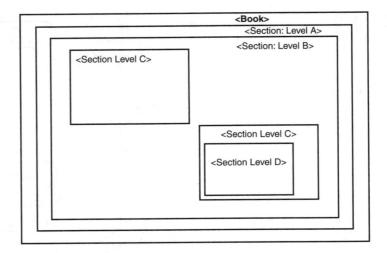

Notelines

This returns us to the `Convert()` method, as shown earlier in Listing 5.5.

```
13:     'next we collect all the contiguous <codeline> lines into a <code> tag
14:     CollectContig outDom, "code"
15:
16:     'ditto for note lines
17:     CollectContig outDom, "note"
```

Having completed our call to `CollectContig` on line 14, we are now ready to call the same method, `CollectContig` on line 17, this time passing in the string "note" rather than "code".

The exact same logic will apply to the noteline entries in the DOM as we've applied to the codeline entries. I won't walk you through it in excruciating detail, as there is no difference whatsoever.

When we are done, we return to line 20 of Listing 5.5 to complete the `Convert()` method, shown here in Listing 5.9.

Listing 5.9   `WordXHTML2XML.cls`

```
20:     outStr = outDom.xml
21:
22:     'if a DTD has been specified, insert the doctype and
        ↪external reference
23:     'seems like there should be a way to do it via the DOM,
        ↪but I can't figure it out
24:     If dtdPath <> "" Then
25:         dtdStr = "<!DOCTYPE book SYSTEM """ & dtdPath &
```

```
                ➥ """>" & vbCrLf
26:              'we want to insert it right after the xml pi
27:              outStr = Replace(outStr, "?>" & vbCrLf, "?>" &
                ➥ vbCrLf & dtdStr, , 1)
28:        End If
29:
30:        'and now we save the results into a file
31:        Open outPath For Output As #1
32:        Print #1, outStr
33:        Close #1
34:  End Sub
```

The next command in `Convert()` is to assign to the local string variable `outStr` the contents of the DOM written out as a Document. We *could* walk the tree, creating text for the output `xml` file for each element we encounter, but there is an easier way.

Instead of walking the DOM ourselves, we can access the `XML` property of the output DOMDocument. By accessing this single property, `msxml` turns our entire structure back to a string so that we can store it as a file.

While this is exposed a property, the object is really linearizing the hierarchy to disk, expressed as a string.

We do not, however, have a `DOCTYPE` element for our DTD. You would think that we could simply call `createDocTypeElement` on the document, but you'd be wrong. For some reason this is not yet available in the XML recommendation.

Our solution is an ugly hack. We access the `XML` property to write the entire file out to a string. Then, on line 24 we manually manipulate that string to insert our `DOCTYPE` element immediately after the XML Programming Instruction. The result is that the output XML document will begin with

```
<?xml version="1.0"?>
<!DOCTYPE book SYSTEM "canon.dtd">
```

At this point our string is complete but it still isn't a file on disk. On line 31 we open a file, on line 32 we write out the XML document string, and on 33 we close that file. This ends the `Convert()` subroutine, and returns us to `control.asp`, the last few lines of which are shown in Listing 5.10.

Listing 5.10 `Control.asp`

```
142:            oH2X.Convert fn0, xmlFN, dtdFN
143:
144:            'and we no longer need the intermediate file
145:            fso.DeleteFile fn0
146:
147:            XHTML2XML = "Converted " & dataPath &
                ➥ ".xhtml" & " to " & xmlFN
148:       End Function
```

We have now returned from Convert on line 142, and we no longer need the intermediate file, which we delete on line 145. Finally, on line 147 we return a success message to the browser.

Next Steps

Our job of converting our Word file to canonical XML is now, finally, complete. Our document now conforms to the canonical DTD.

This process can be repeated for each of the chapters from the book to build up a suite of XML files that we will begin to manipulate in the coming chapters.

Chapter 6

Storing, Rendering, and Displaying The Stories

We have transformed our Word document first to HTML, then to XHTML and now, after a few rounds of manipulation, into our canonical XML, conforming with our DTD.

Now that we have the data in the form we want, what shall we do with it? At this point there are a number of options, and we'll consider a few of them for the remainder of the book.

One task is to divide the book into stories, which we've arbitrarily defined as a D-level heading with its content, or a C-level heading with *its* content. That is, if a C heading contains three D headings, then we have four stories: the C content up to the first D heading, and then each of the three D headings.

While the task of splitting book chapters into stories may appear arbitrary, it is closely related to the more common task of breaking stories out of newsletters, newspapers, directories, and so forth.

In coming chapters we'll explore rendering the XML document in various formats, including high-level browsers (for example, IE 5) and also low-level browsers (for example, Netscape 3) or to print, PDF, and so forth. We will also create a collapsible Table of Contents that we can then use to find stories quickly.

For now, we'll concentrate on splitting the chapters into stories, the atomic units of information that we will then store in a database and display on demand.

Finding Stories from the Inside Out

We will start with the Document Object Model we just built in Chapter 5, and we'll pull it apart, storing the individual stories as we go.

The structure of these documents is fairly complex, but I've drawn a schematic of it shown in Figure 6.1

Figure 6.1

Schematic of document structure.

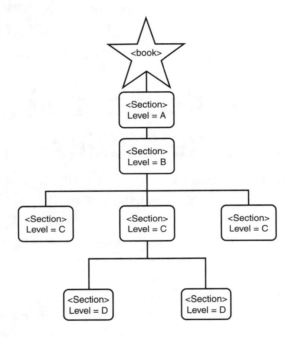

This simplified representation of the Document Object Model shows our root node, <book> at the top, with a single child, a section. Of course, this A-level section has a child title, but we've left that out of the drawing to keep things simple. The A-level section has a B-level child, which in turn has a number of C-level sections as children. The C-level sections will have a number of children, including a title, text, and possibly notes and code. The C-level sections may also contain D-level sections, which in their own turn may have notes, Geek Speak, code, and text as children.

Start with the D-Level Stories

The specification states that the D-level story includes all its contained elements. The C-level story also contains all of *its* elements, but we do not want the D-level stories to appear within the C-level stories.

Thus, if the middle C-level section in Figure 6.1 is "ASP Vs. WebClasses" and it contains text, notes, code, and two D-level sections, we want the D-level sections to be broken out into their own stories.

The trick to making this work is to start from the bottom, or innermost stories: the D-level. We'll move each D-level (and all its children) out of the DOM and into the database. When we then get to the C-level stories, their contained D-level sections will no longer be there, and we can take everything else in the C-level section with impunity.

Implementing Persistence

The code to accomplish this is surprisingly simple. We start, as always in our ASP file `control.asp`. We've looked at this file in earlier chapters, and so I'll show only the relevant function in Listing 6.1.

Listing 6.1   `Control.asp`

```
150:     Function SplitStories()
151:         dim res, oSplit
152:
153:         set oSplit = Server.CreateObject
         ➥("FromScratch.SplitStories")
154:
155:         res = oSplit.SplitStories(dataPath & ".xml", DSN,
         ➥DBUser, DBPass)
156:
157:         SplitStories = "Split " & dataPath & ".xml into " &
         ➥res & " stories"
158:     End Function
```

Once again we begin by instantiating an ActiveX object; this time `FromScratch.SplitStories`. We call the object's `SplitStories` method, passing in the file we want to split.

Note   The script function (`SplitStories`), the object (`FromScratch.SplitStories`), and the object's method (`SplitStories`) all have the same name. This is not a problem; which one is intended is determined by context.

You'll remember that in the user interface you are asked to fill in the Base filename (for example, `Chap3`) which we add to the directory to create the following datapath:

```
dataPath = fso.BuildPath(dataDir, baseName)
```

We now add the extension .xml to create, for example Chap3.xml. We pass this file-name to SplitStories as its only parameter.

Listing 6.2 shows the SplitStories method.

Listing 6.2   `SplitStories.cls`

```
0:
1:  'Takes a path to an XML file in our canonical format and splits
    ➥the file up into "stories"
2:  'A story is defined as the contents of an A-D section, NOT
    ➥including any descendent sections
3:  'The resulting stories are stored in the database
4:  Public Function SplitStories(ByVal xmlPath As String, ByVal DSN
    ➥As String, ByVal DBUser As String, ByVal DBPass As String) As Long
5:      Dim all As New DOMDocument, i As Long,
        ➥sections As IXMLDOMNodeList
6:      Dim c As IXMLDOMElement, level As String, curLev As String,
        ➥curLevIndex As Integer
7:      Dim numStories As Long, storyId As Long
8:
9:      numStories = 0
10:
11:     'open the database so we can store the stories
12:     DBConn.open DSN, DBUser, DBPass
13:
14:     'load the XML up into a DOM
15:     all.async = False
16:     all.Load (xmlPath)
17:
18:     'we begin by looking for all the D sections, then C, etc.
19:     'for each of these, we extract that section's sub-tree
        ➥from the overall document,
20:     'create a new XML fragment from it, and store that
        ➥in the database
21:     For curLevIndex = 3 To 0 Step -1
22:         'this will first do D, then C, B, A
23:         curLev = Chr(Asc("A") + curLevIndex)
24:
25:         'Create a collection of all sections at this level
26:         Set sections = all.selectNodes("//section[@level = """ &
            ➥curLev & """]")
27:
28:         'we step thru the collection backwards, so that our removals
            ➥don't upset the indexing
29:         For i = sections.length - 1 To 0 Step -1
30:             StoreStory sections(i)
31:             numStories = numStories + 1
32:         Next
33:     Next
34:
35:     DBConn.Close
```

```
36:
37:     SplitStories = numStories    'return number of stories
38: End Function
```

On line 4 we receive a single parameter: the path to the xml file. A number of local variables are declared, and on line 9 numStories is initialized to zero; this will count the stories found so that we can report the results.

On line 12 we make a connection through ODBC to our database.

Note   Directions for setting up ODBC are given in Chapter 2, "Moving from HTML to XHTML."

You will, of course, need a database, which you can restore from the files on our Web site, or create yourself. I'll review the structure of the database later in this chapter.

On line 15 we set the DOMDocument's async property to False. As discussed in previous chapters, this will cause the program to wait until the entire document is loaded before proceeding. On line 16 we load the DomDocument with the contents of the file that was passed in as a parameter (xmlPath). The effect of this is to create the DOMDocument for our XML file.

The bulk of the work is done on lines 21–33.

Lines 21 and 23 are a hack to enable us to "count down" from D to C to B and then to A. We start with the ASCII value for the letter "A" and add 3 to it, to give us D. The next time through we add only 2 (giving us C), then 1, and finally zero. Here's how: The curLevIndex is initialized to 3 and added to the integer value of the ASCII character "A"; the resulting value is then evaluated as a character and that character is assigned to the local variable curLev.

EXCURSION

Visual Basic: The Asc() function takes a string and returns the integer value representing the first letter in the string. Chr() returns a string representing the integer provided.

With curLev now holding the letter "D" it is time to find all the sections whose attribute is level="D". We declare a collection to hold these sections, named (surprise!) sections. This is declared on line 5 as an IXMLDomNodeList, that is, a collection of Nodes.

On line 26 we set `sections` to the result of calling `selectNodes` on our DomDocument. The method `selectNodes` takes as a parameter an XSL pattern.

> This method is the DOM equivalent to the template command in XSL.

We build the pattern with our `curLev` variable. If `curLev` has the value "D" then our `selectNodes` parameter will be `//section[@level="D"]`.

> We're using `//` to indicate all descendents rather than `/`, which would search only immediate children.

This searches all descendents of the root for elements of type `section` that have an attribute `level` whose value is `"D"`, and places them in the `sections` collection.

On lines 29–32 we step through the `sections` collection, and for each section in the collection we call `StoreStory`.

The outer `for-` loop then repeats, this time adding 2 to the value of `"A"` and setting `CurLevel` to `"C"`. Once these sections are gathered into the sections collection, we step through the collection, again calling `StoreStory`. We then repeat this for the B-level and A-level. Note that there will be only a single B-level and a single A-level section to store from each chapter.

Writing the Stories to the Database

Each time through the inner `for` loop shown on lines 29–31, we call `StoreStory`, passing in an individual section. The code for `StoreStory` is shown in Listing 6.3.

Listing 6.3 `SplitStories.cls`

```
0:  'Store the subtree identified by the caller in the db
1:  Private Function StoreStory(c As IXMLDOMElement) As Long
2:      Dim newStoryEl As IXMLDOMElement, parent As IXMLDOMElement
3:      Dim storyId As Long, parentId As Variant, title As String
4:      Dim newStory As New DOMDocument
5:
6:      'add the xml pi
7:      newStory.appendChild newStory.createProcessingInstruction(
          ➥"xml", "version=""1.0""")
8:
9:      'we create a new XML element to hold the story
```

```
10:        Set newStoryEl = newStory.createElement("story")
11:        newStory.appendChild newStoryEl
12:
13:        'we get the storyId from the id of the section
14:        storyId = c.getAttribute("id")
15:
16:        'and the parentId is the id of the parent section, if any
17:        Set parent = c.parentNode
18:        parentId = parent.getAttribute("id")
19:        If IsNull(parentId) Then parentId = 0
20:
21:        'we'll store the title also as a separate field, so it is
            ➥easy to search for
22:        title = c.selectSingleNode("title").Text
23:
24:        'just in case there are any reserved characters,
            ➥we'd better quote them
25:        title = HTMLQuote(title)
26:
27:        'now insert the desired subtree to form the body of the story
28:        'note that since we are not copying, we are actually removing
            ➥c from its original parent
29:        'which is what we want, so that later selections at higher
            ➥levels won't include the children
30:        newStoryEl.appendChild c
31:
32:        'and store the XML, along with the extracted metadata,
            ➥in the database
33:        'first delete any previous version
34:        DBConn.Execute "delete from stories where StoryId = " & storyId
35:        DBConn.Execute "insert into Stories(StoryId, ParentId,
            ➥SectionLevel, Title, XML, TaglessText) Values(" _
36:            & storyId & ", " & parentId & ", " _
37:            & DBQuote(c.getAttribute("level")) & ", " & _
                ➥DBQuote(title) & ", " _
38:            & DBQuote(newStory.xml) & ", " & _
                ➥DBQuote(newStory.Text) & ")"
39:
40:        StoreStory = storyId     'return the story id of the stored story
41: End Function
```

On line 1 we see the signature of the StoreStory method; it takes a single parameter, a DomElement. Our goal is to create a new, complete XML document from this story, and then store that document in the database.

We begin on line 4 by creating the new DOMDocument, which we'll call newStory. On line 7 we add the standard Processing Instruction to our new DOMDocument.

On line 10 we create a new element of type story, named newStoryEl. Notice that we create that element by calling createElement on newStory.

As mentioned in previous chapters, the only object you create with the new keyword is DomDocument; all the rest of the objects are created with factory methods of the document, such as createElement. CreateElement, in fact, only associates the new element with the Document; it does not insert it into the tree. That is an additional step, shown here on line 11 with the call to appendChild.

We now have a DOMDocument, newStory, with a single node (the Processing Instruction), and an orphan element newStoryEl. On line 11 we add newStoryEl to newStory. The DomDocument newStory now has two nodes: the processing instruction and the "story" element.

Inserting the Story

We are ready to insert this story into the database, but before doing so, we'll assign a number of values to local variables, so that we can quickly fill in the various fields of the story record (for example, title, parentID, and so forth).

The element c, you will remember, was the element passed into storeStory from SplitStories. Let's assume, for the moment, that it is a D-level element. On line 14 we ask that D-level element for its "id" attribute. Every section has an "id" which is unique across the entire book, so that we can uniquely identify each section in the database. This "id" was added when we created the XML file, as described in Chapter 4. We'll hold this id in the local variable storyID.

Keeping Track of the id

We also want to keep track of the id of this story's parent, so that we can re-create the book structure if we need to. If this is a D-level section, its parent will be the C-level section to which it was attached in the canonical XML file. We set the local variable parent to the parent element by accessing c's parentNode property. All elements can tell you their parent, as well as their previous and next siblings.

On line 18 we ask the parent for its id and store that value in the local variable parentID. If that value is NULL, we set it to zero on line 18. The top level section in this file has no parent, and our convention is to give this the ID of 0. When we make the Table of Contents, when we find sections whose parent is zero, we will know they are the start of the chapter.

On line 22 we call c.selectSingleNode.

selectSingleNode is exactly like selectNodes except that it returns only the first node it finds, and returns it directly to an element rather than in a collection. We use it here because we know there is only one, and thus this is a convenient shortcut.

On line 22 `selectSingleNode` asks c to return the single node that matches the pattern passed as a parameter. `selectSingleNode` takes an XSL-style pattern as its parameter. In this case we pass in the exact name of the node we're looking for, "title". `selectSingleNode` will return the first node that matches our pattern; in this case there is only one node that will match: the title for this D-level element.

Once we have the title element, we use the text property, which returns the concatenation of all descendent text nodes under that element.

 Note

If the title were originally `"The <b>American</b> Dream"` then the title element would have three children: two text nodes and a bold element. The bold element would have a text node: `"American"`, The text property of `title` would walk this sub-tree, concatenate the text elements, and return the string `"The American Dream"`.

On line 25 we pass the `title` to a helper routine we've written called `HTMLQuote`, which is shown in Listing 6.4. The text property resolves entities. If there were an ampersand in the original text it would have been stored when we created the XML document as `&amp;`. The text property would now helpfully return this as `&`, but we need to force it back to `&amp;`.

Listing 6.4 `mUtil.bas`

```
0:  'expands the reserved characters into their entity representation
1:  Public Function HTMLQuote(ByVal s As String) As String
2:      s = Replace(s, "&", "&amp;")     'must be first
3:      s = Replace(s, "<", "&lt;")
4:      s = Replace(s, ">", "&gt;")
5:      s = Replace(s, "'", "&apos;")
6:      s = Replace(s, """", "&quot;")
7:      HTMLQuote = s
8:  End Function
```

`HTMLQuote`, as you can see, replaces reserved characters such as < and > with their entity representations, `&lt;` and `&gt;` respectively.

Returning to Listing 6.3, on line 30 we append c, the element passed in from `SplitStories`, to our new element `newStoryEl`. This *moves* c from its old position in the original DOMDocument, to this new element in the new DOMDocument. It is as if we clipped it out of the old tree and moved it to this new tree.

It is important to realize that when we move c it brings along with it all its descendents. Thus, if c is a D-level element and it has child nodes, such as Notes, text, code, and so forth, they've all been moved, lock, stock and barrel out from their old DOM and into the new.

The net effect is that we now have a new DOMDocument that represents the story, consisting of the contents of our D-Level section. Equally important, the section has been removed from the original DOMDocument. This is what we want; when we finish processing all the D-level sections and turn to processing the C-level sections, there will be no D-level sections left within them; that is exactly what the spec calls for.

Creating the Database

The next step, as shown on lines 34–38, is to store this new story in our database. We use a very simple database structure, which you can replicate either by using the script provided on the CD, or by following these steps:

1. Open SQL Server 7 Enterprise Manager.
2. Navigate to your list of databases, and right-click to choose New Database, as shown in Figure 6.2.

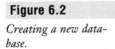

Figure 6.2

Creating a new database.

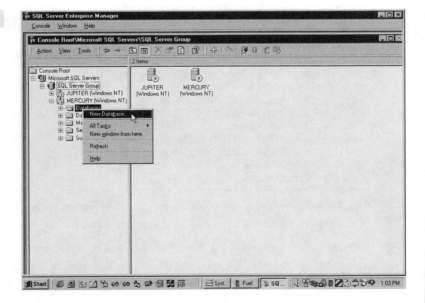

3. Name your database "XWDFS" (for XML Web Documents from Scratch) and choose all the database defaults.

4. When the database is created, navigate to it, expand to find the tables and right-click on tables to choose New Table, as shown in Figure 6.3.

Figure 6.3

Creating a new table.

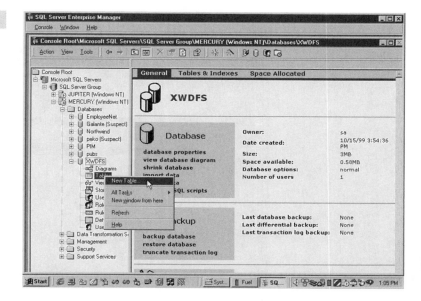

5. Call the new table "Stories."
6. Add the following fields as shown in Figure 6.4.

- StoryID, an integer
- ParentID, an integer
- SectionLevel, a character of length 1
- Title, a varChar of length 500
- XML, of type text
- TaglessText, of type text

Uncheck Allow Nulls on every field and make StoryID the primary key for the table. Save the new table.

That's it. This one table will be sufficient to store our stories. Returning to Listing 6.3, on line 34 we delete any existing entry for our new story. If we're updating, we want to be sure to remove any old data; if we have no old data this does nothing. On lines 35–38 we insert the new record.

```
34:    DBConn.Execute "delete from stories where StoryId = " & storyId
35:    DBConn.Execute "insert into Stories(StoryId, ParentId,
       ➥SectionLevel, Title, XML, TaglessText) Values(" _
```

```
36:          & storyId & ", " & parentId & ", " _
37:          & DBQuote(c.getAttribute("level")) & ", " &
             ➥DBQuote(title) & ", " _
38:          & DBQuote(newStory.xml) & ", " &
             ➥DBQuote(newStory.Text) & ")"
```

Figure 6.4

Designing "Stories."

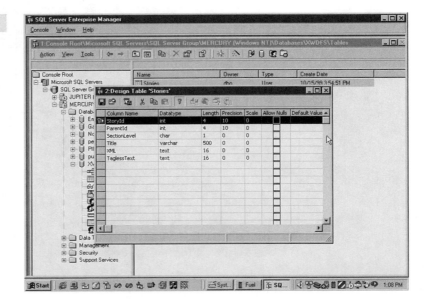

We pass in the `storyID`, `ParentID`, and `Title` that we obtained earlier on lines 14–22. We have not placed the element's section level in a local variable, so we obtain that value in line on line 37 by calling `getAttributes` on c itself.

The string values are processed by a second utility function we've written, `DBQuote`, shown in Listing 6.5.

Listing 6.5 `mUtil.bas`

```
0:   'formats a string so it can be passed as a SQL argument
1:   Public Function DBQuote(s As String)
2:       DBQuote = "'" & Replace(s, "'", "''") & "'"
3:   End Function
```

`DBQuote` simply replaces all single quotes with double single quotes and returns the entire string within single quotes. For example, if we wanted to enter the word `don't` into the database, we would need to enter `'don''t'`.

Finally, returning to line 40 of Listing 6.3, we return the `storyID` to the calling function, `SplitStories`.

```
40:      StoreStory = storyId      'return the story id of the stored story
```

This returns us to line 30 of Listing 6.2, where you'll find that we don't actually use that ID at all; we returned it entirely as a convenience during debugging.

On line 31 of Listing 6.2 we increment our count of stories. We loop through lines 29–31 for each section in the collection. When we finish, we return to the outer loop, which returns us to line 21 where we step down to the next set of sections; that is we move from the D-level to the C-level, then to B-level and A-level.

When we finally fall through the outer loop on line 33, that is when we've finished splitting stories and we've accounted for all the elements in the XML document. We close our database connection and return the number of stories we've found.

```
30:                StoreStory sections(i)
31:                numStories = numStories + 1
32:          Next
33:      Next
34:
35:      DBConn.Close
36:
37:      SplitStories = numStories    'return number of stories
```

This returns control to line 157 of `control.asp`, shown in Listing 6.1 and reproduced here for your convenience.

Listing 6.1   `Control.asp`

```
150:     Function SplitStories()
151:         dim res, oSplit
152:
153:         set oSplit = Server.CreateObject(
             ➥"FromScratch.SplitStories")
154:
155:         res = oSplit.SplitStories(dataPath & ".xml")
156:
157:         SplitStories = "Split " & dataPath & ".xml into " &
             ➥res & " stories"
158:     End Function
```

You will remember that we were in the script function `SplitStories` within `control.asp`. On line 155 the number of stories is returned to the local variable `res`, and the function returns the string `"Split " & dataPath & ".xml into " & res & " stories"` so that if we were processing `Chap3.xml` and it was split into 16 stories, we would be able to display the string "Split chap3.xml into 16 stories".

This string is returned to line 50 of `Control.asp` where it is written to the client's browser.

```
50:      Response.Write SplitStories()
```

What We've Accomplished

Now that we've seen the details, let's jump up a few thousand feet to get a better overview. `Control.asp` has called its internal function `SplitStories`, which has invoked the `SplitStories` method on our ActiveX object, passing in the file we want to split (`Chap3.xml`).

The `SplitStories` method was shown in Listing 6.2. It opened a connection to the database, and then set up a loop to work through each of the D-level, C-level, B-level, and A-level sections; working from the bottom (D-level) upwards to the A-level. As each section was found it was fed to `StoreStories`, shown in Listing 6.3.

`StoreStories` extracted the necessary information and then stored the story in the Database. Split stories kept track of how many stories were stored, and then reported back to `Control.asp`, which printed the information to the page.

When we're done, our input DOMDocument (based on, for example, `chap3.xml`) is empty, and each of the stories has been stashed in the database.

 **Note**   While the DOMDocument has been emptied, the original file, for example, `Chap3.xml`, is untouched. It is only the in-memory representation that has been affected.

Displaying the Story

Now that we've stored the stories in the database, how do we display them?

Because our document is now in XML, we can display it in any number of formats. Of course, a natural first approach will be to display it in HTML.

Converting from our Canonical format to HTML is, in some ways, like stepping back through the looking glass. We will, for the most part, simply reverse the conversions we created in the transition from HTML to XML.

It is somewhat simpler going back, however, as we have done a lot of work already to create a robust structure. Many of the conversions are simple mappings from our canonical tags to `<div>` tags in HTML.

It is important to realize that we could, of course, convert to any number of HTML styles, depending both on which browsers we wish to support and also on presentation/style decisions made by, for example, a graphic artist.

Converting to HTML

Converting our stories to HTML will help us in our ultimate goal of building an application that lets us review the topics in the left frame and view the details of each story in the right frame, as shown in Figure 6.5.

Figure 6.5

Viewing the details of each story in the frame.

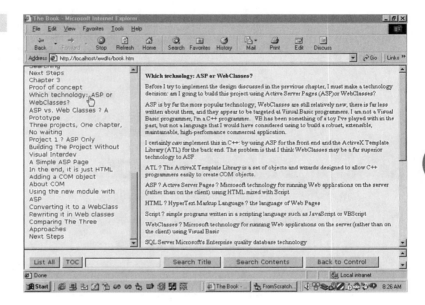

For now, however, we are interested only in the right frame. This view of the story is created by showstory.asp. We can call that page directly, by passing in the id of the story we're interested in. For example, if we navigate to the URL ...ShowStory.asp?StoryID=3002 we see story 3002 as it is stored in the database, as shown in Figure 6.6.

This raises two important questions: How did we get this story out of the database and how did we display an XML page as HTML? Answering these two questions will be the focus of the remainder of this chapter.

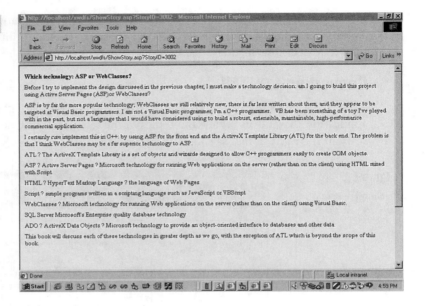

Figure 6.6

Story 3002 as stored in the database.

Retrieving a Story from the Database

Listing 6.6 is the complete ShowStory.asp file.

Listing 6.6   ShowStory.asp

```
0:  <!-- #include file ="include.asp" -->
1:  <%
2:      'ShowStory.asp - retrieves the XML for single story from
        ➥the database,
3:      'converts it into HTML via an XSL stylesheet, and displays
        ➥the results
4:
5:      dim storyId, xml, oXSL
6:
7:      storyId = Request("storyId")
8:
9:      'get the XML from the database
10:     set rs = DBConn.Execute("select xml from stories where
        ➥storyId = " & storyId)
11:     xml = rs("xml").value
12:     rs.close
13:
14:     'transform to HTML via the XSL stylesheet
15:     set oXSL = Server.CreateObject("FromScratch.XSLTransform")
16:     oXSL.InputXML = xml
17:     oXSL.XSLFile = fso.BuildPath(codeDir, "Story2HTML.xsl")
18:     oXSL.Transform
```

```
19:
20:        'display the HTML
21:        response.write oXSL.OutputXML
22:  %>
```

As you can see, there is not much to it. It begins on line 0, by including the file
include.asp, shown in Listing 6.7.

Listing 6.7 `include.asp`

```
0:   <%
1:        'General include file for XWDFS
2:
3:        Option Explicit
4:
5:        Dim DBConn, rs, fso, DSN, DBUser, DBPass, codeDir,
           ➥dataDir, baseName, dataPath
6:
7:        'retrieve the params from the cookie
8:        codeDir = GetInput("CodeDir")
9:        dataDir = GetInput("DataDir")
10:       DSN = GetInput("DSN")
11:       DBUser = GetInput("DBUser")
12:       DBPass = GetInput("DBPass")
13:       baseName = GetInput("BaseName")
14:
15:       'we almost always need a database connection
16:       set DBConn = Server.CreateObject("ADODB.Connection")
17:       DBConn.Open DSN, DBUser, DBPass
18:
19:       'and also a File System Object to manipulate directories
20:       set fso = Server.CreateObject("Scripting.FileSystemObject")
21:
22:       dataPath = fso.BuildPath(dataDir, baseName)
23:
24:       Function GetInput(name)
25:           GetInput = Request.Cookies("XWDFS")(name)
26:       End Function
27:
28:  %>
```

Include.asp exists only to manage a number of constants needed by the ASP pages
used in this application. It has only a single function, GetInput, shown on lines
24–26, which simply returns a cookie based on a name provided as a parameter.

Notice that the entire include file is within <% %> script designations on lines 0 and
28. There is no HTML here, just server-side VBScript. This is true for showStories
as well. After the very first line in which include.asp is included, the rest of the file,
from line 1 through line 22, is server-side script.

On line 7 of Listing 6.6 we pick up the story `id` passed in as a parameter (the `StoryID=3002` shown in the URL). The work is accomplished on lines 10 through 12.

```
10:      set rs = DBConn.Execute("select xml from stories where
         ↪storyId = " & storyId)
11:      xml = rs("xml").value
12:      rs.close
```

On line 10 we execute an SQL statement against our database, requesting the `xml` field from the story matching the `storyID` provided. On line 11, we assign to our local variable `xml` the text stored in the `xml` field. This is, of course, the very text stored in the database from the output DOM we just finished working with earlier in this chapter. In short, the variable `xml` now has the XML string that represents the story, ready to be read into a DOMDocument.

Instantiating the Input XML DOMDocument

The task for the next few lines, lines 15–18, is to instantiate the input XML DOMDocument from the XML we retrieved from the database, and transform that XML to HTML by using (you guessed it!) an XSL stylesheet.

```
15:      set oXSL = Server.CreateObject("FromScratch.XSLTransform")
16:      oXSL.InputXML = xml
17:      oXSL.XSLFile = fso.BuildPath(codeDir, "Story2HTML.xsl")
18:      oXSL.Transform
```

On line 15 we create our familiar ActiveX object. On line 16 we set its `InputXML` property to the `xml` string we just retrieved from the database. On line 17 we set its `XSLFile` property to the appropriate XSL stylesheet, "`Story2HTML.XSL`", which we will discuss in just a moment. Finally on line 18 we call `Transform`.

When we are done, on line 21 we will write to the client browser, passing in the `OutputXML` property of the output DOMDocument.

Using XSL to Render HTML

Let's dive just a bit deeper into the manipulation of `FromScratch.XSLTransform`. Returning to line 16 of Listing 6.5 shows us the following:

```
16:      oXSL.InputXML = xml
```

This property is implemented as shown in Listing 6.8.

Listing 6.8   `XSLTransform.cls`

```
0:   Property Let InputXML(ByVal newValue As String)
1:       'load the string into a new DOM
```

```
2:          Set myInputDOM = ParseIntoDOM(newValue, False, "Input
           ➥from XML")
3:    End Property
4:
```

All of the work is on line 2, where we invoke `ParseIntoDom`, passing in that XML string, along with the parameters `False` and `"Input from XML"`. The implementation of `ParseIntoDom` has been seen before, but it is reproduced here as Listing 6.9.

Listing 6.9 `XSLTransform.cls`

```
0:   'worker function to read an input source into a new DOM
1:   'if isURL is true, then data is the text of a URL;
     ➥else data is an XML string
2:   Private Function ParseIntoDOM(data As String,
     ➥isURL As Boolean, src As String) As DOMDocument
3:       Dim dom As New DOMDocument, result As Boolean
4:       dom.async = False
5:       If isURL Then
6:           result = dom.Load(data)
7:       Else
8:           result = dom.loadXML(data)
9:       End If
10:      If Not result Then
11:          ReportParseError src, dom
12:      End If
13:      Set ParseIntoDOM = dom
14:  End Function
```

We see that `isURL` is false and `src` is the string `"Input from XML"` while the first parameter, `data` is the XML we retrieved from the database.

On line 3 we create the new DOMDocument, and on line 5 we test the input to see if it is from a URL. As it is not, we proceed on line 8 to call `loadXML` on our new DOMDocument, passing in the string retrieved from the database. Hey! Presto! The input DOMDocument springs into existence.

Returning to Listing 6.5 on line 18 we call `Transform`. Again, we've seen this code before, but as it is brief, I've reproduced it here as Listing 6.10.

Listing 6.10 `XSLTransform.cls`

```
0:   'the function that does the work - actually transforms input
     ➥via XSL to output
1:   Public Sub Transform()
2:       Set myOutputDOM = New DOMDocument
3:       myInputDOM.transformNodeToObject myXSLDOM, myOutputDOM
4:       If myOutputDOM.parseError.errorCode <> 0 Then
         ➥ReportParseError "Output", myOutputDOM
5:   End Sub
```

A new empty DOMDocument is created for the output. We then call transformNodeToObject on the inputDomDocument, passing in the XSL stylesheet and the newly created output DOMDocument.

The XML to HTML Stylesheet

All of this has been rather mechanical. We obtain the HTML as a text string from the database, create an XML DomDocument from that file, and then call transformNodeToObject on that DOMDocument, passing in our XSL stylesheet. As you can see, the real work, the hard work, is in crafting that stylesheet.

Implementing the XSL Transformation

For most of the text we receive from the input DOMDocument, we'll want to render exactly as it is, in the output document. On the way, however, we must handle a number of challenges: How should we display section headings and titles? How do we want to render notes? What style do we want to apply to code?

In addition, we must undertake certain transformations to render our XML elements in standard HTML. For example, we must convert space runs and tab elements to non-breaking spaces.

Listing 6.11 is the complete StoryToHTML stylesheet, which we will review in detail.

Listing 6.11   StoryToHTML.xsl

```
0:    <?xml version="1.0"?>
1:    <xsl:stylesheet
2:        xmlns:xsl="http://www.w3.org/TR/WD-xsl"
3:        xmlns="http://www/w3/org/TR/REC-html40"
4:        result-ns="">
5:
6:        <!-- default rule for text nodes - just output the text -->
7:        <xsl:template match="text()">
8:            <xsl:value-of/>
9:        </xsl:template>
10:
11:       <!-- the root node - output the structure of the HTML page
          ➥and begin the recursion -->
12:       <xsl:template match="/">
13:       <html>
14:       <head>
15:       <style>
16:           * {font-family:Georgia; font-size:10pt; margin-bottom:6pt;}
17:           .unknown {color:red;}
18:           .code {background-color:lightgrey;padding:3pt;}
```

```
19:           .textcode {font-family: Courier New; font-size:10pt; }
20:           .codeline, .codeline b{font-family: Courier New;
              ➥font-size:9pt; line-height:9pt; margin-bottom:0; }
21:           .sectionHeader {font-weight:bold}
22:           .LH, .FN {font-style:italic;}    <!-- listing
              ➥header, figure caption -->
23:           .note {background-color:lightgreen; margin:0 4em; padding:3pt;}
24:           .noteline, .noteline b, .noteline i, .noteHeader
              ➥{font-family:Verdana; font-size:8pt;}
25:           .noteline {margin-left:2em;}
26:           .noteHeader {font-weight: bold;}
27:           .summary {font-style:italic; font-size:8pt;
              ➥margin-bottom:0;}
28:       </style>
29:       </head>
30:           <xsl:apply-templates/>
31:       </html>
32:       </xsl:template>
33:
34:       <!-- sentinel for any left over tags -->
35:       <xsl:template match="*">
36:           <div class="unknown">
37:               !!<xsl:node-name/>!!
38:               <xsl:apply-templates />
39:           </div>
40:       </xsl:template>
41:
42:       <!--
43:           The top level element - might be story or book
              ➥depending on who's calling
44:           Just wraps the content inside <body> tags
45:           Then finishes with some summary info about numbers
              ➥of nodes of different kinds
46:         -->
47:       <xsl:template match="story¦book">
48:       <body>
49:           <xsl:apply-templates/>
50:           <div class="summary">
51:               Section summary
52:               <br/><xsl:eval>this.selectNodes("//div").length
                  ➥</xsl:eval> paragraphs
53:               <br/><xsl:eval>this.selectNodes("//code").length
                  ➥</xsl:eval> code blocks
54:               <br/><xsl:eval>this.selectNodes("//note").length
                  ➥</xsl:eval> notes
55:           </div>
56:       </body>
57:       </xsl:template>
58:
59:       <!--
60:           Sections just map into DIVs with their own class.
              ➥We'll keep the level attribute in case we ever
```

continues

Listing 6.10   Continued

```
61:              want to do formatting based on it
62:        -->
63:      <xsl:template match="section">
64:      <div class="section"><xsl:attribute name="level">
         ➥<xsl:value-of select="@level"/></xsl:attribute>
65:          <xsl:apply-templates/></div>
66:      </xsl:template>
67:
68:      <!--
69:          Our basic text paragraph element. We maintain the
             ➥class attribute, which is really the same
70:          as the original Word style name
71:        -->
72:      <xsl:template match="div">
73:          <div>
74:              <xsl:attribute name="class"><xsl:value-of select=
                 ➥"@class"/></xsl:attribute>
75:              <xsl:apply-templates/>
76:          </div>
77:      </xsl:template>
78:
79:      <!-- we ignore PD - these are publishing directions,
         ➥e.g. "begin note" -->
80:      <xsl:template match="div[@class='PD']">
81:      </xsl:template>
82:
83:      <!--
84:          These are our specialized content types for code
             ➥blocks and notes.
85:          We just change them into divs with corresponding styles
86:        -->
87:      <xsl:template match="codeline¦code¦noteline">
88:      <div><xsl:attribute name="class"><xsl:node-name/>
         ➥</xsl:attribute><xsl:apply-templates/></div>
89:      </xsl:template>
90:
91:      <!-- The note element is a little special, because we
         ➥want to put in a header that says "Note" -->
92:      <xsl:template match="note">
93:          <div class="note">
94:          <div class="noteHeader">Note</div>
95:          <xsl:apply-templates/>
96:          </div>
97:      </xsl:template>
98:
99:      <!-- Titles for sections also map into their own div class -->
100:     <xsl:template match="title">
101:         <div class="sectionHeader">
102:             <xsl:apply-templates/>
103:         </div>
104:     </xsl:template>
```

```
105:
106:     <!-- underline elements are used to denote code in the text -
         ➡turn these into their own special spans -->
107:     <xsl:template match="u">
108:         <span class="textcode"><xsl:apply-templates/></span>
109:     </xsl:template>
110:
111:     <!-- handle vanilla HTML-like tags -
         ➡just map them to the same thing -->
112:     <xsl:template match="b|i|sub|sup|br">
113:         <xsl:element>
114:             <xsl:apply-templates/>
115:         </xsl:element>
116:     </xsl:template>
117:
118:     <!-- spaceruns and tabs get mapped into sequences of  s.
         ➡We approximate tabs with 4 spaces -->
119:     <xsl:template match="spacerun">
120:         <span><xsl:eval>Repeat(" ",
             ➡this.getAttribute("len"))</xsl:eval></span>
121:     </xsl:template>
122:
123:     <xsl:template match="tab">
124:         <span><xsl:eval>Repeat(" ", 4)</xsl:eval></span>
125:     </xsl:template>
126:
127:     <!-- translate special chars into entities for display
         ➡in HTML - we use numbered entities so we don't have to
128:         explicitly define them - may only work in IE -->
129:     <xsl:template match="char">
130:         <xsl:choose>
131:             <xsl:when test="@type[. = 'emDash']">&#8212;</xsl:when>
132:             <xsl:when test="@type[. = 'bullet']">&#8226;</xsl:when>
133:             <xsl:when test="@type[. = 'ellipsis']">&#8230;</xsl:when>
134:             <!-- we'll just use 2 nbsps for emSpace -
             ➡#8195 doesn't seem to work as documented -->
135:             <xsl:when test="@type[. = 'emSpace']">  </xsl:when>
136:             <xsl:when test="@type[. = 'smartApos']">&#146;</xsl:when>
137:             <xsl:when test="@type[. = 'smartLQuote']">&#147;</xsl:when>
138:             <xsl:when test="@type[. = 'smartRQuote']">&#148;</xsl:when>
139:             <xsl:otherwise><span class="unknown">char:
             ➡<xsl:value-of select="@type"/></span></xsl:otherwise>
140:         </xsl:choose>
141:     </xsl:template>
142:
143:
144: <xsl:script>
145: <![CDATA[
146:     // returns a string consisting of n copies of t
147:     function Repeat(t, n)
148:     {
149:         var r = "";
```

continues

Listing 6.10   Continued

```
150:          while (n-- > 0)
151:              r += t;
152:          return r;
153:      }
154: ]]>
155: </xsl:script>
156:
157: </xsl:stylesheet>
```

Getting Started

Our XSL stylesheet begins on line 0 by properly identifying itself with a Processing Instruction. The stylesheet element then identifies the namespaces we'll be using. Line 2 identifies the xsl namespace, as described in previous chapters. Line 3 declares the html namespace, and note again that this is unnamed (xmlns is not followed by a colon and an identifier). This indicates that if no namespace is specified, then we mean HTML. Finally, the output namespace is set to empty, indicating that it will use the unnamed namespace, in this case HTML. Our output DOMDocument will be an HTML document, so this is correct.

The HTML Header

On line 12 we match the root element.

```
12:      <xsl:template match="/">
```

When we do, we add a number of elements to the output DOMDocument. These are the headings we want in our HTML file, and include the standard <html> and <head> elements as well as a <style> element. The <style> element will provide CSS (Cascading Style Sheet) styling for the HTML document.

The XML document passed in will have a root element of either <book> or <story>. The XSL to handle these is identical, as shown on lines 47–57.

```
47:      <xsl:template match="story¦book">
48:      <body>
49:          <xsl:apply-templates/>
50:          <div class="summary">
51:              Section summary
52:              <br/><xsl:eval>this.selectNodes("//div").
                 ➥length</xsl:eval> paragraphs
53:              <br/><xsl:eval>this.selectNodes("//code").
                 ➥length</xsl:eval> code blocks
54:              <br/><xsl:eval>this.selectNodes("//note").
                 ➥length</xsl:eval> notes
55:          </div>
56:      </body>
57:      </xsl:template>
```

We replace the story or book element with an HTML body element, and then call apply-templates to pick up all the elements within the book or story. We'll come back to lines 50–54 shortly.

Because XSL is declarative, rather than functional, we are best served not by walking down the XSL file line-by-line, but rather by considering the various tasks we wish to accomplish, and focusing on how this is done with XSL.

Handling Sections

You will remember that the XML document is divided into sections, which represent the A-, B-, C-, and D-level headings. Each section has associated with it a title, and any number of text, notes, and code elements.

On lines 63–66 we process the sections as shown in the match statement of the template element.

```
63:     <xsl:template match="section">
```

When sections are matched, we create a new <div> element for the output HTML DOMDocument. We hard-code the first attribute, class to "section". We also want to preserve the level attribute, so we create a new attribute (using xsl:attribute) and set its value using the value-of statement as we've seen previously.

```
64:     <div class="section"><xsl:attribute name="level">
        ➥<xsl:value-of select="@level"/></xsl:attribute>
```

 **Note**   Remember that the @ sign in the xsl-pattern indicates matching on an attribute name.

On line 65 we call apply-templates to ensure that we recurse into the sections, so that we will process each of their contained elements.

In effect, each section will begin with a div identifying the section, and between the opening <div> and its end tag </div> will be the title, and all the text, notes, and code of that section.

The title is the first visible element in the section. Lines 99–104 match title elements and create a div with the attribute sectionHeader.

```
 99:    <!-- Titles for sections also map into their own div class -->
100:    <xsl:template match="title">
101:        <div class="sectionHeader">
102:            <xsl:apply-templates/>
103:        </div>
104:    </xsl:template>
```

The attribute `class="sectionheader"` will be used by the browser to match the Cascading Style Sheet selector `sectionHeader` shown on line 21.

```
21:            .sectionHeader {font-weight:bold}
```

The effect is that the `sectionHeader` will use the default style, shown on line 16

```
16:            * {font-family:Georgia; font-size:10pt; margin-bottom:6pt;}
```

but will modify that default style to set the font-weight to bold.

On line 102 we call `apply-templates`, which will pick up the text from the title. On lines 6–9 we designate that any element of type text will be mapped *as is* to the output DOMDocument; that is text will just be carried over.

```
7:            <xsl:template match="text()">
8:                <xsl:value-of/>
9:            </xsl:template>
```

It is this text which will be rendered in bold. We took this exact idiom apart in the previous discussion of XSL so I won't belabor it here.

The bulk of the text in the input document is in `<div>` elements, each representing a paragraph of text. On lines 72–77 we handle these elements, simply creating a new `div` element for the output HTML and copying over the `class` attribute intact.

```
72:            <xsl:template match="div">
73:                <div>
74:                    <xsl:attribute name="class"><xsl:value-of
                        ↪select="@class"/></xsl:attribute>
75:                    <xsl:apply-templates/>
76:                </div>
77:            </xsl:template>
```

Rendering Code

Our specification details that when we display code it should be set off from the main body of text. To accomplish this, we'll create a `<div>` for our `<code>` and `<codeline>` elements. Each will have its own `class` attribute, and thus each will match a specific CSS `selector`.

On line 87 we match on any one of `codeline`, `code` or `noteline`

```
87:        <xsl:template match="codeline¦code¦noteline">
```

Our action on each of these is to create a `div` element, with an attribute `class`. The value assigned to the class is the `node-name` we've matched (for example, `codeline` or `code`, or `noteline`). We then call `apply-templates` to ensure that we recurse into these elements.

```
87:        <xsl:template match="codeline¦code¦noteline">
88:        <div><xsl:attribute name="class"><xsl:node-name/>
           ➥</xsl:attribute><xsl:apply-templates/></div>
89:        </xsl:template>
```

Code elements will thus be converted to `<div>` elements with an attribute `class` whose value is `code`. On line 18 we see that the style for code elements is to change the background color and to create 3pt padding.

```
18:            .code {background-color:lightgrey;padding:3pt;}
```

Thus, as we render the code in HTML it will be set against a light-colored background, and will stand out from the body of the text.

Handling Notes

Our strategy for notes is very similar, and we have already seen that line 87 matches `noteline` elements.

Note elements must be matched separately, however, because we want to write the word `Note` at the top of the note, before displaying the contents of the note itself. We see this implemented on lines 92–97.

```
92:        <xsl:template match="note">
93:            <div class="note">
94:            <div class="noteHeader">Note</div>
95:            <xsl:apply-templates/>
96:            </div>
97:        </xsl:template>
```

When we match a note, we create an outer `div` whose class is set to `note`. On line 23, we declare the style for that class.

```
23:            .note {background-color:lightgreen; margin:0 4em; padding:3pt;}
```

We immediately declare an inner `div` with the class `noteHeader` whose contents is the word `Note`. `NoteHeader` shares its style with `noteline` and bold and italic notelines, as shown on line 24.

```
24:            .noteline, .noteline b, .noteline i, .noteHeader
           ➥{font-family:Verdana; font-size:8pt;}
25:            .noteline {margin-left:2em;}
26:            .noteHeader {font-weight: bold;}
```

We also see special (cascading) styles for noteline (which gets a left margin) and note header (which is rendered in bold).

Inline Code

When I wrote the original Word document, I underlined certain words within paragraphs if they referred to code. For example, in Chapter 3, I wrote "Remember to substitute your own computer's name as the Server in line 5" (currently it is set to `myServer`).

The underline indicates to the editor that this is code, to be set in a special font. When this was saved in HTML, the underline was preserved, as shown from the following excerpt from `Chap3.htm`:

```
1989:   <p class=FT>Remember to substitute your own
        ➥computer's name as the Server in
1990:   line 15 (currently it is set to <u>myServer</u>).</p>
```

In all our conversions—to XHTML, to the intermediate XML file, and to our final canonical XML form—the underline element was preserved and it is thus preserved in the database.

Now, when we write this *back* to HTML, we've decided to acknowledge the actual meaning of this underline as being a code excerpt. We will change our "u" elements (that is, underlined elements) to spans with the class "`textcode`".

```
107:        <xsl:template match="u">
108:            <span class="textcode"><xsl:apply-templates/></span>
109:        </xsl:template>
```

By setting the class to "textcode" we instruct the browser to apply the style designated in the textcode selector, shown on line 19.

```
19:            .textcode {font-family: Courier New; font-size:10pt; }
```

The effect of this is seen in Figure 6.7, in which I show both the browser and the source HTML.

Note

One could argue that we've got this exactly backward. When we transformed to XML we ought to have saved these entries not as u elements, but rather as `textCode` elements. This would give us the ability to use stylesheets or not on the way out.

We've kept it the way I've shown you to demonstrate a number of points:

1. The line between syntax and semantics is not always bright and shining.

2. There is more than one way to accomplish the same goal.

3. Often, you don't get it exactly right the first time.

That third point is no joke; when working with XML and XSL, as with any complex language, judgment is involved. You will be continually called upon to decide when it is worthwhile to transform a given tag into a semantically richer tag; the answer is not always obvious.

Figure 6.7

Viewing the source.

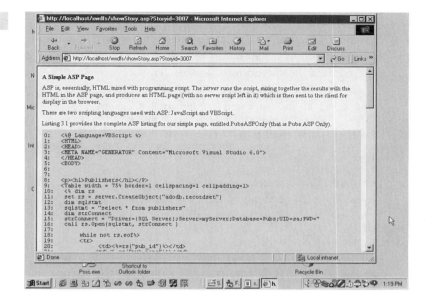

Vanilla HTML

Our XML document consists of a number of other elements that must be transformed into HTML.

The simplest of these are the XML tags that have direct matches in HTML, and that can be passed along as they are, as shown on lines 112–116.

```
111:        <!-- handle vanilla HTML-like tags -
            ➥just map them to the same thing -->
112:        <xsl:template match="b|i|sub|sup|br">
113:            <xsl:element>
114:                <xsl:apply-templates/>
115:            </xsl:element>
116:        </xsl:template>
```

For each of these elements we declare a new element in the output DOMDocument, copying over the contents. Here's how: The xsl:element element returns the current element. Thus, if we match a <b> element, xsl:element puts a <b> element into the output DOMDocument. Within the open and close xsl:element tags we see the xsl:apply-templates tag, which copies in the contents of the <b> element.

Spaceruns and Tabs

The original Word document had multiple spaces at various parts of the document. When Word saved these to HTML it saved them using a single space followed by a run of hexadecimal a0 characters. We converted these to our spacerun elements, whose attribute tells how many spaces are needed.

Spaceruns

We now would like to replace these with a sequence of non-breakable spaces (which HTML will not collapse into a single space). The HTML markup for this is . We convert the spacerun to   elements on lines 118–121.

```
118:      <!-- spaceruns and tabs get mapped into sequences
➥of  s. We approximate tabs with 4 spaces -->
119:      <xsl:template match="spacerun">
120:          <span><xsl:eval>Repeat(" ",
          ➥this.getAttribute("len"))</xsl:eval></span>
121:      </xsl:template>
```

On line 119 we match any spacerun element. On line 120 use the xsl:eval element to evaluate the contents of the eval element as script. Thus, whatever is between <xsl:eval> and </xsl:eval> will be treated as script, and the result will be placed as the contents of the span.

The script calls the Repeat function, passing in the numeric entity equivalent of   as the first parameter, and the value of the attribute "len" of the current element (the spacerun).

We see Repeat() implemented on lines 144–155.

```
144:   <xsl:script>
145:   <![CDATA[
146:      // returns a string consisting of n copies of t
147:      function Repeat(t, n)
148:      {
149:          var r = "";
150:          while (n-- > 0)
151:              r += t;
152:          return r;
153:      }
154:   ]]>
155:   </xsl:script>
```

The script is bounded by xsl:script tags, and the contents of the script are held within a CDATA block so that the XSL parser will not parse reserved characters such as the > in line 150. This function does nothing more than create a string of n copies (the second parameter: the length of the spacerun) of t (the character passed in:).

Tabs

Lines 123–125 do for tabs exactly as lines 119–121 did for spaces.

```
123:      <xsl:template match="tab">
124:          <span><xsl:eval>Repeat(" ", 4)</xsl:eval></span>
125:      </xsl:template>
```

Once again we call the repeat function, this time handing in the hard-wired value of 4 for the length. Each tab is thus transformed into four non-breaking space characters.

Special Characters

Our XML document has a number of `char` elements that represent characters that require special handling in HTML and other markup languages. The `char` element is language-agnostic and semantically meaningful. By language-agnostic I mean that the `char` element is not specific to a particular markup language; it is a canonical format for these special characters. By semantically meaningful, I mean that the `char` element is self-describing. For example, when I see a `char` element with the attribute `type=emdash` it is immediately obvious what it is, rather than if I saw an element whose value was, for example, —.

There are great advantages to storing these `char` elements as we have in our database, but now that we're creating an HTML document we must convert them back into the entities required by HTML.

On line 129 we match any `char` element. On line 130 we set up a `choose` block so that we can match on the attribute for the type of character we're considering.

```
129:        <xsl:template match="char">
130:            <xsl:choose>
```

Lines 131–138 implement the transformation of all of the special types we know about.

```
131:                <xsl:when test="@type[. = 'emDash']">&#8212;</xsl:when>
132:                <xsl:when test="@type[. = 'bullet']">&#8226;</xsl:when>
133:                <xsl:when test="@type[. = 'ellipsis']">&#8230;</xsl:when>
134:                <!-- we'll just use 2 nbsps for emSpace -
                    ➥#8195 doesn't seem to work as documented -->
135:                <xsl:when test="@type[. = 'emSpace']">  </xsl:when>
136:                <xsl:when test="@type[. = 'smartApos']">&#146;</xsl:when>
137:                <xsl:when test="@type[. = 'smartLQuote']">&#147;</xsl:when>
138:                <xsl:when test="@type[. = 'smartRQuote']">&#148;</xsl:when>
```

For example, when the special character is of type `bullet`, the transformation on line 132 will be accomplished; the output DOMDocument will include the string •, the entity for a bullet.

On line 139 we see the `xsl:otherwise` element, which will match if none of the other `when` statements does. This again is a trap in the code to mark characters we weren't expecting. In this case we will create a span with a class attribute of `unknown`, whose contents are the word `char:` followed by the value of the `type` attribute.

The unknown class displays the text in red, as shown on line 17

```
17:            .unknown {color:red;}
```

The `choose` statement is closed on line 140, and the template element is closed on line 141.

Handling Production Directives

We have matched all the elements we know about and want to process except Production Directives. These are elements in our XML document that were created to hold special instructions originally intended for the Macmillan editors. We do not want to display these in our output HTML, but we also don't want them caught by our "unknown" elements trap, so on lines 79–81 we'll match them explicitly but take no action with them.

```
79:         <!-- we ignore PD - these are publishing directions,
       ➥ e.g. "begin note" -->
80:         <xsl:template match="div[@class='PD']">
81:         </xsl:template>
```

The Document Summary

At the bottom of every story, we place a short summary noting how many paragraphs are in the story, and how many code blocks and notes, as shown in Figure 6.8.

Figure 6.8

A short summary noting paragraph amount.

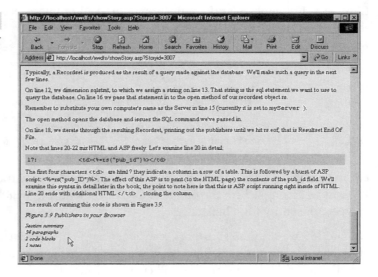

The implementation of this summary takes us back to lines 47–57. We said earlier that when we match the story or book, we create the body tag. Within the body is the HTML produced by apply-templates (and thus processing all the other elements in the document). Before we close the <body> tag on line 56 we create a new div with a class summary

```
47:        <xsl:template match="story¦book">
48:        <body>
49:            <xsl:apply-templates/>
50:            <div class="summary">
51:                Section summary
52:                <br/><xsl:eval>this.selectNodes("//div").length
                   ➥</xsl:eval> paragraphs
53:                <br/><xsl:eval>this.selectNodes("//code").length
                   ➥</xsl:eval> code blocks
54:                <br/><xsl:eval>this.selectNodes("//note").length
                   ➥</xsl:eval> notes
55:            </div>
56:        </body>
57:        </xsl:template>
```

The .summary selector on line 27 sets the style for the summary to italic 8 point with no bottom margin.

```
27:            .summary {font-style:italic; font-size:8pt; margin-bottom:0;}
```

We print the words Section summary followed by the details of how many paragraphs, code blocks, and notes were found. To be honest, this has little real-world value, but it does demonstrate that you can access, and display, meta-data about the documents stored in the database.

We compute these figures with the selectNodes method. Note that the method must be called on an element, in this case we call it on the current element using the keyword *this*.

The current element here is the top level element: either story or book. On line 52 we pass as the parameter to selectNodes the XSL-pattern "//div". This will find every div element that is a descendent of the current element, in other words, every div in the book or story. What is returned is a collection, and we access the length property of that collection which tells us how many objects (for example, how many <div> elements) are in that collection. Finally, we print that value by using the <xsl:eval> element.

<xsl:eval> hands its contents to a scripting engine, and returns the result as a string, which is inserted in the output DOMDocument.

Next Steps

We've chopped each chapter into stories, stored those stories in the database, and then rendered the stories in HTML. Our next step is to build a Table of Contents to serve in the left pane of our application.

Creating Components Using XML and XSL with DHTML

So far we've seen how to turn an HTML document into an XHTML document. From there we have used both the XML Document Object Model and XSL to create an XML document that we've manipulated and stored in the database. In this chapter we'll return to the database, extract pieces of the data, and create a dynamic, collapsible Table of Contents, as shown in Figure 7.1.

Figure 7.1

The Table of Contents.

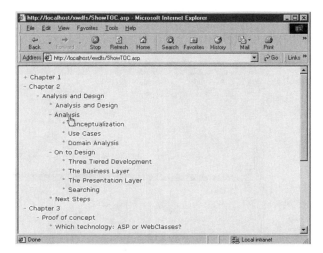

Notice the plus (+) and minus (-) signs next to the topics. Those with + signs are collapsed; clicking on the plus signs will open the topics below them, as shown by those with minus signs. Under the heading `Chapter 2`, the highlighted topic "Analysis and Design" is collapsed, while the next topic, "Analysis" is expanded. Items with asterisks (*) are leaves (that is to say topics with no children).

We'll examine the code we used to create this in detail. We'll then look at a few other ways to accomplish exactly the same work.

Strategy

Our first solution to this problem will be to extract data from the database to create a simple XML DOMDocument that reflects the original structure of the sections, as described in previous chapters. We'll then feed that XML document to an XSL stylesheet that will produce an HTML file, which we can view in a browser. That HTML file will include JavaScript to create the dynamic table of contents.

You'll remember that an A-level section contains a B-level section, which may contain (among other things) any number of C-level sections, which in their turn may contain any number of D-level sections.

We've flattened this structure into records in our database, but we've kept enough information to re-create it, which we'll do now. Once we have an XML DOMDocument with this structure, we'll display it as an HTML page using XSL.

You will remember that in our database we have only one table, and it has only a few fields, as shown in Figure 7.2.

Figure 7.2

The Stories Table.

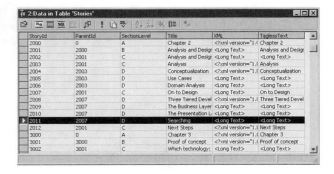

Each record has a `StoryID` that uniquely identifies the story, and a `ParentID`, which is the `storyID` of the containing section. Thus, for example, in Figure 7.2 we see that the highlighted record for Story 2011 (a D-level section) has the parent 2007. If we look up four lines, we find that 2007 is a C-level section. This makes sense; a D-level section would be contained within a C-level. In our Table of Contents we'll want to indent this D-level section within the containing C-level section.

Story 2007 in turn has a `parentID` of 2001. We find 2001 on the second line. The `SectionLevel` field reveals that this is a B-level section whose `parentID` is 2000.

2000 is an A-level section, which is, as you may remember, a chapter. All A-level entries have a `parentID` of 0.

Re-Creating the Hierarchy

Knowing this structure, we'll extract each record and rebuild the original relationships among the sections. For this document, however, we need only enough information to create the Table of Contents. The actual story itself, along with the notes, code, and so forth, are not (yet) needed.

We will therefore create a new element, `listing`, which will hold the information we need: the storyID and the level, along with the `title` that we will display. Once we've created a DOMDocument that reflects these relationships, we can display it in our browser by using XSL to build an HTML page.

To summarize, our strategy is to extract from the database the minimum information necessary to create an XML Document consisting of `<listing>` elements; each of which will have a level and a title, and `listing` elements may be nested one within the other. We'll use XSL to build the Table of Contents from this new XML DOM.

ShowTOC.ASP

The ASP page responsible for searching the database and generating the Table of Contents is ShowTOC.ASP as shown in Listing 7.1.

Listing 7.1 `ShowTOC.asp`

```
0:  <!-- #include file ="include.asp" -->
1:  <%
2:      'ShowTOC.asp - creates the XML for the TOC from the database
3:      'then converts it into HTML via an XSL stylesheet and
        ➥displays the results
4:      dim oxsl:, tocXML
5:
6:      'create the toc - beginning at the root (storyId = 0)
7:      tocXML =  "<?XML version='1.0'?>" & vbCrLf _
8:              & "<toc>" & vbCrLf  & DoTOCSection(0) & "</toc>"
9:
10:     'transform to HTML via the XSL stylesheet
11:     set oxsl: = Server.CreateObject("FromScratch.xslTransform")
```

continues

Listing 7.1   Continued

```
12:        oxsl:.InputXML = tocXML
13:        oxsl:.xslFile = fso.BuildPath(codeDir, "Toc2HTML.xsl")
14:        oxsl:.Transform
15:
16:        'display the HTML
17:        response.write oxsl:.OutputXML
18:
19:
20:        Function DoTOCSection(id)
21:            'handle one section element for MakeTOC
22:            dim s, rs
23:
24:            'get all the children of the given storyId
25:            set rs = DBConn.Execute("select StoryId, SectionLevel,
           ➡Title from Stories where ParentId = " & id & " order by
           ➡StoryId")
26:            do until rs.eof
27:                'for each one, create an XML element that contains
               ➡the particulars
28:                s = s & "<listing id=""" & rs("storyId") & """
               ➡level=""" & rs("SectionLevel") & """">"  & vbCrLf
29:                s = s & "<title>" & rs("Title") & "</title>" & vbCrLf
30:                'recurse into my children
31:                s = s & DoTOCSection(rs("StoryId"))
32:                s = s & "</listing>" & vbCrLf
33:                rs.MoveNext
34:            loop
35:            rs.Close
36:
37:            'return the resulting string
38:            DoTOCSection = s
39:        End Function
40:    %>
```

This time we create an XML document in a way different from any we've seen before. In the past, we've created our DOMDocument from a file, or by transforming another DOMDocument, or we've created it using XSL. This time, all the work is done in the ASP file. We'll read data from the database, construct the string in memory, and then create the DOMDocument from that.

On line 0 include.asp is included, as we've seen previously. Line 1 begins the script portion of the ASP file. The actual work begins on line 7 where tocXML is assigned a string.

```
7:        tocXML = "<?XML version='1.0'?>" & vbCrLf _
8:                & "<toc>" & vbCrLf  & DoTOCSection(0) & "</toc>"
```

`tocXML` is the string from which we'll create the XML DOMDocument as shown on lines 11 and 12.

```
11:    set oxsl: = Server.CreateObject("FromScratch.xslTransform")
12:    oxsl:.InputXML = tocXML
```

Returning to line 7, we see that the first text in the string is our standard heading for an XML document: the processing instruction `<?XML version='1.0'?>`, as we would expect. This is followed by `vbCrLf`, forcing a new line character into the file, leaving the processing instruction alone on the first line of our XML file.

Next in the string is a `<toc>` tag, which again is set alone on a line. This is followed by a call to the `DoTOCSection` method, to which we'll return in a moment. Finally, the `<toc>` tag is closed and the string is ended. That's it. From this string we'll create the input document.

Obviously the work of creating the body of the XML document lies in the `DoTOCSection` method, which we find on lines 20–39.

You'll note that when we call this function, we pass in the value `0`. On line 20, the parameter is named `id`. You may remember that when we created the stories, and saved them in the database, each top-most section (the A-level tag) was assigned the `parentID` of 0. This is not a coincidence.

On line 25 we search the database. Given a `storyID`, we create a collection of stories, which are the children of that ID.

```
25:   set rs = DBConn.Execute("select StoryId, SectionLevel,
    ➥Title from Stories where ParentId = " & id & " order by StoryId")
```

Let's take another look at the records in our database, as shown in Figure 7.3.

Figure 7.3

The Stories Table, revisited.

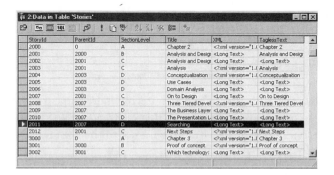

We see that each record has a `StoryID`, and that every record also points to a `ParentID` (the `storyID` of the containing section), except A-level stories, which have a `ParentID` of 0.

Now let's open the Query Analyzer and execute the same search as executed by the ASP page, starting, as we do on line 7 with `ParentID 0` (zero):

```
select StoryId, SectionLevel, Title from Stories where
ParentId = 0 order by StoryId
```

Figure 7.4 shows the results when this query is run against the database after adding stories from the first three chapters.

Figure 7.4

Selecting the A level.

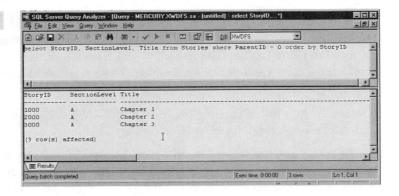

As you can see, the result is to return the records for the A-level headers, as we'd expect.

On line 26 we begin a loop, working our way through each of these records.

```
26:    do until rs.eof
```

We declared a variable s on line 22 which will be used to build up a string, which on line 38 will be the return value of this function. In effect, whatever we put in that string will be inserted into our XML document between the `<toc>` and `</toc>` tags.

On line 28 we add to the s string

```
28: s = s & "<listing id=""" & rs("storyId") & """
level=""" & rs("SectionLevel") & """>"  & vbCrLf
```

The `<listing>` tag is given the attribute id where the current record's storyID is used. In the case of our first record, this is storyID `2000`. This listing tag is also given a second attribute, level, which is set to the SectionLevel returned from the query (in this case "A").

On line 29, we add the title to the string

```
29:          s = s & "<title>" & rs("Title") & "</title>" & vbCrLf
```

Again, because we are building an XML document, the title is within `<title>` tags, and the value is the field retrieved from the query.

At this point, the first time through, s looks like this:

```
<listing id="1000" level="A">
<title>Chapter 1</title>
```

On line 31 we add to s the result of recursively calling DoTOCSection, passing in the *current* storyID (1000). This bit of recursion is the secret to creating the entire table of contents.

DoTOCSection will now search the database to find all records whose *parentID* is 2000. This search produces a single record, with an ID of 2001 (the B-level section).

When we return to line 31, s will look like this:

```
<listing id="2000" level="A">
<title>Chapter 2</title>
<listing id="2001" level="B">
<title>Analysis and Design</title>
```

Note, that when we opened listing 2001, we have not yet closed listing 2000. Thus, listing 2001 is *contained within* listing 2000.

When we reach a leaf, we are ready to close up our open listings. This completes the containment, with D-level listings within C-level, which are within B-level and so forth.

You can see the effect of this by following these steps:

1. Open ShowToc.ASP in an editor.
2. Navigate to line 34 and insert a new line below so that your code looks like this:

```
        loop
    Response.Write(s)
        rs.Close
```

3. Save this file and open ShowTOC.ASP in a browser.
4. Show the source HTML.

The result is shown in Figure 7.5.

Each A-level section will find its B-level, which in turn will find all its C-level sections, each of which will find all their D-level.

The recursion continues until every record has been added to our string. Then, on line 35, we close the recordSet and on line 38 we return the string. This brings us back to line 8, where we place a </toc> endtag.

Figure 7.5

The results of the actions taken upon ShowTOC.ASP.

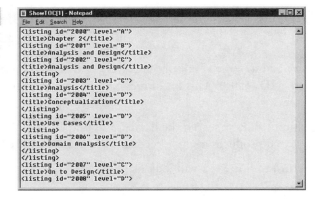

```
ShowTOC[1] - Notepad
File Edit Search Help
<listing id="2000" level="A">
<title>Chapter 2</title>
<listing id="2001" level="B">
<title>Analysis and Design</title>
<listing id="2002" level="C">
<title>Analysis and Design</title>
</listing>
<listing id="2003" level="C">
<title>Analysis</title>
<listing id="2004" level="D">
<title>Conceptualization</title>
</listing>
<listing id="2005" level="D">
<title>Use Cases</title>
</listing>
<listing id="2006" level="D">
<title>Domain Analysis</title>
</listing>
</listing>
<listing id="2007" level="C">
<title>On to Design</title>
<listing id="2008" level="D">
```

On line 11 we create the FromScratch.xslTransform object we've seen before, and on line 12 we set its InputXML property to the string we just created. This calls ParseIntoDOM as we've seen in earlier chapters, and a new XML DOMDocument is created, containing the XML from the string in tocXML.

Transforming the XML to the Table of Contents

Now that we have our XML document we can begin the process of creating a Table of Contents for display. To accomplish this, we'll rely on XSL, which will transform our XML into HTML, and along the way we'll write out the client-side script we require.

Before we can undertake to use XSL to transform our XML into HTML, we must know what the HTML will look like. Building a collapsible TOC is a non-trivial task, so we begin by getting it to work in HTML. Once we know what HTML and script we need, it will be easier to create the XSL.

Building the TOC in HTML

The collapsible TOC will list the title of each "story." We'll prepend this text with one of three symbols: a plus sign if it has children and is collapsed, a minus sign if it has children and is expanded, or an asterisk if it is a leaf. We saw this in Figure 7.1.

To get this started, I'll create the scripts to manipulate the listings. Once this works, I'll be able to go back to XSL and create the scripts, HTML, and data all from the XML DOMDocument created from the database.

Listing 7.2 shows the HTML required to accomplish this design goal.

Listing 7.2 TOC.htm

```
0:   <html>
1:       <head>
2:       <style>
3:           * {font-family:Verdana; font-size:10pt;}
4:           .listing {margin-bottom:3pt; cursor:hand;}
5:           .expand {color:red;}
6:       </style>
7:       <script>
8:       <!--
9:       function Expand()
10:      {
11:          // get to the "owning" div
12:          var e = window.event.srcElement.parentElement.
             ➥parentElement;
13:          var sign = e.children(0).children(0);
             ➥// the plus/minus sign span
14:
15:          // if we were expanded, then hide the contents
16:          // don't do anything if there's no sign (ie. leaf node)
17:          switch (sign.innerText)
18:          {
19:          case '-':
20:              sign.innerText = '+';
21:              for (var i = 1; i < e.children.length; i++)
22:                e.children(i).style.display="none";
23:              break;
24:          case '+':
25:              sign.innerText = '-';
26:              for (var i = 1; i < e.children.length; i++)
27:                e.children(i).style.display="";
28:              break;
29:          }
30:      }
31:      function Highlight(on)
32:      {
33:          // change the background as the mouse
             ➥passes over selections
34:          event.srcElement.style.backgroundColor =
             ➥(on ? "yellow" : "");
35:          return false;
36:      }
37:      function ShowStory()
38:      {
39:          // cause the rh frame to display the selected story –
             ➥we have the story id as the listing element's id
40:          var srcId = event.srcElement.id;
41:
42:          // tack on options to control the "mode" of display,
             ➥based on checkboxes in BookControls.htm
```

continues

7

Listing 7.2   Continued

```
43:             var NonCSS = parent.frames.bottom.NonCSS.checked;
44:             var CodeBlocks = parent.frames.bottom.CodeBlocks.checked;
45:
46:             parent.frames.rh.location.href = "ShowStory.asp?StoryId="
                ➥+ srcId + (NonCSS ? "&NonCSS=y" : "") +
                ➥(CodeBlocks ? "&CodeBlocks=y" : "");
47:             return false;
48:         }
49:         -->
50:     </script>
51:     </head>
52:     <body>
53:         <div>
54:             <div class="listing" style="margin-left:0em">
55:                 <span class="expand" onclick="Expand()">-</span>
56:                 <span onmouseover="Highlight(true)"
57:                     onmouseout="Highlight(false)"
58:                     onclick="ShowStory()" id="1000">Chapter 1</span>
59:             </div>
60:             <div>
61:                 <div class="listing" style="margin-left:2em">
62:                     <span class="expand" onclick="Expand()">-</span>
63:                     <span onmouseover="Highlight(true)"
64:                         onmouseout="Highlight(false)"
65:                         onclick="ShowStory()" id="1001">
                            ➥Getting Started</span>
66:                 </div>
67:                 <div>
68:                     <div class="listing" style="margin-left:4em">
69:                     <span class="expand" onclick="Expand()">-</span>
70:                     <span onmouseover="Highlight(true)"
71:                         onmouseout="Highlight(false)"
72:                         onclick="ShowStory()" id="1002">How this book
                            ➥is organized</span>
73:                     </div>
74:                     <div>
75:                     <div class="listing" style="margin-left:6em">
76:                     <span class="expand" onclick="Expand()">*</span>
77:                     <span onmouseover="Highlight(true)"
78:                     onmouseout="Highlight(false)"
79:                     onclick="ShowStory()" id="1003">Unabashedly
                        ➥Microsoft Only</span>
80:                     </div>
81:                 </div>
82:             </div>
83:         </body>
84: </html>
```

If you put this code into a file (without the line numbers, of course) and save it as an HTML file, you can view it in your browser and see that the contents do in fact expand and collapse, as shown in Figure 7.6.

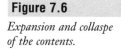

Figure 7.6

Expansion and collaspe of the contents.

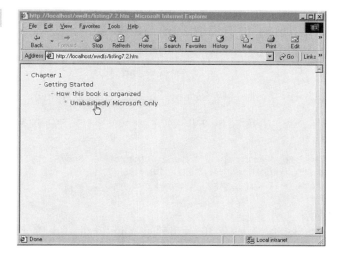

To make this magic work, we need three client-side scripts, shown on lines 9–50. We'll examine them in increasing order of complexity, starting with the simplest: `Highlight()`.

Highlight

Highlight, shown on lines 31–36, does nothing but access the element that fired the event handler, and set its background color to yellow if the parameter passed is "on" or else to the empty string (and thus the default background color).

The default background color is set in the style element within the head element, shown on lines 2–6. Line 3 shows that the default text style is 10 point Verdana.

```
3:          * {font-family:Verdana; font-size:10pt;}
```

We see, for example on lines 56 and 57 that Highlight is set as an event handler for `mouseover` and `mouseout` for the title.

```
56:                <span onmouseover="Highlight(true)"
 57:                    onmouseout="Highlight(false)"
```

This is repeated for each title, as shown on lines 64, 65, 70, 71, 77, and 78.

We call `highlight(on)` when the mouse is over the title, and that sets the background color to yellow, restoring it to default when we mouseout.

Show Story

Somewhat more complex is the `ShowStory()` event handler, which is called when the user clicks on a particular title, as shown for example on line 58.

```
58:                    onclick="ShowStory()" id="1000">Chapter 1</span>
```

This invokes the ShowStory method shown on lines 37–48. Every title has an id, and for example on line 40 we access that ID. We do this by asking for the id of the srcElement (that is the source element) of the event.

```
40:          var srcId = event.srcElement.id;
```

We'll skip over lines 42–44 for now and come back to them in a later chapter.

On line 46 we set the right-hand pane to ShowStory.asp, to which we pass the id as a parameter.

```
46:          parent.frames.rh.location.href = "ShowStory.asp?StoryId=" +
            ➥srcId + (NonCSS ? "&NonCSS=y" : "") +
            ➥(CodeBlocks ? "&CodeBlocks=y" : "");
```

Expand

Expand, shown on lines 9–30, is the heart and soul of the collapsible Table of Contents. On line 55, for example, we assign this event handler to the onclick event of our minus sign.

```
55:              <span class="expand" onclick="Expand()">-</span>
```

Every title in our HTML page will be within two div elements: an outer and an inner div. The inner div will be of class listing and will hold display information such as how far to indent. The outer div will be the point of control for collapsing and expanding the title.

To make this work, when you click on a minus sign of a particular title, we must gain access to the outer div of that title. On line 12 we do so by getting the grandparent of the srcElement.

```
12:          var e = window.event.srcElement.parentElement.parentElement;
```

Let's break this down. We get an event, which we can refer to as window.event. We can get to the element that fired the event (the click on the minus sign) by window.event.srcElement. We can get to the parent of that srcElement (that is the inner div) by window.event.srcElement.parentElement, and we get to its outer div by window.event.srcElement.parentElement.parentElement.

We assign that outerdiv element to the local variable, e. We then ask e for the first child of its first child (remember, in JavaScript collections are zero-based; the first element is element 0). That first child of the first child is the minus (or plus) sign, and we assign that to the variable sign.

```
13:          var sign = e.children(0).children(0);
            ➥// the plus/minus sign span
```

This code relies on an intimate understanding of the DOM we've created, but that is safe because this is the self-same code which created the DOM, and so we know just where to find the plus or minus sign.

In DHTML an element's inner text is the actual text displayed for that element. In the case of `sign.innerText` this will be the '-' or '+' sign itself. On line 17, we switch on that value and take action accordingly.

It may be confusing that we use `switch` here, rather than `xsl:choose`. Remember that at this point we are in client-side JavaScript, which will be sent to the browser and processed there.

If we have a minus sign, the case on lines 19–23, then we change it to a plus sign (`innerText` is read/write in DHTML, and this is why we say you need IE4 or better to use this application!). We then iterate through all the descendents of this element and set their display property to "none."

It is important to note the distinction between setting display to "none" versus setting the visibility property. When you set display="none" no room for the invisible elements is reserved. In IE4 or better, this causes the page to redraw without these elements; in effect the TOC closes up.

If, on the other hand, we currently have a plus sign, as shown on lines 24–28, we change the sign to minus, and we iterate through all these elements and change the display to an empty string; that is we make them visible and they are allocated room, the Table of Contents expands.

Creating the HTML from XML Using XSL

Now that our HTML works, we want to create an XSL file that will output the HTML we need from the XML we have. We'll call that file `TOC2HTML.xsl`, which we see invoked on line 13 of `ShowTOC.ASP`.

```
13:    oxsl:.xslFile = fso.BuildPath(codeDir, "Toc2HTML.xsl")
```

The effect of applying this XSL file against the XML file we built from the database ought to be very similar to the HTML we just examined. Let's take a look at the XSL file in detail, as shown in Listing 7.3.

Listing 7.3   `TOC2HTML.xsl`

```
 0:    <?XML version="1.0"?>
 1:    <!-- we use this style sheet to display the table of contents -->
 2:    <xsl:stylesheet
 3:        xmlns:xsl:="http://www.w3.org/TR/WD-xsl:"
 4:        xmlns="http://www/w3/org/TR/REC-html40"
 5:        result-ns="">
 6:
 7:        <!-- default rules -->
 8:        <xsl:template match="text()"><xsl:value-of/></xsl:template>
 9:
10:        <xsl:template match="/">
11:            <xsl:apply-templates />
12:        </xsl:template>
13:
14:        <!-- Our base element. Create the HTML structure, including
         ➥the scripts needed to expand/contract the elements -->
15:        <xsl:template match="toc">
16:        <html>
17:        <head>
18:        <style>
19:            * {font-family:Verdana; font-size:10pt;}
20:            .listing {margin-bottom:3pt; cursor:hand;}
21:            .expand {color:red;}
22:        </style>
23:        <script><xsl:comment><![CDATA[
24:        function Expand()
25:        {
26:            var e = window.event.srcElement.parentElement.
            ➥parentElement;    // get to the "owning" div
27:            var sign = e.children(0).children(0);
            ➥// the plus/minus sign span
28:
29:            // if we were expanded, then hide the contents
30:            // don't do anything if there's no sign (ie. leaf node)
31:            switch (sign.innerText)
32:            {
33:            case '-':
34:                sign.innerText = '+';
35:                for (var i = 1; i < e.children.length; i++)
36:                  e.children(i).style.display="none";
37:                break;
38:            case '+':
39:                sign.innerText = '-';
40:                for (var i = 1; i < e.children.length; i++)
41:                  e.children(i).style.display="";
42:                break;
43:            }
44:        }
45:        function Highlight(on)
46:        {
```

```
47:             event.srcElement.style.backgroundColor =
                ➥(on ? "yellow" : "");
48:             return false;
49:         }
50:     function ShowStory()
51:     {
52:         var srcId = event.srcElement.id;
53:         var UseCSS = parent.frames.bottom.UseCSS.checked;
54:         parent.frames.rh.location.href = "ShowStory.asp?StoryId="
            ➥+ srcId + (UseCSS ? "" : "&NonCSS=y");
55:         return false;
56:     }
57:     ]]></xsl:comment></script>
58:     </head>
59:     <body>
60:         <xsl:apply-templates />
61:     </body>
62:     </html>
63:     </xsl:template>
64:
65:     <xsl:script>
66:         // global for maintaining the current indent level
67:         var indent = 0;
68:     </xsl:script>
69:
70:     <!-- Each story has a listing element, that are nested
        ➥based on the book structure -->
71:     <xsl:template match="listing">
72:         <div>
73:             <!-- This inner div controls the indenting level -->
74:             <div class="listing">
75:                 <xsl:attribute name="style">margin-left:<xsl:eval>
                    ➥indent</xsl:eval>em</xsl:attribute>
76:                 <!-- The region that contains the +-
                    ➥sign for expanding -->
77:                 <span class="expand" onclick="Expand()">
78:                     <xsl:choose>
79:                         <!--
80:                             If I have any listing nodes as children,
                            ➥then I am not a leaf, and so output a minus sign
81:                             for the expand/contract control. If I
                            ➥am a leaf, then just use a small dot
82:                         -->
83:                         <xsl:when test="listing">-</xsl:when>
84:                         <xsl:otherwise>&#183;</xsl:otherwise>
85:                     </xsl:choose></span>
86:                 <!--
87:                     This span holds the story title, and has mouse
                    ➥events to color it as the mouse moves over it
88:                     Clicking in this span will display the story in
                    ➥the rh pane, which is why we need the id attrib
```

continues

Listing 7.3   Continued

```
89:                    -->
90:                    <span onmouseover="Highlight(true)"
                    ➥onmouseout="Highlight(false)"
                    ➥onclick="ShowStory()">
91:                      <xsl:attribute name="id"><xsl:value-of select=
                      ➥"@id"/></xsl:attribute>
92:                      <xsl:value-of select="./title"/></span>
93:                    </div>
94:                    <!--
95:                      bump up the indent before we recurse, then restore
                      ➥ it when we're done
96:                      we have to use a global since there's no good way
                      ➥to pass in an argument
97:                    -->
98:                    <xsl:eval>indent += 2;"";</xsl:eval>
99:                    <xsl:apply-templates />
100:                   <xsl:eval>indent -= 2;"";</xsl:eval>
101:               </div>
102:          </xsl:template>
103:
104:          <!-- We don't have to do anything with titles, since we
             ➥retrieved its value when processing the listing element -->
105:          <xsl:template match="title">
106:          </xsl:template>
107:
108:     </xsl:stylesheet>
```

By this time you ought to be more comfortable scanning an XSL document, and I won't review in detail the same material we've discussed earlier in the book. On line 0 we see, for example, the standard processing instruction, and on lines 2–5 we create the namespaces. Line 8 handles text elements, and lines 10–12 match the root element and recurse into our input XML DOMDocument.

The first new element we see is on line 15, where we match on the toc element we created on line 8 of Listing 7.1.

```
15:        <xsl:template match="toc">
```

On lines 16–63 we write out HTML. The effect is that the TOC element is replaced by all the HTML we need at the top of our Table of Contents HTML document. Let's look at this in some detail.

Line 17 and 18 create the expected html and head tags. Lines 18–22 establish three styles. The first, shown on line 19, will be the default style for our new HTML document. The second, on line 20, will be the style assigned to any element marked with the attribute class="listing". Finally, on line 21 we create a style for the plus and minus signs called expand.

Line 23 creates a `script` element in the output DOMDocument. This will create client-side script in the HTML file, which will be run in the user's browser.

```
23:        <script><xsl:comment><![CDATA[
```

XSL comments are not passed along to the output HTML. If we want a comment in HTML (which we do) then we must use the `xsl:comment` element to create one. We want to put our script in a comment in the HTML file, because some browsers can't handle script, and they'll ignore it if it is in a comment.

At the end of line 23 we add a `<![CDATA[` tag, which tells the XSL parser that the contents of the comment are not to be parsed (and thus, we can include otherwise restricted characters such as the > and < signs).

Lines 23–57 are the client-side script to handle the expansion and contraction of elements in the table of contents. This is exactly the script we examined in our HTML file, transposed right into our XSL document, and marked with CDATA so it won't be processed, but merely passed along to the output HTML.

On line 57 we close the CDATA element, we close the `xsl:comment` element, and we close the HTML script element. On line 58 we close the `head` element for the HTML document.

Lines 59–63 ensure that the remaining output will be bracketed within `body` tags, and that the entire HTML document will end with a closing `</html>` tag.

Creating the Listing Elements

What goes within that body tag is decided by the remainder of the XSL page.

Lines 65–68 create a global variable for use in the remainder of the document. To do so, we open an `xsl:script`, but the only work we do in the script is to create the variable `indent` and initialize it to `0` (zero). We'll see what this is for in just a moment.

```
65:        <xsl:script>
66:            // global for maintaining the current indent level
67:            var indent = 0;
68:        </xsl:script>
```

You will remember that in Listing 7.1 we created listing elements. On line 71 of Listing 7.2 we match those listing elements.

```
71:        <xsl:template match="listing">
```

For each listing found we will add to the output document a `div` element, which we'll refer to as the "outer div" because within that element we'll create a second, "inner" `div` element. This inner `div` will have the attribute `class` with the hard-wired value `listing`. The effect is that the inner `div` will use the style for listing, which we added earlier, on line 20 (each listing has a 3 point bottom margin and sets the cursor to hand).

You will remember that in our HTML document, we created indentation for contained elements by using a style element. We see this for example on lines 54 and 61 of Listing 7.2:

```
54:<div class="listing" style="margin-left:0em">
61:    <div class="listing" style="margin-left:2em">
```

On line 75 of our XSL file, shown in Listing 7.3, we give the inner div an attribute style whose value will be margin-left: followed by the value of the global variable indent. We then add the letters "em" to the value of that attribute. Thus, at the moment, this would produce

```
<div class="listing" style="margin-left:0em">
```

Look familiar? This is exactly what we saw on line 54 of the HTML.

We next create an element span to hold the plus, minus, or asterisk. The span has a class attribute expand, and an event handler. The effect is that the output document now also includes this tag:

```
<span class="expand" onclick="Expand()">
```

The contents of the span are decided on lines 78–85. We've seen the xsl:choose, xsl:when, and xsl:otherwise elements before.

Each line will be given an asterisk (*) if it is a leaf, or a minus (-) if it has children. No lines will be given plus signs (+) at this time, because our specification states that all topics are fully expanded when first displayed.

On line 83 we use the test=*pattern* attribute of the xsl:when element.

```
83:        <xsl:when test="listing">-</xsl:when>
```

This returns true if searching the children of the current element will find at least one to match the pattern. The pattern we use here is listing; the effect is to match when the current element has children which are also listings (that is, for example, when a C-level has D-level children). If this does match, we output a minus sign (-), otherwise we are a leaf and we output an asterisk. Line 85 closes the xsl:choose and the span.

Our output, for listings with children, will now look like this:

```
<span class="expand" onclick="Expand()">-</span>
```

Next, we need to create a span for the title itself. We output a span element on line 90 with three event handlers.

```
90:                    <span onmouseover="Highlight(true)" onmouseout=
                    ➥"Highlight(false)" onclick="ShowStory()">
```

We add one more attribute to this HTML element span, id whose value is set to the value of the current XML element's attribute id. Thus the span in the output HTML looks like this.

```
<span onmouseover="Highlight(true)" onmouseout="Highlight(false)"
➥onclick="ShowStory()" id = "1000">
```

We follow this by outputting the title. We obtain the title by using the xsl:value-of element with a select attribute that searches for the title element, which is a child of the current element.

Skinning Cats

In XML there is often more than one way to accomplish the same goal. Here we've created our TOC by extracting stories from the database, building an XML DOMDocument by concatenating strings, and then applying an XSL stylesheet.

You will remember, however, that before we put the stories *into* the database, we first created XML files for each chapter. We could, if we chose, create the same dynamic Table Of Contents by going back to these chapters and applying an XSL file against them to create the TOC.

In fact, we have a pair of options. We could, on the one hand, manipulate the chapter's XML file into a Table of Contents DOMDocument indistinguishable from the one created from the database. We then would simply apply the same XSL file as we did in this chapter: Toc2HTML.xsl.

As an alternative, we can manipulate the chapter's XML directly into the requisite html by creating a new XSL file, perhaps called xml2toc2HTML.xsl.

Let's examine these one at a time, to see how this might be done.

From XML to XML

We begin by writing an XSL file which we can apply against chap2.xml and produce an output file to feed to toc2html.xsl. To be clear, the XML file we produce will be identical to the XMLDOMDocument we just created out of the database; this time however we'll create it from Chap2.xml.

To do this, it helps to review the structure of the input XML file (chap2.xml) and then to consider the structure of the input expected by Toc2HTML.xsl.

We know that the XML expected by `Toc2HTML.xsl` is very simple, as illustrated in Figure 7.7.

Figure 7.7

The results of the actions taken upon ShowToc.ASP, revisited.

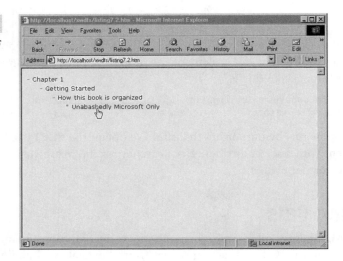

This, remember, was produced by reading from the database and creating a string which was used to create a DOMDocument. That DOMDocument was then fed to `Toc2HTML.xsl`.

`Chap2.xml` is far more complex than this; an excerpt of this is shown in Listing 7.4.

Listing 7.4 `Chap2.xml`

```
 0:  <?XML version="1.0"?>
 1:  <!DOCTYPE book SYSTEM "canon.dtd">
 2:  <book><section level="A" id="2000"><title>Chapter 2</title>
     <section level="B" id="2001"><title>Analysis and Design</title>
     <div class="FT">
 3:  This is not a book on Object-oriented Analysis and Design.
     I already wrote one of those (
 4:          <i>
 5:  Beginning Object-oriented Analysis and Design. Wrox
     Press 1998 ISBN1-861-001-33-9)
 6:          </i>
 7:
 8:  , and it takes a few hundred pages to explain OOA&amp;D
     in any detail.
 9:          </div>
10:             <div class="FT">
11:  That said, we can't examine a program in depth without
     understanding how it will be used, and so we must spend some time on
      analysis. In addition, before we examine the code, we'll want to
     understand the object model we plan to implement.
```

```
12:        </div>
13:             <div class="FT">
14: This chapter will provide a whirl-wind description of the analysis
    ➥ and design of EmployeeNet: an application for managing human resources
    ➥ in a middle-sized corporation. Hang on to your hat, we're going to do
    ➥ this very quickly.
15:        </div>
16:             <section level="C" id="2002"><title>Analysis and
                ➥ Design</title><div class="FT">
17: With a large project such as EmployeeNet, I would expect to invest
    ➥ a significant amount of time on Analysis (understanding the
    ➥requirements) and design (modeling the solution) before beginning
    ➥implementation (writing the code).
18:        </div>
19:             <div class="FT">
20: In 1992 I would have speculated that EmployeeNet was a two year
    ➥project. I would have been wrong, of course; by the time we were done,
    ➥ it would have slipped out to three years!
21:        </div>
22:             <div class="FT">
23: By 1995 I might have known that we had less than a year to build
    ➥ a project like this, because the world is speeding up, and Internet
    ➥ sites had better hit the market in under a year.
24:        </div>
25:             <div class="FT">
26: The tools are getting better, we're all getting smarter about how
    ➥ to build Web applications and the competition is fierce. The time frame
    ➥ keeps shrinking. Today, I believe we must endeavor to get a first
    ➥release out the door in 4-6 months. Perhaps less. To do this, I'd spend
    ➥ about a month on analysis, another month on design and then two months
    ➥coding and a month testing. These estimates make it sound like one phase
    ➥ ends before the other begins which is not true, but they do give a good
    ➥ rough and ready approximation of how I'd divide my time.
27:        </div>
28:             </section><section level="C" id="2003"><title>Analysis
                ➥</title><div class="FT">
29: EmployeeNet will manage the human resources needs of middle-sized
    ➥ corporations. The project is being sponsored by Acme Manufacturing, and
    ➥ we'll build it to meet their needs and then generalize for other
    ➥companies as we go.
30:        </div>
31:             <div class="FT">
32: Acme employs 2,000 people in the manufacture of high-end consumer
    ➥products. Their principal products are the Acme Widget and their world-
    ➥famous Gizmo. They have manufacturing plants in East Podunk and New
    ➥Boondock and their main offices are in Gotham.
33:        </div>
34:             <section level="D" id="2004"><title>
                ➥Conceptualization</title><div class="FT">
35: EmployeeNet will allow the personnel department to track all
    ➥benefits for employees, and will allow employees to review and edit
    ➥their own employment records.
```

continues

Listing 7.4 Continued

```
36:          </div>
37:                    </section><section level="D" id="2005"><title>
                       ➥Use Cases</title><div class="FT">
38:  There was a time when the typical requirements for a software
     ➥project were expressed in terms of capabilities and performance. While
     ➥ this ensured that the resulting system met certain specified
     ➥benchmarks,
39:          <spacerun len="1"/>
40:
41:  it did not ensure that anyone could or would want to use it.
     ➥Typically the user didn't factor into consideration until after the
     ➥ product was out the door.
42:          </div>
43:                    <div class="FT">
44:  Object-oriented analysis begins with a thorough understanding
     ➥ of how the product will be
45:          <i>
46:  used
47:          </i>
48:  . A
49:              <b>
50:  use-case
```

As you can see, we need only a very small percentage of the information in the input XML file to produce our output XML file. Essentially, we need to find the section elements (highlighted in the excerpt) and turn them into listing elements, picking up the titles as we go and maintaining the nesting structure. We can ignore virtually all the remaining elements.

To accomplish this, I will save `Control.asp` as `ControlR2.asp` (revision 2), and I'll add a menu choice for `Make TOC From XML`, as shown in this excerpt:

```
55:      case "Make TOC from XML"
56:          Response.Write MakeTOCFromXML()
```

As you can see, this invokes the script function `MakeTOCFromXML()`, shown in Listing 7.5 (the line numbering indicates that this is an excerpt from the `ControlR2.ASP` file).

Listing 7.5 `ControlR2.asp`

```
180:      Function MakeTOCFromXML()
181:          'convert XML file to TOC Listing file
182:          dim oxsl:, fn
183:
184:          set oxsl: = Server.CreateObject("FromScratch.xslTransform")
185:
186:          'convert xhtml to XML via a stylesheet
187:          oxsl:.InputFile = dataPath & ".xml"
188:          oxsl:.xslFile = fso.BuildPath(codeDir, "XML2TOC.xsl")
```

```
189:
190:            oxsl:.Transform
191:
192:            fn = dataPath & ".toc.xml"
193:            oxsl:.SaveOutputAsFile fn
194:
195:            MakeTOCFromXML = "TOC constructed"
196:        End Function
```

The work of this code is to create an instance of our ActiveX object, as shown on line 184, and provide as input the original chapter's XML file, shown on line 187, as well as the XSL file, shown on line 188.

We then call transform, shown on line 190, which is *exactly* the same method we've called in the past to apply an XSL page against an XML DOMDocument.

The output file chap2.toc.xml is created on lines 192–193. The real work, of course, is done in XML2TOC.xsl, shown in Listing 7.6.

Listing 7.6 XML2TOC.xsl

```
0:   <?XML version="1.0"?>
1:
2:   <!--
3:       Given a chapter's .xml file, (e.g., chap3.xml) create an output
4:       XML which can be read by toc2html.xsl
5:   -->
6:
7:   <xsl:stylesheet
8:       xmlns:xsl:="http://www.w3.org/TR/WD-xsl:"
9:       xmlns="http://www/w3/org/TR/REC-XML"
10:      result-ns="">
11:
12:      <xsl:template match="/">
13:          <xsl:pi name="XML">version="1.0"</xsl:pi>
14:          <xsl:apply-templates />
15:      </xsl:template>
16:
17:      <!-- catch any unknown tags -->
18:      <xsl:template match="*">
19:          <unknown><xsl:attribute name="tag">
          ➥<xsl:node-name/></xsl:attribute>
20:              <xsl:apply-templates />
21:          </unknown>
22:      </xsl:template>
23:
24:      <!-- our top level tag -->
25:      <xsl:template match="book">
26:          <toc>
27:              <xsl:apply-templates/>
28:          </toc>
```

continues

Listing 7.6   Continued

```
29:        </xsl:template>
30:
31:        <!-- tags we can ignore -->
32:        <xsl:template match="head|title|style|body|script|a|
           ↪meta|link|div|b|i|spacerun|tab|note|u|noteline|codeline|code|char">
           ↪<xsl:apply-templates/></xsl:template>
33:
34:        <!-- find the sections, create listings. Then create titles. -->
35:        <xsl:template match="section">
36:            <listing>
37:                <xsl:attribute name="id"><xsl:value-of select="@id"/>
                   ↪</xsl:attribute>
38:                <xsl:attribute name="level"><xsl:value-of select=
                   ↪"@level"/></xsl:attribute>
39:                <title><xsl:value-of select="./title"/></title>
40:                <xsl:apply-templates/>
41:            </listing>
42:        </xsl:template>
43:    </xsl:stylesheet>
```

The first 15 lines should be very familiar by now. Lines 18–23 handle unrecognized tags; if all goes well, these are never invoked.

The work is between lines 24 and 42. Our goal is to match the book element in the XML file and turn it into a toc tag. We then want to match each section, and create the listing elements with the id, level, and title that will constitute our output file, which we can then feed to Toc2HTML.xsl.

Lines 24–29 match the book element (there should be just one), and create our new toc element. Everything we find will be bracketed by the opening <toc> and the closing </toc> element tags.

> **Note**
>
> We know we don't have to match story elements, because our input is always a chapter, for example chap2.xml. We know that these consist of book elements, as described by our canonical DTD.

On line 32 we explicitly ignore all the tags we know about that we're not interested in. Note that we are explicitly ignoring the title tag; this is because the title will be picked up along with the section element, as shown in the final lines of the file. Let's look at these in detail.

On line 35 we match the section element, and we create a listing element in the output DOMDocument. We assign two attributes to the listing: id and level.

These are each picked up directly from the corresponding attributes in the `section` element. We then add a `title` element, searching the current element (`section`) for its immediate children, matching on `title` and then assigning to our new `title` the value of the original `title`.

That's it. When we call `Transform` as shown on line 190 of Listing 7.5, our XML file is transformed according to the rules of our XSL stylesheet, and the resulting file is saved to disk, as shown in Listing 7.7.

Listing 7.7   `TOC.xml`

```
0:   <?xml version="1.0"?>
1:   <toc>
2:       <listing id="1000" level="A">
3:           <title>Chapter x1</title>
4:           <listing id="1001" level="B">
5:               <title>Getting Started</title>
6:               <listing id="1002" level="C">
7:                   <title>How this book is organized</title>
8:                   <listing id="1003" level="D">
9:                       <title>Unabashedly Microsoft Only</title>
10:                  </listing>
11:                  <listing id="1004" level="D">
12:                      <title>About the project: EmployeeNet</title>
13:                  </listing>
14:              </listing>
15:              <listing id="1005" level="C">
16:                  <title>What tools you need</title>
17:                  <listing id="1006" level="D">
18:                      <title>How many machines?</title>
19:                  </listing>
20:                  <listing id="1007" level="D">
21:                      <title>Setting up your development
                          ➥environment</title>
22:                  </listing>
23:              </listing>
24:              <listing id="1008" level="C">
25:                  <title>What do you already need to know?</title>
26:                  <listing id="1009" level="D">
27:                      <title>Scale</title>
28:                  </listing>
29:              </listing>
30:              <listing id="1010" level="C">
31:                  <title>Distributed interNet Applications  N-Tier
                     ➥ development</title>
32:                  <listing id="1011" level="D">
33:                      <title>A brief history</title>
34:                  </listing>
35:                  <listing id="1012" level="D">
36:                      <title>Logical vs. Physical layers</title>
```

continues

Listing 7.7   Continued

```
37:                    </listing>
38:                </listing>
39:                <listing id="1013" level="C">
40:                    <title>Components and Microsoft's Component Object
                     ➥ Model</title>
41:                    <listing id="1014" level="D">
42:                        <title>MTS and COM+</title>
43:                    </listing>
44:                </listing>
45:                <listing id="1015" level="C">
46:                    <title>Next Steps</title>
47:                </listing>
48:            </listing>
49:        </listing>
50:  </toc>
```

This file can now be viewed using the *exact* same Toc2HTML.xsl file as was used when we built this structure from the database.

From XML to HTML

Why bother creating this interim file, however? Why not just output HTML? A few simple changes to our XSL file will accomplish this. We already know just what is needed because we've already written Toc2HTML.xsl. We can combine the logic of XML2TOC.xsl with Toc2HTML.xsl to produce xml2toc2html.xsl!

Let's add another function (and another button) to ControlR2.asp

```
58:            case "Make HTML TOC From XML"
59:                Response.Write MakeTOCFromXML2HTML()
```

The implementation for this function is shown in Listing 7.8.

Listing 7.8   ControlR2.asp

```
199:    Function MakeTOCFromXML2HTML()
200:        'convert XML file to TOC Listing file
201:        dim oxsl:, fn
202:
203:        set oxsl: = Server.CreateObject("FromScratch.xslTransform")
204:
205:        'convert xhtml to XML via a stylesheet
206:        oxsl:.InputFile = dataPath & ".xml"
207:        oxsl:.xslFile = fso.BuildPath(codeDir, "XML2TOC2HTML.xsl")
208:
209:        oxsl:.Transform
210:
211:        fn = dataPath & ".toc.htm"
212:        oxsl:.SaveOutputAsFile fn
213:
```

```
214:            MakeTOCFromXML2HTML = "TOC constructed as HTML"
215:        End Function
```

This function is just like the previous, only this time on line 207 we use a different
XSL stylesheet: xml2toc2html.xsl, as shown in Listing 7.9.

Listing 7.9 XML2TOC2HTML.xsl

```
 0:    <?xml version="1.0"?>
 1:
 2:    <!--
 3:        Given a chapter's .xml file, (e.g., chap3.xml) create a
 4:        dynamic TOC in html
 5:    -->
 6:
 7:    <xsl:stylesheet
 8:        xmlns:xsl="http://www.w3.org/TR/WD-xsl"
 9:        xmlns="http://www/w3.org/TR/REC-html40"
10:        result-ns="">
11:
12:        <xsl:template match="/">
13:            <xsl:apply-templates />
14:        </xsl:template>
15:
16:        <!-- catch any unknown tags -->
17:        <xsl:template match="*">
18:            <unknown><xsl:attribute name="tag">
            ➥<xsl:node-name/></xsl:attribute>
19:                <xsl:apply-templates />
20:            </unknown>
21:        </xsl:template>
22:
23:        <!-- our top level tag -->
24:        <xsl:template match="book">
25:            <html>
26:                <head>
27:                    <style>
28:                        * {font-family:Verdana; font-size:10pt;}
29:                        .listing {margin-bottom:3pt; cursor:hand;}
30:                        .expand {color:red;}
31:                    </style>
32:                    <script><xsl:comment><![CDATA[
33:                        function Expand()
34:                        {
35:                            var e = window.event.srcElement.
                            ➥parentElement.parentElement;    //
                            ➥get to the "owning" div
36:                            var sign = e.children(0).children(0);
                            ➥    // the plus/minus sign span
37:
38:            // if we were expanded, then hide the contents
```

continues

Listing 7.9   Continued

```
39:              // don't do anything if there's no sign (ie. leaf node)
40:                      switch (sign.innerText)
41:                      {
42:                      case '-':
43:                          sign.innerText = '+';
44:                          for (var i = 1; i <
                            ➥e.children.length; i++)
45:                            e.children(i).style.display="none";
46:                          break;
47:                      case '+':
48:                          sign.innerText = '-';
49:                          for (var i = 1; i <
                            ➥e.children.length; i++)
50:                            e.children(i).style.display="";
51:                          break;
52:                      }
53:                  }
54:              function Highlight(on)
55:              {
56:                  // change the background as the mouse
                    ➥passes over selections
57:                  event.srcElement.style.backgroundColor =
                    ➥(on ? "yellow" : "");
58:                  return false;
59:              }
60:              function ShowStory()
61:              {
62:                  // cause the rh frame to display the
                    ➥selected story -
                    ➥we have the story id as the listing element's id
63:                  var srcId = event.srcElement.id;
64:
65:
66:                  // tack on options to control the "mode"
                    ➥of display, based on checkboxes in
                    ➥BookControls.htm
67:                  // var NonCSS = parent.frames.bottom.
                    ➥NonCSS.checked;
68:                  // var CodeBlocks = parent.frames.bottom.
                    ➥CodeBlocks.checked;
69:                  // parent.frames.rh.location.href =
                    ➥"ShowStory.asp?StoryId=" + srcId +
                    ➥(NonCSS ? "&NonCSS=y" : "") +
                    ➥(CodeBlocks ? "&CodeBlocks=y" : "");
70:
71:                  parent.location.href = "ShowStory.asp?StoryId=" +
                    ➥srcId;
72:                  return false;
73:              }
74:          ]]></xsl:comment></script>
75:      </head>
```

```
76:                <body>
77:                    <xsl:apply-templates />
78:                </body>
79:            </html>
80:        </xsl:template>
81:
82:        <!-- tags we can ignore -->
83:        <xsl:template match="head|title|style|body|script|a|meta|link|
           ➥div|b|i|spacerun|tab|note|u|noteline|codeline|code|char">
           ➥<xsl:apply-templates/></xsl:template>
84:
85:        <xsl:script>
86:            // global for maintaining the current indent level
87:            var indent = 0;
88:        </xsl:script>
89:
90:
91:        <!-- find the sections, create listings.
        ➥ Then create titles. -->
92:        <xsl:template match="section">
93:
94:            <div>
95:                <!-- This inner div controls the indenting level -->
96:                <div class="listing">
97:                    <xsl:attribute name="style">margin-left:<xsl:eval>
                       ➥indent</xsl:eval>em</xsl:attribute>
98:                <!-- The region that contains the +- sign for
                   ➥expanding -->
99:                <span class="expand" onclick="Expand()">
100:                    <xsl:choose>
101:                        <!--
102:                            If I have any listing nodes as children,
                               ➥then I am not a leaf,
                               ➥and so output a minus sign
103:                            for the expand/contract control. If I am
                           ➥ a leaf, then just use a small dot
104:                        -->
105:                        <xsl:when test="section">-</xsl:when>
106:                        <xsl:otherwise>*</xsl:otherwise>
107:                    </xsl:choose></span>
108:                <!--
109:                    This span holds the story title, and has mouse
                       ➥events to color it as the mouse moves over it
110:                    Clicking in this span will display the story in
                       ➥ the rh pane, which is why we need the id attrib
111:                -->
112:                <span onmouseover="Highlight(true)" onmouseout=
                   ➥"Highlight(false)" onclick="ShowStory()">
113:                    <xsl:attribute name="id"><xsl:value-of select=
                       ➥"@id" /></xsl:attribute>
114:                    <xsl:value-of select="./title" /></span>
```

continues

Listing 7.9　Continued

```
115:                  </div>
116:                  <!--
117:                      bump up the indent before we recurse, then
                         ➥restore it when we're done
118:                      we have to use a global since there's no
                         ➥good way to pass in an argument
119:                  -->
120:                  <xsl:eval>indent += 2;"";</xsl:eval>
121:                      <!-- all we care about is section elements -
                         ➥we've already handled the title element above -->
122:                      <xsl:apply-templates select="section" />
123:                  <xsl:eval>indent -= 2;"";</xsl:eval>
124:              </div>
125:          </xsl:template>
126:      </xsl:stylesheet>
```

Although this is a long listing, there are few surprises. Our goal is to do the work originally done in the two previous XSL files. This new file represents a simple join of their logic.

The first 10 lines establish the XSL file and namespaces. Note that the output namespace is HTML as you'd expect; our final product from this XSL file is an HTML file we can view in a browser.

The logic in lines 12 through 21 is the same as in previous files, so I won't belabor the point. On line 24 we match on book, which again we can be guaranteed, as the input document will be a chapter, such as chap1.xml.

On matching book, this time we do not create a toc element, but rather we output to our HTML DOMDocument the necessary HTML that we saw previously in Toc2HTML.xsl. Thus we see the same style and script that we saw in the previous analysis. This covers lines 23 through 80.

On line 83 we match and ignore exactly the same elements we matched and ignored in xml2toc.xsl.

On line 92 we match on section, and here the logic becomes a combination of the two previous approaches. We match on section, because that is what we have in the XML file, and we output the inner and outer div elements that we require for the dynamic TOC. This logic is unchanged through line 125, and on line 126 we close off our XSL stylesheet.

As you can see, there is nothing novel in our use of XSL, but what is new here is that we're getting our input directly from the chapter's XML file, and our output is an HTML file we can browse.

Next Steps

We've seen that XSL combined with manipulation of the DOMDocument affords us great flexibility in our ability to transform XML in any number of different ways. Now that we have all of the individual pieces working, it is time to assemble our application, which we will do in the next chapter.

Chapter 8

Building the Application and Adding Missing Functionality

We now have nearly all the pieces working for our application. It is time to put them together and fill in the missing functionality.

The Application

You will remember from Chapter 1, "Getting Started with XML," that the application, BiblioTech, is a simple browser-based search engine that retrieves stories or sub-chapters from books I've written.

We envisioned using this to find appropriate explanations of concepts and to grab source code that can be cut and pasted into email messages.

BiblioTech will provide a list of all the topics in a book, either in list form or as a collapsible Table of Contents. Each topic will be active; clicking on the topic will display the related article. In addition, the user can search for words, either in the title or, ultimately, anywhere in the text.

Figure 8.1 shows how the application looks when you first fire it up.

Figure 8.1

BiblioTech.

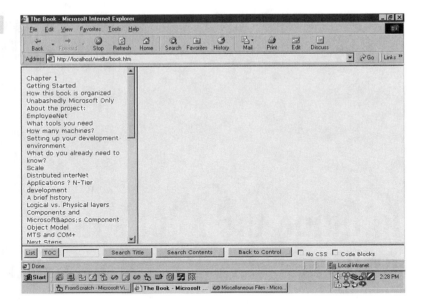

Figure 8.1

BiblioTech.

 Note

Que's publishing requirements dictate an 800x600 resolution, and so I've truncated the List All button and shortened the text field for this illustration.

You will remember that the purpose of this application is to assist the author in answering reader inquiries. We want to be able to search for stories based on words in the text or in the title, and we want to ensure that we can clip segments of code to the Windows clipboard so that we can paste them into return messages. In addition, we want to be able to use this application in down-level browsers, in case we're ever stuck running it with IE3!

Listing Stories

You can scroll through the list of topics, highlight a topic by hovering over it, and click it to display the story, as shown in Figure 8.2.

You can also choose to see the stories listed as a collapsible Table of Contents, as shown in Figure 8.3, by clicking the TOC button.

A new feature is the capability to search for an article by its title or by its contents, by filling in the text box and then clicking the appropriate button, as illustrated in Figure 8.4.

Figure 8.2

Display a story.

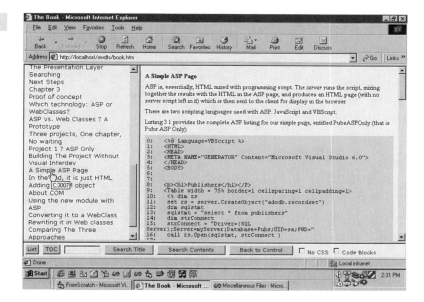

Figure 8.3

Table of contents.

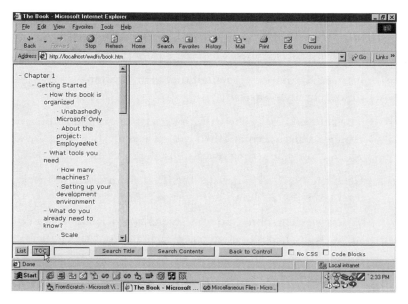

8

Figure 8.4

Searching.

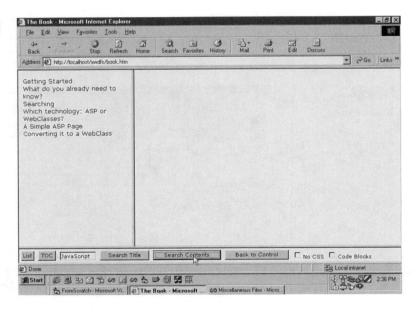

Here we've searched for the word JavaScript in the contents of all the stories, and the application has listed all the stories with that word anywhere in the text.

Down-Level Browsers and Clipping Code

To support browsers that do not support Cascading Style Sheets, we added a check box: "No CSS". To understand the effect of this check box, let's look at how cascading stylesheets are used when the button is _not_ checked.

Figure 8.5 shows a segment of the story "A Simple ASP Page" displayed with Cascading Style Sheets.

The code is actually shown with a gray background and the note with a green background. This is accomplished with cascading style sheets, as shown in Figure 8.6, which shows the source revealed by the right frame.

Checking No CSS eliminates the CSS, and utilizes the display functionality of down-level browsers, as shown in Figure 8.7.

When we view source, no CSS styling is provided, but we do see that in this version we are using tables to align our output and font tags to manage the rendering of the text.

Figure 8.5

Display with Cascading Style Sheets.

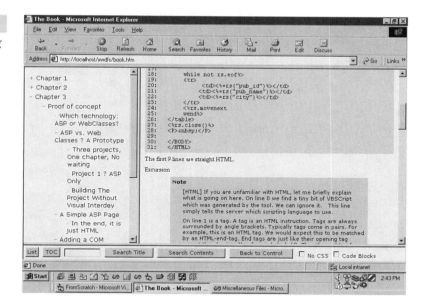

Figure 8.6

Source Code.

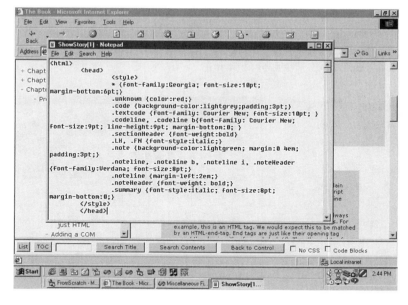

8

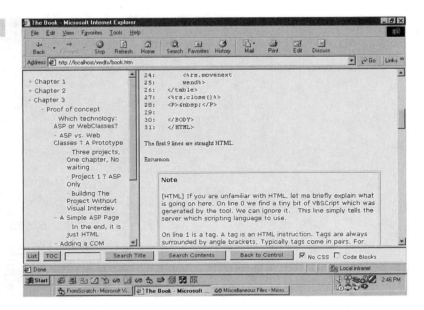

In addition to the check box to turn off CSS styling, we have added a check box marked Code Blocks. This adds the capability to clip code to the clipboard right from the display. Checking Code Blocks causes the display to include a button on each code block, as shown in Figure 8.8.

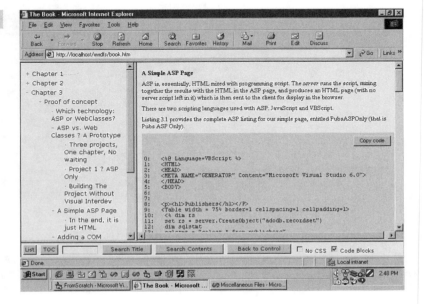

Clicking Copy Code in the code listing causes the code to be copied to the clipboard *without the line numbers* and with no HTML markup. The point of this is to put clean code on the clipboard, ready to be pasted into a development environment. For example, we can paste the code into a source code editor, as shown in Figure 8.9.

Figure 8.9

Pasting the source code.

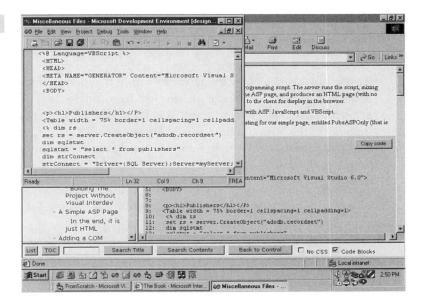

Examining the Application in Detail

We've seen much of the functionality for this application in previous chapters. Putting it all together into this frame-based application, adding the searching, the non-CSS functionality, and the code blocks are all new. The rest of this chapter will examine this new functionality in detail.

You run this application by clicking `Go To Book Application` on `Control.asp` or by navigating directly to `book.htm`. The file `book.htm`, which manages the application, is a very simple frameset, as illustrated in Listing 8.1.

Listing 8.1   `book.htm`

```
0:  <HTML>
1:  <HEAD>
2:  <META NAME="GENERATOR" Content="Microsoft Developer Studio">
3:  <META HTTP-EQUIV="Content-Type" content="text/html;
    ↪charset=iso-8859-1">
4:  <TITLE>The Book</TITLE>
5:  </HEAD>
```

continues

Listing 8.1   Continued

```
 6:   <frameset rows="*,32">
 7:       <frameset cols="30%,*">
 8:           <frame name="lh" src="StoryList.asp"/>
 9:           <frame name="rh"/>
10:       </frameset>
11:       <frame name="bottom" src="BookControls.htm"/>
12:   </frameset>
13:   </HTML>
```

As you can see, the outer frameset has within it an inner frameset, which in turn holds two frames. The first is lh, (for **l**eft-**h**and side) which is initialized to StoryList.asp. The second frame is rh (for **r**ight-**h**and side). Also within the outer frameset is the bottom frame named (appropriately) bottom, which is initialized with BookControls.htm. The right-hand frame, rh, initially has no page at all, and is therefore blank.

There are a number of things to explore in this application, but the control center is BookControls.htm, so let's start there, as shown in Listing 8.2.

Listing 8.2   BookControls.htm

```
 0:   <HTML>
 1:   <HEAD>
 2:   <META HTTP-EQUIV="Content-Type" content="text/html;
      ➥charset=iso-8859-1">
 3:   <style>
 4:   * {font-family:Verdana; font-size:8pt; margin:2;}
 5:   </style>
 6:   </HEAD>
 7:   <script>
 8:   </script>
 9:   <BODY>
10:   <input type="button" value="List All"
      ➥onclick="parent.frames.lh.document.location.href='StoryList.asp'">
11:   <input type="button" value="TOC"
      ➥onclick="parent.frames.lh.document.location.href='ShowTOC.asp'">
12:   <input id="searchText" size=20>
13:   <input type="button" value="Search Title"
14:       onclick="parent.frames.lh.document.location.href=
          ➥'StoryList.asp?searchTitle=' + searchText.value">
15:   <input type="button" value="Search Contents"
16:       onclick="parent.frames.lh.document.location.href='StoryList.asp?
          ➥searchContents=' + searchText.value">
17:   <input type="button" value="Back to Control"
      ➥onclick="parent.location.href='Control.asp'">
18:   <input type="checkbox" id="NonCSS">No CSS
19:   <input type="checkbox" id="CodeBlocks">Code Blocks
20:   </BODY>
21:   </HTML>
```

The first few lines are standard HMTL. We create a button on line 10 for "List All" (shown as List in Figure 8.1 to save space), and its onClick event is set to display StoryList.asp in the left-hand frame.

On line 11 we see a button marked TOC, which displays ShowToc.asp in the left-hand frame. With these two buttons, it is possible to toggle back and forth between a simple list of all the topics and an indented Table of Contents. We've seen ShowTOC.asp, but StoryList is new.

We'll examine StoryList.asp in just a moment, but note that on line 12 there is an input field. On line 13 we create a button called Search Title, which also calls StoryList, but this time passes in the string SearchTitle= concatenated with the value of whatever text is in the text field.

In addition, on line 15 is a button called SearchContents, which also is identical to line 14, but this time passes in the string SearchContents= with the contents of the text field concatenated.

The effect is that StoryList can be called in one of three ways: alone, with SearchTitle=, or with SearchContents=.

StoryList.asp

We'll return to the final lines of Listing 8.2 later in this chapter, but let's take a look first at how StoryList works, as shown in Listing 8.3.

Listing 8.3 StoryList.asp

```
0:  <!-- #include file ="include.asp" -->
1:  <HTML>
2:  <HEAD>
3:  <META HTTP-EQUIV="Content-Type" content="text/html;
    ➥charset=iso-8859-1">
4:  <style>
5:  * {font-family:Verdana; font-size:10pt;}
6:  .story {cursor: hand;}
7:  </style>
8:  </HEAD>
9:  <script>
10: function Highlight(on)
11: {
12:     // change the background as the mouse passes over selections
13:     event.srcElement.style.backgroundColor = (on ? "yellow" : "");
14:     return false;
15: }
16: function ShowStory()
17: {
```

continues

Listing 8.3   Continued

```
18:        // cause the rh frame to display the selected story -
           ➥we have the story id as the listing element's id
19:        var srcId = event.srcElement.id;
20:
21:        // tack on options to control the "mode" of display,
           ➥based on checkboxes in BookControls.htm
22:        var NonCSS = parent.frames.bottom.NonCSS.checked;
23:        var CodeBlocks = parent.frames.bottom.CodeBlocks.checked;
24:
25:        parent.frames.rh.location.href = "ShowStory.asp?StoryId=" +
           ➥srcId + (NonCSS ? "&NonCSS=y" : "") +
           ➥(CodeBlocks ? "&CodeBlocks=y" : "");
26:        return false;
27:    }
28:    </script>
29:    <BODY>
30:    <%
31:        'construct a SQL WHERE clause based on the search arguments
32:        dim where
33:
34:        'default to all stories
35:        where = ""
36:
37:        'search by title
38:        if Request("searchTitle") <> "" then
39:            where = "where title like '%" &
               ➥Replace(Request("searchTitle"), "'", "''") & "%'"
40:        end if
41:
42:        'search by text within the bodies
43:        if Request("searchContents") <> "" then
44:            where = "where TaglessText like '%" &
               ➥Replace(Request("searchContents"), "'", "''") & "%'"
45:        end if
46:
47:        'get the selected stories and list their titles.
           ➥make the id of each element be the story id
48:        set rs = DBConn.Execute("select StoryId, SectionLevel,
           ➥Title from Stories " & where & " order by StoryId")
49:        do until rs.eof
50:    %>
51:    <div><span class="story" id="<% =rs("StoryId") %>"
       ➥title="<% =rs("SectionLevel") & ":" & rs("StoryId") %>"
52:        onmouseover="Highlight(true)" onmouseout="Highlight(false)"
           ➥onclick="ShowStory()"><% =rs("Title") %></span></div>
53:    <%
54:            rs.MoveNext
55:        loop
56:    %>
57:    </BODY>
58:    </HTML>
```

This file is divided into three sections: client-side script, server-side script, and HTML. The latter two sections overlap a bit, as server-side script and HTML are intermixed in ASP files.

We begin on lines 4–7 with a short CSS style section in which we set the default style (using *) and the style for stories (which sets the cursor to hand on mouseOver).

Lines 9–28 show the client-side script section, which consists of two methods: Highlight and ShowStory. These are essentially the same as we saw in the previous chapter.

Highlight() is used to add color to the story title on mouseOver; ShowStory is used to select the story when the title is clicked. Each of these is set as an event handler on lines 51–52. We'll return to these lines shortly.

ShowStory begins on line 19 by determining the ID of the element that invoked the handler: that is, the title that was clicked. On line 22 we can see whether the NonCSS check box is checked, and on line 23 we can see the CodeBlocks check box.

Line 25 is where the work is done. We set the right-hand frame to display the ShowStory.asp page, passing in to that page the parameter StoryID set to the id we extracted on line 19, followed by either or both of two possible flags. If NonCSS is checked, then the parameter string is appended with "&NonCSS=y" and if CodeBlocks is checked, then the parameter string is appended with "&CodeBlocks=y".

> **Note**
>
> The ternary operator (?) is a JavaScript, Java, and C++ construct. It consists of three terms: the test, the return for true, and the return for false. In the case shown, for example, we test the value of NonCSS; if it is true we return the string "&NonCSS=y"; if it is false we return the empty string.
>
> When you invoke an ASP page with a string such as "ShowStory.asp?StoryID=5&NonCSS=y" the ASP Request Object QueryString collection will contain two entries: StoryID and NonCSS. The value of the former will be 5 and the value of the latter will be y.

On line 30 we begin server-side script which builds a SQL statement to execute on the server, depending on the value of the SearchTitle and SearchContents variables in the ASP Request object. These values are set when StoryList is invoked by bookControls.htm as shown on line 14 of Listing 8.2.

```
14: onclick="parent.frames.lh.document.location.href='StoryList.asp?
    ➥searchTitle=' + searchText.value">
```

8

The SQL statement itself is invoked on line 48, returning records each with three fields: StoryID, SectionLevel, and Title. On lines 49–55 we iterate through these records, creating a <div> for each record to hold the titles of each story. It is here that we set the event handlers.

Implementing XSL for Down-Level Browsers

Let's review: book.htm and bookControl.htm work with ShowTOC or StoryList to create a list of titles in the right-hand frame.

When the user clicks on a particular story, ShowStory is called, and the state of the two check boxes is passed in as a parameter. When we examined ShowStory in the previous chapter we ignored these parameters, assuming they were blank (representing that the check boxes were unchecked).

Let's take a look at what happens when the NonCSS check box *is* checked, requesting that we display the story without the use of Cascading Style Sheets. Because ShowStory.asp is brief, I've reproduced it in full in Listing 8.4.

Listing 8.4   **ShowStory.asp**

```
0:  <!-- #include file ="include.asp" -->
1:  <%
2:      'ShowStory.asp - retrieves the XML for
        ➥single story from the database,
3:      'converts it into HTML via an XSL stylesheet,
        ➥and displays the results
4:
5:      dim storyId, xml, oXSL, styleSheetName
6:
7:      storyId = Request("storyId")
8:
9:      'get the XML from the database
10:     set rs = DBConn.Execute("select xml from stories
        ➥where storyId = " & storyId)
11:     xml = rs("xml").value
12:     rs.close
13:
14:     'transform to HTML via the XSL stylesheet
15:     set oXSL = Server.CreateObject("FromScratch.XSLTransform")
16:     oXSL.InputXML = xml
17:     styleSheetName = "Story2HTML.xsl"
18:     if Request("NonCSS") <> "" then styleSheetName =
        ➥"Story2HTMLNonCSS.xsl"
19:     oXSL.XSLFile = fso.BuildPath(codeDir, styleSheetName)
20:     oXSL.Transform
21:
22:     'display the HTML
23:     response.write oXSL.OutputXML
24:  %>
```

You will remember that we extract the story from the database on lines 7–12, and then we read it from the database record into an XMLDOMDocument on lines 15–16.

On line 17 we set the XSL stylesheet to Story2HTML.xsl as we saw previously. On line 18, however, we check the NonCSS Request variable.

```
18:      if Request("NonCSS") <> "" then styleSheetName =
    ➥"Story2HTMLNonCSS.xsl"
```

Last time we assumed it was empty and thus had no impact. This time let's assume the check box was checked, and this variable now has the value "y"; in this case the variable styleSheetName is changed to Story2HTMLNonCSS.xsl, which invokes a different XSL stylesheet, as shown in Listing 8.5.

Listing 8.5   `Story2HTMLNonCSS.xsl`

```
 0:   <?xml version="1.0"?>
 1:   <!-- Stylesheet for displaying XML stories, but for a down-level
    ➥ browser - no use of styles -->
 2:   <xsl:stylesheet
 3:       xmlns:xsl="http://www.w3.org/TR/WD-xsl"
 4:       xmlns="http://www/w3/org/TR/REC-html40"
 5:       result-ns="">
 6:
 7:       <!-- default rule for text nodes - just output the text -->
 8:       <xsl:template match="text()">
 9:           <xsl:value-of/>
10:       </xsl:template>
11:
12:       <!-- the root node - output the structure of the HTML page
    ➥ and begin the recursion -->
13:       <xsl:template match="/">
14:       <html>
15:           <xsl:apply-templates/>
16:       </html>
17:       </xsl:template>
18:
19:       <!-- sentinel for any left over tags -->
20:       <xsl:template match="*">
21:           <div><font color="red">
22:               !!<xsl:node-name/>!!
23:               <xsl:apply-templates />
24:           </font></div>
25:       </xsl:template>
26:
27:       <!--
28:           The top level element - might be story or book
    ➥depending on who's calling
29:           Just wraps the content inside <body> tags
```

continues

Listing 8.5   Continued

```
30:            Then finishes with some summary info about numbers
               ➥of nodes of different kinds
31:        -->
32:     <xsl:template match="story¦book">
33:     <body>
34:         <font face="Georgia" size="2">
35:         <xsl:apply-templates/>
36:         <p><i>
37:             Section summary
38:             <br/><xsl:eval>this.selectNodes("//div").length
                ➥</xsl:eval> paragraphs
39:             <br/><xsl:eval>this.selectNodes("//code").length
                ➥</xsl:eval> code blocks
40:             <br/><xsl:eval>this.selectNodes("//note").length
                ➥</xsl:eval> notes
41:         </i></p></font>
42:     </body>
43:     </xsl:template>
44:
45:     <!-- We don't need to do anything special at the section level -->
46:     <xsl:template match="section">
47:         <xsl:apply-templates/>
48:     </xsl:template>
49:
50:        <!--
51:            Our basic text paragraph element. We maintain the class attribute,
               ➥which is really the same
52:            as the original Word style name
53:        -->
54:     <xsl:template match="div">
55:         <p>
56:             <xsl:apply-templates/>
57:         </p>
58:     </xsl:template>
59:
60:     <xsl:template match="div[@class='LH'] ¦ div[@class='FN']">
61:         <p>
62:             <i><xsl:apply-templates/></i>
63:         </p>
64:     </xsl:template>
65:
66:     <!-- we ignore PD - these are publishing directions,
        ➥e.g. "begin note" -->
67:     <xsl:template match="div[@class='PD']">
68:     </xsl:template>
69:
70:        <!--
71:            These are our specialized content types for
               ➥code blocks and notes.
72:            Each now needs its own font commands
```

```
73:      -->
74:      <xsl:template match="codeline">
75:          <div><xsl:apply-templates/></div>
76:      </xsl:template>
77:
78:      <xsl:template match="noteline">
79:          <p><xsl:apply-templates/></p>
80:      </xsl:template>
81:
82:      <xsl:template match="code">
83:          <p><font face="Courier New"><xsl:apply-templates/></font></p>
84:      </xsl:template>
85:
86:      <!-- The note element is a little special, because we want
      ➥ to put in a header that says "Note" -->
87:      <xsl:template match="note">
88:          <center><table border="1" cellpadding="5" width="90%">
          ➥<tr><td><font face="Verdana" size="2">
89:          <b>Note</b>
90:          <xsl:apply-templates/>
91:          </font></td></tr></table></center>
92:      </xsl:template>
93:
94:      <!-- Titles for sections are bolded -->
95:      <xsl:template match="title">
96:          <div><font size="3"><b><xsl:apply-templates/></b></font></div>
97:      </xsl:template>
98:
99:      <!-- underline elements are used to denote code in the text - turn
      ➥these into their own special spans -->
100:     <xsl:template match="u">
101:     <span><font face="Courier New"><xsl:apply-templates/></font></span>
102:     </xsl:template>
103:
104:     <!-- handle vanilla HTML-like tags –
      ➥just map them to the same thing -->
105:     <xsl:template match="b|i|sub|sup|br">
106:         <xsl:element>
107:             <xsl:apply-templates/>
108:         </xsl:element>
109:     </xsl:template>
110:
111:     <!-- spaceruns and tabs get mapped into sequences of
      ➥ s. We approximate tabs with 4 spaces -->
112:     <xsl:template match="spacerun">
113:         <span><xsl:eval>Repeat(" ",
          ➥this.getAttribute("len"))</xsl:eval></span>
114:     </xsl:template>
115:
116:     <xsl:template match="tab">
```

8

continues

Listing 8.5   Continued

```
117:            <span><xsl:eval>Repeat(" ", 4)</xsl:eval></span>
118:        </xsl:template>
119:
120:        <!-- translate special chars into entities for
             display in HTML - we use numbered entities so we don't
121:            have to explicitly define them -->
122:        <xsl:template match="char">
123:            <xsl:choose>
124:                <xsl:when test=".[@type = 'emDash']">&#8212;</xsl:when>
125:                <xsl:when test=".[@type = 'bullet']">&#8226;</xsl:when>
126:                <xsl:when test=".[@type = 'ellipsis']">&#8230;</xsl:when>
127:                <!-- we'll just use 2 nbsps for emSpace -
                     #8195 doesn't seem to work as documented -->
128:                <xsl:when test=".[@type = 'emSpace']"> 
                      </xsl:when>
129:                <xsl:when test=".[@type = 'smartApos']">&#146;</xsl:when>
130:                <xsl:when test=".[@type = 'smartLQuote']">&#147;</xsl:when>
131:                <xsl:when test=".[@type = 'smartRQuote']">&#148;</xsl:when>
132:                <xsl:otherwise><span class="unknown">char: <xsl:value-of
                     select="@type"/></span></xsl:otherwise>
133:            </xsl:choose>
134:        </xsl:template>
135:
136: <xsl:script>
137: <![CDATA[
138:     // returns a string consisting of n copies of t
139:     function Repeat(t, n)
140:     {
141:         var r = "";
142:         while (n-- > 0)
143:             r += t;
144:         return r;
145:     }
146: ]]>
147: </xsl:script>
148:
149: </xsl:stylesheet>
```

I've printed the entire stylesheet here, though little of it is different from
StoryToHTML.XSL considered in the previous chapter. This will provide context for
the changes, which are shown in bold.

The first and most obvious change to note is that the <html> tag shown on lines 14
and 16 now contains nothing but the values returned by invoking apply-templates.
In the previous version we found an extensive set of style elements.

Not surprisingly, in this version we must set the font explicitly, as shown for example
on line 34. We then find that while we were able to use <div> elements with the class

attribute in the previous version, here we will use <p> elements, and explicit formatting, such as the use of the <i> element shown on line 36. Because we do not have the ability to change the formatting based on the class of the element, we must search for specific elements within the source document and set the formatting appropriately. Thus, on lines 60–64 we set all the LH and FN elements to be displayed in italics.

On lines 87–92 we place the notes within a box by creating a table with a border. Inline code is denoted by changing the font to Courier New as shown on lines 100–102.

In short, while we have to be a bit clever about how we manipulate the HTML for down-level browsers, there are no great surprises here. You can easily imagine creating a series of similar XSL stylesheets to transform to any number of output specifications.

Implementing CodeBlocks

The XSL stylesheet to implement CodeBlocks is a bit more complicated. To begin to write such a stylesheet, we must first consider what we want in the HTML page it produces.

Our goal is to create a button that will copy the code to the clipboard. Let's make life tolerable and posit that the specification calls for IE5. Attempting this feat for IE4 and Netscape, would be, if not impossible, at least unpleasant. You could, of course, write your own custom client object, but it turns out to be pretty easy to let IE5 do the work for you.

Creating Codeblocks in HTML

Here's our approach. You will remember from the previous chapter that when we display code in HTML, we create an outer <div> with the attribute class whose value is code, and an inner <div> for each line of code, as shown in this excerpt from the resulting HTML:

```
<div class="code"><div class="codeline">
```

To manage the button, we'll add to the outer <div> a button whose value (and thus text) will be Copy Code. We'll attach an event handler for clicking the button that will call a client-side script function CopyCode, and we'll pass in a unique identifier for the block of code. The resulting HTML will look like this:

```
<div class="code"><table width="100%"><tr><td align="right">
➥<input type="button" value="Copy code" class="button"
➥onclick="CopyCode('CodeBlock84542208')"/> </td></tr></table>
```

Note that the button has been placed inside a table so that we can make it flush right. The CopyCode method is passed a unique identifier: the word CodeBlock followed by a unique identifying number. We'll see where this identifier comes from in just a moment.

When the button is clicked, the CopyCode method will be called, as shown in Listing 8.6.

Listing 8.6

```
0:   <html>
1:       <head>
2:           <style>
3:           * {font-family:Georgia; font-size:10pt; margin-bottom:6pt;}
4:           .unknown {color:red;}
5:           .code {background-color:lightgrey;padding:3pt;}
6:           .textcode {font-family: Courier New; font-size:10pt; }
7:           .codeline, .codeline b{font-family: Courier New;
               ➥font-size:9pt; line-height:9pt; margin-bottom:0; }
8:           .sectionHeader {font-weight:bold}
9:           .LH, .FN {font-style:italic;}
10:          .note {background-color:lightgreen; margin:0 4em; padding:3pt;}
11:          .noteline, .noteline b, .noteline i, .noteHeader
               ➥{font-family:Verdana; font-size:8pt;}
12:          .noteline {margin-left:2em;}
13:          .noteHeader {font-weight: bold;}
14:          .summary {font-style:italic; font-size:8pt; margin-bottom:0;}
15:          .button {font-family: Arial; font-size:8pt;}
16:      </style>
17:          <script><!--
18:          function CopyCode(id)
19:          {
20:              // find the appropriate block of text
21:              var d = theCodeData.selectSingleNode("//codeblock
                   ➥[@id='" + id + "']");
22:              // extract the code by concatenating all the text -
                   ➥ this also resolves the HTML quoting
23:              var s = d.text;
24: // stash the text in an element, so we can create a text range
25:              trElement.innerText = s;
26:              // the only way I know of to get something on the
                   ➥clipboard is to exec a command on a text range
27:              var tr = trElement.createTextRange();
28:              tr.execCommand("Copy");
29:          }
30:      --></script>
31:      </head>
```

Listing 8.6 is the head section of the HTML file. It includes the style section as well as the client-side script, in this case the CopyCode method.

`CopyCode` relies on the existence of an XML island in the HTML document. As stated in the first chapter, an XML island is a Microsoft innovation, supported in IE5, to embed XML within an HTML file. You establish an XML island with the HTML tag `<xml>`. We see this later in the HTML file, as shown in Listing 8.7. We'll need to examine Listing 8.6 and Listing 8.7 at the same time to understand how this works.

Listing 8.7

```
 0:               <div class="summary">
 1:                   Section summary
 2:                   <br/>34 paragraphs
 3:                   <br/>2 code blocks
 4:                   <br/>1 notes
 5:               </div>
 6:               <xml id="theCodeData"><codedata>
 7:                   <codeblock id="CodeBlock84542208">
 8: &lt;%@ Language=VBScript %&gt;
 9: &lt;HTML&gt;
10: &lt;HEAD&gt;
11: &lt;META NAME="GENERATOR" Content="Microsoft Visual Studio 6.0"&gt;
12: &lt;/HEAD&gt;
13: &lt;BODY&gt;
14:
15:
16: &lt;p&gt;&lt;h1&gt;Publishers&lt;/h1&gt;&lt;/P&gt;
17: &lt;Table width = 75% border=1 cellspacing=1 cellpadding=1&gt;
18: &lt;% dim rs
19: set rs = server.CreateObject("adodb.recordset")
20: dim sqlstmt
21: sqlstmt = "select * from publishers"
22: dim strConnect
23: strConnect = "Driver={SQL Server};
     ➥Server=myServer;Database=Pubs;UID=sa;PWD="
24: call rs.Open(sqlstmt, strConnect )
25:
26:     while not rs.eof%&gt;
27:     &lt;tr&gt;
28:         &lt;td&gt;&lt;%=rs("pub_id")%&gt;&lt;/td&gt;
29:         &lt;td&gt;&lt;%=rs("pub_name")%&gt;&lt;/td&gt;
30:         &lt;td&gt;&lt;%=rs("city")%&gt;&lt;/td&gt;
31:     &lt;/tr&gt;
32:     &lt;%rs.movenext
33:     wend%&gt;
34: &lt;/table&gt;
35: &lt;%rs.close()%&gt;
36: &lt;P&gt; &lt;/P&gt;
37:
38: &lt;/BODY&gt;
```

continues

8

Listing 8.7   Continued

```
39:    &lt;/HTML&gt;
40:    </codeblock>
41:                <codeblock id="CodeBlock84549536">
42:        &lt;td&gt;&lt;%=rs("pub_id")%&gt;&lt;/td&gt;
43:    </codeblock>
44:            </codedata></xml>
45:        <input type="hidden" id="trElement"/>
46:      </body>
47:    </html>
```

On line 6 of Listing 8.7, we see the XML island defined with the xml element

```
6:          <xml id="theCodeData">
```

theCodeData is the id or identifying name of the XML island. Within the HTML, we can refer to the XML island by the id theCodeData. Between the opening xml tag on line 6, and the closing xml tag on line 44, we are within an island of XML, and all the elements must be XML elements, not HTML.

The very first XML element we see is also on line 6; it is the XML element <codedata>. The codedata element is used to contain our reserved area of code, and it provides the XML-required single top-level element, just as book and story did in the previous chapters.

Within the codedata element will be contained one or more codeblock elements. Each codeblock element in turn holds a specific block of code. Each codeblock is identified by a unique id, so that we can refer to it individually. Within the code block is the code without line numbers and with no HTML tags. It is the contents of the codeblock that will be copied to the clipboard.

We're going to set aside for now the question of how we create the XML island with its contained codedata and codeblock elements; we'll return to that when we look at the XSL stylesheet. For now, we assume that the XML island exists. Returning to Listing 8.6 and the implementation of CopyCode, on line 21 we see that we can call selectSingleNode on the XML island.

Note

Remember that theCodeData is an element of type XML, which is itself an *HTML* element, and thus can be called within a DHTML script.

SelectSingleNode however is not an HTML method; it is an XML method. How is it that we're calling an XML method on an HTML element? It turns out that the default property of the XML element is XMLDocument. This property returns a reference to the underlying XML DOMDocument.

> Thus calling `theCodeData.SelectSingleNode` is exactly like calling `theCodeData.XMLDocument.selectSingleNode`.
>
> So we're not calling `SelectSingleNode` on the island, we're calling it on `XMLDocument`, which is an XML object.
>
> While we're being picky, we can call `theCodeData` directly because DHTML assumes the default object `document.all`. Thus, this innocent statement `theCodeData.SelectSingleNode` turns out to be shorthand for
>
> `document.all.theCodeData.XMLDocument.SelectSingleNode`

We pass an XQL (XML Query Language) statement in to `selectSingleNode`, which looks for the first `codeblock` element within the descendants (not just the immediate children) of XMLDocument with an attribute `id` set to the id we passed in as a parameter of `CopyCode`. In short, this finds the `codeblock` with the matching id.

On line 23 we extract the text from that matching codeblock. You'll note in the comment on line 22 that calling the `text` property also resolves the HTML quoting, so that, for example, `&lt;` is returned as < just as we want it to be.

Lines 25–28 are IE5-specific Tomfoolery necessary to copy the text to the clipboard. On line 25 we set the hidden element `trElement` to the string using the DHTML `innerText` property. On line 27 we call `createTextRange` on that element, returning a text range on which we then call `execCommand`, which executes the `Copy` command and copies the text to the clipboard.

Creating the HTML with XSL

Now that we know what the final HTML should look like, it is easier to create our XSL Stylesheet. Again, we begin with `Story2HTML.xsl` and we modify it to create `Story2HTMLCodeBlocks.xsl`, as shown in Listing 8.8.

Listing 8.8   `Story2HTMLCodeBlocks.xsl`

```
0:   <?xml version="1.0"?>
1:   <!-- Stylesheet for displaying XML stories augmented to keep
     ➥a unadorned version of code blocks as an XML island -->
2:   <xsl:stylesheet
3:       xmlns:xsl="http://www.w3.org/TR/WD-xsl"
4:       xmlns="http://www/w3/org/TR/REC-html40"
5:       result-ns="">
6:
7:       <!-- default rule for text nodes - just output the text -->
8:       <xsl:template match="text()">
9:           <xsl:value-of/>
```

continues

Listing 8.8   Continued

```
10:     </xsl:template>
11:
12:     <!-- the root node - output the structure of the HTML page
        ⮕and begin the recursion -->
13:     <xsl:template match="/">
14:     <html>
15:     <head>
16:     <style>
17:         * {font-family:Georgia; font-size:10pt; margin-bottom:6pt;}
18:         .unknown {color:red;}
19:         .code {background-color:lightgrey;padding:3pt;}
20:         .textcode {font-family: Courier New; font-size:10pt; }
21:         .codeline, .codeline b{font-family: Courier New;
            ⮕font-size:9pt; line-height:9pt; margin-bottom:0; }
22:         .sectionHeader {font-weight:bold}
23:         .LH, .FN {font-style:italic;}      <!-- listing header,
            ⮕ figure caption -->
24:         .note {background-color:lightgreen; margin:0 4em; padding:3pt;}
25:         .noteline, .noteline b, .noteline i, .noteHeader
            ⮕{font-family:Verdana; font-size:8pt;}
26:         .noteline {margin-left:2em;}
27:         .noteHeader {font-weight: bold;}
28:         .summary {font-style:italic; font-size:8pt; margin-bottom:0;}
29:         .button {font-family: Arial; font-size:8pt;}
30:     </style>
31:     <script><xsl:comment><![CDATA[
32:         function CopyCode(id)
33:         {
34:             // find the appropriate block of text
35:             var d = theCodeData.selectSingleNode
                ⮕("//codeblock[@id='" + id + "']");
36:             // extract the code by concatenating all the
                ⮕ text - this also resolves the HTML quoting
37:             var s = d.text;
38:             // stash the text in an element, so we can
                ⮕create a text range
39:             trElement.innerText = s;
40:             // the only way I know of to get something on the
                ⮕clipboard is to exec a command on a text range
41:             var tr = trElement.createTextRange();
42:             tr.execCommand("Copy");
43:         }
44:     ]]></xsl:comment></script>
45:     </head>
46:         <xsl:apply-templates/>
47:     </html>
48:     </xsl:template>
49:
50:     <!-- sentinel for any left over tags -->
51:     <xsl:template match="*">
```

```
52:            <div class="unknown">
53:                !!<xsl:node-name/>!!
54:                <xsl:apply-templates />
55:            </div>
56:      </xsl:template>
57:
58:      <!--
59:          The top level element - might be story or book
                ➥depending on who's calling
60:          Just wraps the content inside <body> tags
61:          Then follows with some summary info about numbers
                ➥of nodes of different kinds
62:          The last piece is a set of <XML> islands that stores
                ➥ a copy of any code blocks to
63:          allow copying of unformatted code to the clipboard
64:        -->
65:      <xsl:template match="story|book">
66:      <body>
67:          <xsl:apply-templates/>
68:          <div class="summary">
69:              Section summary
70:              <br/><xsl:eval>this.selectNodes("//div").length
                ➥</xsl:eval> paragraphs
71:              <br/><xsl:eval>this.selectNodes("//code").length
                ➥</xsl:eval> code blocks
72:              <br/><xsl:eval>this.selectNodes("//note").length
                ➥</xsl:eval> notes
73:          </div>
74:          <!-- create an XML island that contains the code for each
                ➥ code block that happens to be in this document -->
75:          <xml id="theCodeData"><codedata>
76:              <xsl:for-each select="//code">
77:                  <codeblock>
78:                      <!-- give each <codeblock> a unique id that
                            ➥can be referenced from the visible
                            ➥rendering -->
79:                      <xsl:attribute name="id">CodeBlock<xsl:eval>
                            ➥uniqueID(this)</xsl:eval></xsl:attribute>
80:                      <!-- for each codeline, we want to insert
                            ➥the text, but we have a lot of extra white
                            ➥ space, so use some script -->
81:                      <xsl:apply-templates select="*">
82:                          <xsl:template match="codeline">
83:                              <xsl:eval>Expand(this)</xsl:eval>
84:                          </xsl:template>
85:                      </xsl:apply-templates>
86:                  </codeblock>
87:              </xsl:for-each>
88:          </codedata></xml>
89:          <!-- and we need an element on which we can construct a
                ➥ textRange, so we can copy to the clipboard -->
```

continues

Listing 8.8   Continued

```
 90:            <input type="hidden" id="trElement" />
 91:        </body>
 92:    </xsl:template>
 93:
 94:    <!--
 95:        Sections just map into DIVs with their own class.
             ➥We'll keep the level attribute incase we ever
 96:        want to do formatting based on it
 97:      -->
 98:    <xsl:template match="section">
 99:    <div class="section"><xsl:attribute name="level">
        ➥<xsl:value-of select="@level"/></xsl:attribute>
100:            <xsl:apply-templates/></div>
101:    </xsl:template>
102:
103:    <!--
104:        Our basic text paragraph element. We maintain the class
             ➥ attribute, which is really the same
105:        as the original Word style name
106:      -->
107:    <xsl:template match="div">
108:        <div>
109:            <xsl:attribute name="class"><xsl:value-of
                ➥select="@class"/></xsl:attribute>
110:            <xsl:apply-templates/>
111:        </div>
112:    </xsl:template>
113:
114:    <!-- we ignore PD - these are publishing directions,
        ➥ e.g. "begin note" -->
115:    <xsl:template match="div[@class='PD']">
116:    </xsl:template>
117:
118:    <!--
119:        These are our specialized content types for code blocks
             ➥and notes.
120:        We just change them into divs with corresponding styles
121:      -->
122:    <xsl:template match="codeline¦noteline">
123:    <div><xsl:attribute name="class"><xsl:node-name/>
        ➥</xsl:attribute><xsl:apply-templates/></div>
124:    </xsl:template>
125:
126:    <!-- we now make a special case of code as well,
        ➥so we can put in the link to copy the unadorned
        ➥code to the clipboard -->
127:    <xsl:template match="code">
128:        <div class="code">
129:        <!-- right justify the button -->
130:        <table width="100%"><tr><td align="right">
```

```
131:                    <input type="button" value="Copy code" class="button">
132:                    <!-- when clicked, we want to call our (DHTML) script
                        ➥ routine with the id of the appropriate code
                        ➥block -->
133:                    <xsl:attribute name="onclick">CopyCode('CodeBlock
                        ➥<xsl:eval>uniqueID(this)</xsl:eval>')
                        ➥</xsl:attribute>
134:                    </input>
135:               </td></tr></table>
136:               <xsl:apply-templates/>
137:               </div>
138:          </xsl:template>
139:
140:          <!-- The note element is a little special, because we
             ➥ want to put in a header that says "Note" -->
141:          <xsl:template match="note">
142:              <div class="note">
143:              <div class="noteHeader">Note</div>
144:              <xsl:apply-templates/>
145:              </div>
146:          </xsl:template>
147:
148:          <!-- Titles for sections also map into their own div class -->
149:          <xsl:template match="title">
150:              <div class="sectionHeader">
151:                  <xsl:apply-templates/>
152:              </div>
153:          </xsl:template>
154:
155:          <!-- underline elements are used to denote code in the text -
             ➥ turn these into their own special spans -->
156:          <xsl:template match="u">
157:              <span class="textcode"><xsl:apply-templates/></span>
158:          </xsl:template>
159:
160:          <!-- handle vanilla HTML-like tags - just map them to the
             ➥ same thing -->
161:          <xsl:template match="b¦i¦sub¦sup¦br">
162:              <xsl:element>
163:                  <xsl:apply-templates/>
164:              </xsl:element>
165:          </xsl:template>
166:
167:          <!-- spaceruns and tabs get mapped into sequences of  s.
             ➥ We approximate tabs with 4 spaces -->
168:          <xsl:template match="spacerun">
169:              <span><xsl:eval>Repeat(" ", this.getAttribute("len"))
                 ➥</xsl:eval></span>
170:          </xsl:template>
171:
172:          <xsl:template match="tab">
```

8

continues

Listing 8.8   Continued

```
173:            <span><xsl:eval>Repeat(" ", 4)</xsl:eval></span>
174:        </xsl:template>
175:
176:    <!-- translate special chars into entities for display in HTML
        ➥ - we use numbered entities so we don't have to
177:        explicitly define them -->
178:    <xsl:template match="char">
179:        <xsl:choose>
180:            <xsl:when test=".[@type = 'emDash']">&#8212;</xsl:when>
181:            <xsl:when test=".[@type = 'bullet']">&#8226;</xsl:when>
182:            <xsl:when test=".[@type = 'ellipsis']">&#8230;</xsl:when>
183:            <!-- we'll just use 2 nbsps for emSpace - #8195 doesn't
                ➥seem to work as documented -->
184:            <xsl:when test=".[@type = 'emSpace']">
                ➥  </xsl:when>
185:            <xsl:when test=".[@type = 'smartApos']">&#146;</xsl:when>
186:            <xsl:when test=".[@type = 'smartLQuote']">&#147;</xsl:when>
187:            <xsl:when test=".[@type = 'smartRQuote']">&#148;</xsl:when>
188:            <xsl:otherwise><span class="unknown">char:
                ➥<xsl:value-of select="@type"/></span></xsl:otherwise>
189:        </xsl:choose>
190:    </xsl:template>
191:
192: <xsl:script>
193: <![CDATA[
194:    // returns a string consisting of n copies of t
195:    function Repeat(t, n)
196:    {
197:        var r = "";
198:        while (n-- > 0)
199:            r += t;
200:        return r;
201:    }
202:
203:    // format a codeline for copying (vs. display), eliminating
        ➥ all extra whitespace, but putting in the space runs
204:    // this is like a mini- apply-templates, but all in script
205:    function Expand(me)
206:    {
207:        var s = "";
208:        var children = me.childNodes;
209:        var c;
210:
211:        // we walk thru all children of the codeline node
212:        while(c = children.nextNode())
213:        {
214:            switch(c.nodeName)
215:            {
216:                case "spacerun":
217:        // we want to expand these to the appropriate number of spaces
```

```
218:                          s += Repeat(" ", c.getAttribute("len"));
219:                          break;
220:
221:                   case "#text":
222:         // text nodes just get concatenated, but we want to get rid of
     ➥all leading and trailing
223:         // whitespace, which the various transformations have added
224:                          s += Trim(c.nodeValue);
225:                          break;
226:
227:                   default:
228:                          // flag any other nodes which might be in here
229:                          s += "!" + c.nodeName + "!";
230:                }
231:          }
232:          // remove leading line number
233:          s = s.replace(/^\d+:/, "");
234:          return s;
235:     }
236:
237:     // remove any leading and trailing whitespace
238:     function Trim(s)
239:     {
240:          s = s.replace(/^\s*/, "");
241:          return s.replace(/\s*$/, "");
242:     }
243: ]]>
244: </xsl:script>
245:
246: </xsl:stylesheet>
```

I've highlighted in bold those areas of the stylesheet which are different from what we've seen so far. The goal of each of these changes is to support the codeblock manipulation in HTML.

The first significant addition is on lines 31–44 where we provide the CopyCode function. This is exactly the code we just reviewed. We insert it into the HTML file as we do all client-side script: by enclosing it in HTML <script> tags, protecting it from down-level browsers with comments, and protecting it from the XSL parser by enclosing it in a CDATA section. This is covered in detail in previous chapters, so I won't belabor it here.

The XML island to hold the actual codeData is shown on lines 74–92. We insert an xml element on line 75, hard-coding its attribute id to "theCodeData", as will be expected by the client-side script.

On line 76 we begin an XSL for-each loop. This will iterate through every matching element: in this case every element within the current scope of type code. The double slash, you will remember, finds all descendents, not just the immediate children.

The immediate scope of this search is the current element, which we see on line 65 is the story or book element—that is, the entire document.

On line 77 we declare a codeblock element to house each code segment found. We assign this codeblock element an attribute id on line 79. The value of that attribute is the string CodeBlock followed by the result of calling the XSL function uniqueID. We pass into uniqueID the current element (the matching code element).

uniqueID is a powerful little function. It returns a value that is guaranteed to be unique for each element in the document being parsed. The valuable aspect of this function, however, is that it is also guaranteed to return the *same* unique identifier every time it is given a particular element. Thus, if I call uniqueID again with the same element, I'll get back the same value. This will be very important later in this file.

Still within the codeblock that we're creating, on line 81 we call apply-templates. This time we add a select statement, but the search is for * which finds all *elements* (but not all nodes!).

We match on codeLine elements twice: once to stash the code into an XML island without formatting or code numbers, and then again to format it for display.

On line 82 we match any element of type codeLine and we pass it to the method Expand, placing the result into the element. The job of Expand is to remove extra leading and trailing whitespace, while preserving the internal whitespace. We see it implemented on lines 205–235.

Note This match of codeline on line 82 is within the scope of the apply-templates element on line 81, which in turn is within the scope of the for-each loop. The second match of codeline is on line 122, which is within the top-level or default scope of the stylesheet.

On line 207 we initialize a string s to empty, and on line 208 we retrieve all the childNodes from the passed in element. We expect that the only childNodes will either be text (the text of the element) or spacerun nodes that we created. We want to preserve the spaceruns but we want to eliminate all other leading or trailing whitespace.

When the nodename method is called on an element it returns the tagname of that element, when it is called on a text node, returns the string #text.

When we match `spacerun` elements, on line 216, we add the appropriate number of spaces to the string. When we match `#text`, we add the text to our string after running it through our `trim` method, shown on lines 238–243. Trim uses the JavaScript `replace` statement to remove leading and trailing whitespace.

Note

replace takes two parameters, the original string and the replacement string. In Java and JavaScript, regular expressions are delimited by forward slash (/) characters rather than double quotes.

The ^ character indicates the beginning of the line. The \s character indicates whitespace and the * indicates "zero or more", thus /^\s*/ can be read "Find any whitespace characters starting at the beginning of the line until a non-whitespace character is found" and the second parameter " " tells you to replace these spaces with an empty string.

The second replace, called on line 241, does the same, except that it works at the end of the line ($) rather than the start of the line.

Note that as usual we insert a trap for any unexpected `childNode` elements (other than `spacerun` and `text`) on lines 227–229.

This expanded text is returned on line 83 and inserted into the output DOMDocument. We close off the match on line 84, we close the `apply-templates` on line 85, and we end the `codeblock` on line 86. This is repeated for each element found and then the `for-each` is closed on line 87. The `codeData` tag is closed on line 88, as is the XML island itself.

We are therefore now able to insert the `codeData` into the HTML along with the script to manipulate it. The only missing piece is to create the button on each displayed code section. This we do on lines 126–138.

Until now we've not had to call out the `code` element; we handled it just as we did the `note` section. We now match it individually on line 127. For each `code` element found we create an outer `div` element on line 128 and then we create a table so that we can right-justify the button. On line 131 we create the button and on line 133 we give that button an attribute with the click event handler.

Here's the tricky (and interesting!) part: The event handler is to call `CopyCode` with an identifier. We create the identifier by adding the string `CodeBlock` and then calling `uniqueID`, passing in the element itself. As stated earlier, this is guaranteed to return the *same* unique number as it will when called on line 79! This makes the link between the button and the block of code at the end of the file.

8

When we examine the source of the HTML produced by this XSL file, we'll see that the id attached to the codeblock will be the exact same id as attached to the appropriate button! Try it yourself: Use the application to create the page as shown in Figure 8.10.

Figure 8.10

With code blocks.

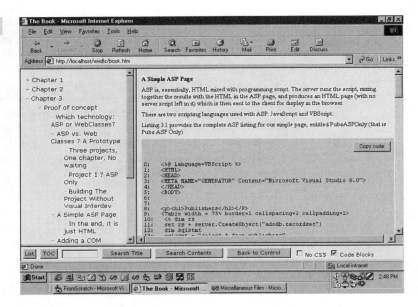

While this is displayed in your browser, open the source and search for CodeBlock. You'll find the HTML to create the button. Now search for the ID shown; you'll find it in the XML island at the end of the file.

Next Steps

The purpose of this discussion was to demonstrate that the XSL stylesheet provides great flexibility in the output it produces. We can create HTML for down-level browsers, or DHTML for up-level browsers to add additional functionality to the data in our database. Creating XSL stylesheets, which output PDF or other formatted data, is as simple as identifying the output you require and writing the appropriate elements to your output document.

In the next chapter we'll look at a utility Mike created (XSL Helper) which can assist in making this task easier.

Chapter 9

Using XSL Helper for Creation and Maintenance of XSL Documents

In this chapter, we'll take a look at XSL Helper, a utility written by Mike Kraley to assist in the creation and maintenance of XSL documents.

Facilitating XSL Creation

XSL Helper was designed to facilitate the creation and debugging of XSL pages. Part of the difficulty in creating XSL pages is that you are trying to keep the interactions among four different entities in mind at the same time. The four entities are as follows:

1. The original XML document which serves as the source or input document.
2. The XSL Stylesheet you're creating, which will modify the source document to produce the output document.
3. The output document, which is produced by applying the XSL Stylesheet to the source document.
4. The display of the output document (for example, in a browser) which represents the user's view of the result of applying the XSL Stylesheet to the source document.

XSL Helper displays all four of these views to you simultaneously. So, for example, if I were creating story2HTML.xsl, my input document might be chap3.xml and my output document might be chap3.html.

XSL Helper displays `chap3.xml` in the upper-left pane, `story2HTML.xsl` in the upper-right pane, `chap3.xml` "as HTML" in the lower-left pane, and `chap3.xml` as it would be seen in a browser in the lower-right pane. All of this is illustrated in Figure 9.1.

Figure 9.1

XSL Helper.

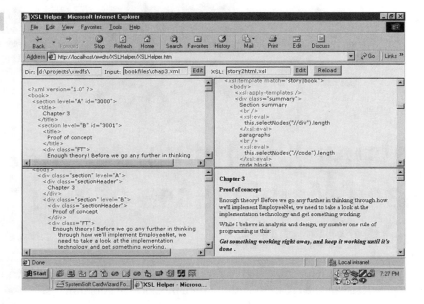

In addition to the four views, there is a small top frame filled with text boxes and buttons. To use XSL Helper, you enter into the first text box the path to the directory in which you store your XML objects and ASP pages. In the second text box you enter the file you want to use as input (in the example shown `chap3.xml`), and in the third text box you enter the XSL Stylesheet you are developing or testing (in the example shown `story2html.xsl`).

Clicking Reload causes XSL Helper to read the input file and display it in the upper-left frame. It displays an HTML representation of the actual XML code, as we'll describe shortly. Similarly, XSL Helper reads the XSL file you've supplied, and displays that in the upper-right frame.

The result of the XSL transformation is, in this case, an HTML document, which is displayed in the lower-left frame. Finally, that resulting HTML is rendered in the lower-right frame exactly as it would be in an IE5 browser.

Both the input file and the XSL file can be edited *in place* by clicking the appropriate Edit button in the top frame.

Much of the rest of this chapter will review how XSL Helper is implemented. Along the way we'll take a look at client-side XML processing.

Note

XSL Helper absolutely demands IE5. You may find that the security built into IE5 restricts your use of this file. To alleviate this, you may need to click on the menu choice Tools/InternetOptions and choose the Security tab.

When XSL Helper is loaded, you can find the zone by looking at the lower-right corner of the browser. On my machine, this shows Local Intranet; yours may be different. You may need a custom security setting to allow you to enable the ActiveX Controls used in XSL Helper. I set mine to Enable, and this seems to have solved the problem, though these are notoriously difficult to get right.

In addition, XSL Helper uses the file system object. This should not be a problem as you've already used VB6 throughout the exercises in this book, and the VB installation installs the file system object.

Implementing XSL Helper

You will note in Figure 9.1 that the actual file navigated to by the browser is `XSLHelper.htm`. This file contains the framesets, which contain the four frames we see displayed in Figure 9.1. The code for this file is shown in Listing 9.1.

Listing 9.1 `XSLHelper.htm`

```
 0:  <HTML>
 1:  <HEAD>
 2:  <META HTTP-EQUIV="Content-Type" content="text/html;
     ➥charset=iso-8859-1">
 3:  <TITLE>XSL Helper</TITLE>
 4:  </HEAD>
 5:  <frameset frameborder=1 border=0 rows="28,*">
 6:      <frame name=Header src="XSLHHeader.htm">
 7:      <frameset frameborder=1 rows="50%,50%" cols="50%,50%">
 8:          <frame name=Input>
 9:          <frame name=StyleSheet>
10:          <frame name=OutputSource>
11:          <frame name=Output>
12:      </frameset>
13:  </frameset>
14:  </HTML>
```

There are two framesets in this file. The outer frameset contains a single frame, `Header`. The outer frameset also contains the inner frameset, which in turn holds four additional frames: `Input`, `StyleSheet`, `OutputSource`, and `Output`. These correspond to the upper-left, upper-right, lower-left, and lower-right frames, respectively.

Note that none of these frames has content except for `Header`, which displays `XSLHHeader.htm`, shown in Listing 9.2. It is this document which does the work, and we'll examine it in detail.

Listing 9.2 `XSLHHeader.htm`

```
0:   <HTML>
1:   <HEAD>
2:       <META HTTP-EQUIV="Content-Type" content="text/html;
     ➥charset=iso-8859-1">
3:       <style>
4:       * {font-family:Verdana;font-size:8pt;}
5:       </style>
6:   </HEAD>
7:   <script>
8:       var fso = new ActiveXObject("Scripting.FileSystemObject");
9:
10:      // this is the main function, called by pressing the Reload button
11:      function Refresh()
12:      {
13:          // remember our parameters in a cookie,
             ➥so we don't have to keep typing them in
14:          var cs = "Params=" + escape(Input.value) + "¦"
             ➥+ escape(StyleSheet.value);
15:          cs += "¦" + escape(Dir.value)
16:          var expDate = new Date();
17:          expDate.setFullYear(expDate.getFullYear()+1);
18:          cs += ";expires=" + expDate.toGMTString();
19:          document.cookie = cs;
20:
21:          // clear out the contents of the four frames
22:          parent.frames.Input.document.clear();
23:          parent.frames.StyleSheet.document.clear();
24:          parent.frames.OutputSource.document.clear();
25:          parent.frames.Output.document.clear();
26:
27:          // create XML documents for the input xml and the stylesheet
28:          var XMLInput = new ActiveXObject("Microsoft.XMLDOM");
29:          var XMLStyleSheet = new ActiveXObject("Microsoft.XMLDOM");
30:          XMLInput.async=false;
31:          XMLStyleSheet.async=false;
32:
33:          // parse the XML for the input and the stylesheet,
             ➥checking and reporting if errors
34:          XMLInput.loadXML(ReadFile(Input.value));
35:          if (XMLInput.parseError.reason)
36:              ReportParseError("input file", XMLInput);
37:          XMLStyleSheet.loadXML(ReadFile(StyleSheet.value));
38:          if (XMLStyleSheet.parseError.reason)
39:              ReportParseError("style sheet", XMLStyleSheet);
40:
41:          // render the input files, transforming them with our
             ➥standard ShowXML.xsl to an HTML version
42:          var s = XMLInput.transformNode(XMLDisplayStyle.XMLDocument);
43:          parent.frames.Input.document.body.innerHTML = s;
44:          s = XMLStyleSheet.transformNode(XMLDisplayStyle.XMLDocument);
45:          parent.frames.StyleSheet.document.body.innerHTML = s;
```

```
46:
47:            // now do the desired transform, and check for errors
48:            var XMLOutput = new ActiveXObject("Microsoft.XMLDOM");
49:            XMLOutput.async = false;
50:            XMLInput.transformNodeToObject(XMLStyleSheet, XMLOutput);
51:            if (XMLOutput.parseError.reason)
52:                ReportParseError("output", XMLOutput);
53:
54:            // and render the output -
              ➥once transformed into HTML and once as is
55:            s = XMLOutput.transformNode(XMLDisplayStyle.XMLDocument);
56:            parent.frames.OutputSource.document.body.innerHTML = s;
57:            parent.frames.Output.document.write(XMLOutput.xml);
58:        }
59:
60:    // report the details of a parsing error
61:    // call with a string that identifies the document
       ➥and the DOM document itself
62:    function ReportParseError(src, dom)
63:        {
64:            var s = "Error parsing " + src + ": " + dom.parseError.reason;
65:            s += "\nline: " + dom.parseError.line;
66:            s += "\npos: " + dom.parseError.linepos;
67:            s += "\nsrc: " + dom.parseError.srcText;
68:            alert(s);
69:        }
70:
71:    // allow the user to edit the contents of the specified frame
72:    function Edit(n)
73:        {
74:            // get a reference to the specified frame
75:            var d = parent.frames(n).document;
76:
77:            // read the contents of the file as a string
78:            var s = ReadFile(document.all(n).value);
79:
80:            // now set the contents of the frame to be one large <textarea>
81:            d.body.style.margin=0;
82:            d.body.innerHTML = "<textarea id=EditText style='width:100%;
              ➥height:98%;border:0;font-family:Verdana;
              ➥font-size:8pt;'>" + "</textarea>";
83:
84:            // set the contents of the text area to the
              ➥contents of the file
85:            d.all("EditText").value = s;
86:
87:            // display the Save and Cancel buttons and hide the Edit button
88:            var prefix = n.substr(0,2);
89:            document.all(prefix + "Save").style.display="";
90:            document.all(prefix + "Cancel").style.display="";
91:            document.all(prefix + "Edit").style.display="none";
```

continues

Listing 9.2   Continued

```
92:          }
93:
94:          // read the contents of the specified file as a string
95:          function ReadFile(fn)
96:          {
97:              var f = fso.OpenTextFile(BuildPath(Dir.value, fn), 1);
98:              var s = f.ReadAll();
99:              f.Close();
100:             return s;
101:         }
102:
103:         // save the edited file to disk
104:         function Save(n)
105:         {
106:             // open the appropriate file name for writing
107:             var f = fso.CreateTextFile(BuildPath(Dir.value,
                 ➥document.all(n).value), true);
108:
109:             // and write the contents of the textarea
110:             f.Write(parent.frames(n).document.all("EditText").value);
111:             f.Close();
112:
113:             // Cancel handles the common tasks to getting
                 ➥back to the pre-Edit state
114:             Cancel(n);
115:         }
116:
117:         // user has pressed the cancel button –
             ➥get back to the original state
118:         function Cancel(n)
119:         {
120:             // hide the Save and Cancel buttons, show the Edit button
121:             var prefix = n.substr(0,2);
122:             document.all(prefix + "Save").style.display="none";
123:             document.all(prefix + "Cancel").style.display="none";
124:             document.all(prefix + "Edit").style.display="";
125:
126:             // and act as if Reload has been pressed –
                 ➥this will refresh all frames
127:             Refresh();
128:         }
129:
130:         // create a file path from the given directory and file name
131:         function BuildPath(d, f)
132:         {
133:             return fso.BuildPath(d, f);
134:         }
135: </script>
136:
137: <script for=window event=onload>
```

```
138:        // initialize the button visibility
139:        InSave.style.display="none";
140:        InCancel.style.display="none";
141:        StSave.style.display="none";
142:        StCancel.style.display="none";
143:
144:        // restore values from cookie
145:        var crumbs = document.cookie.split(";");
146:        if (crumbs[0])
147:        {
148:            var nv = crumbs[0].split("=");
149:            if (nv[0] == "Params")
150:            {
151:                var cs = nv[1].split("|");
152:                Input.value = unescape(cs[0]);
153:                StyleSheet.value = unescape(cs[1]);
154:                Dir.value = unescape(cs[2]);
155:            }
156:        }
157: </script>
158:
159:
160: <BODY style='margin:2 5;'>
161:
162: <!-- this XML island holds our standard "view XML as HTML" style
     ➥sheet which we reuse many times and don't have to change -->
163: <xml id="XMLDisplayStyle" src="ShowXML.xsl" ></xml>
164:
165: <!-- the UI -->
166: Dir: <input id=Dir>
167: Input: <input id=Input>
168: <input type=button id=InEdit value=Edit onclick="Edit('Input')">
169: <input type=button id=InSave value=Save onclick="Save('Input')">
170: <input type=button id=InCancel value=Cancel onclick="Cancel('Input')">
171:
172: XSL: <input id=StyleSheet>
173: <input type=button id=StEdit value=Edit onclick="Edit('StyleSheet')">
174: <input type=button id=StSave value=Save onclick="Save('StyleSheet')">
175: <input type=button id=StCancel value=Cancel
     ➥onclick="Cancel('StyleSheet')">
176:
177: <input type=button id=Reload value=Reload onclick="Refresh()">
178: </BODY>
179: </HTML>
```

9

XSLHHeader.htm is divided into two sections: the header and the body. The header runs from line 1 through line 159. The body begins on line 160. We'll begin our analysis on line 166.

On lines 166–177 the controls are created and assigned their various handler methods. Both the Input and XSL text fields have three buttons associated with them (Edit, Save, and Cancel). When the page is first loaded, the onLoad method will execute, and the Save and Cancel buttons will be hidden, as shown on lines 139–142.

```
139:      InSave.style.display="none";
140:      InCancel.style.display="none";
141:      StSave.style.display="none";
142:      StCancel.style.display="none";
```

If the user clicks Edit, then the Save and Cancel buttons will be displayed. We'll see this later in the chapter.

The user will enter the appropriate filenames (or they will be restored from cookies) and then he'll click Reload. The Reload button was created on line 177, and has associated with it the Refresh method, which is where all the heavy lifting is done.

```
177:  <input type=button id=Reload value=Reload onclick="Refresh()">
```

What Refresh() Does

The job of Refresh is to clear the frames and then fill them with the documents as described earlier. It does this by creating an XML DOMDocument for the input XML file and another XML DOMDocument for the stylesheet. It parses both the input XML file and the XSL Stylesheet (which of course is itself an XML file), checking for errors and reporting any problems.

We want to be able to look at the contents of these XML files in the upper frames. The easiest way to do this is to convert them to HTML files and display them using standard browser technology. To accomplish this, the Refresh method uses ShowXML.xsl. This is a simple XSL Stylesheet that we've created to render an XML file in a browser. We'll consider this file in detail in just a moment.

With the XML source file and XSL Stylesheet rendered, the next step is to accomplish the transformations dictated by the XSL Stylesheet, report any errors encountered, and then display the resulting output file. In fact this output is rendered twice: once to display the HTML tags and the second time to display the output as it would be viewed in a browser.

How Refresh() Works

The steps for Refresh are as follows:

1. Pick up the parameters entered by the user and store them in a cookie.
2. Clear the frames.
3. Display the input XML file and the XSL Stylesheet in their respective frames.

4. Do the transformations on the input file specified by the Stylesheet.

5. Display the resulting output file, both as HTML and as it would be seen in a browser.

Pick Up the Parameters

XSL Helper requires three pieces of information, or "parameters." These are: the input file (chap3.xml), the StyleSheet (story2HTML.xsl), and the output file (chap3.html). After a while it becomes tedious to continually re-enter these, so we've decided to stash them away with cookies as a convenience. Rather than fussing with the cookie collections, we just concatenate all three pieces of information into a delimited string on line 14, and we'll save that string as a single cookie.

 Note
escape() is a JavaScript method which encodes text strings so that they can be safely stored as a cookie. Escaped strings can be returned to normal strings by using unescape(), as shown later in this file.

On lines 16 and 17 the expiration date for the cookie we're about to create is set to a full year from now and the document's cookie collection is set to hold the cookie with the file parameters on line 19.

```
19:        document.cookie = cs;
```

On lines 22–25 we clear each of the frames in preparation for rendering the four views.

Display the Input XML and the XSL Stylesheet

On lines 28 and 29 we create two new objects, each is of type XMLDom, and each will hold an XMLDOMDocument.

```
28:    var XMLInput = new ActiveXObject("Microsoft.XMLDOM");
29:    var XMLStyleSheet = new ActiveXObject("Microsoft.XMLDOM");
```

After setting their async property to false (as discussed in previous chapters, this causes the program to block until the documents are fully loaded), we are ready to load in the XML documents from their respective files.

On line 34 we fill the first XMLDOMDocument with the input (source) document.

```
34:        XMLInput.loadXML(ReadFile(Input.value));
```

This invokes the ReadFile() method, shown on lines 95–100, which simply creates a new file-system object and reads in the contents of the file, returning the contents as a string.

9

The call to `loadXML` causes this string to be read into the XMLDOMDocument. If there are parse errors, we'll report these errors to the user with the method `ReportParseError`, shown on lines 62–68.

This method, `ReportParseError`, creates a string from the `parseError` object of the DOMDocument and puts that string into an alert box. It is worth taking a moment to review this simple method, as it reveals the details that are available to you from the DOMDocument's built-in error reporting mechanism.

```
64:    var s = "Error parsing " + src + ": " + dom.parseError.reason;
65:    s += "\nline: " + dom.parseError.line;
66:    s += "\npos: " + dom.parseError.linepos;
67:    s += "\nsrc: " + dom.parseError.srcText;
68:    alert(s);
```

Returning to line 37, we then load the XSL Stylesheet with the same mechanism, reporting any parse errors for the stylesheet as well.

```
37:        XMLStyleSheet.loadXML(ReadFile(StyleSheet.value));
38:        if (XMLStyleSheet.parseError.reason)
39:            ReportParseError("style sheet", XMLStyleSheet);
```

With these two files loaded, each in its own DOMDocument, we are ready to display them in the browser.

The goal is that the browser will display the XML exactly as it might look in our text editor. If you were just to feed the XML to the browser, it would try to interpret the XML; this is not what we want. We want instead for the browser to display the XML as content, almost as a picture of the file.

To do this, we need the XML to be transformed into a string of HTML that can be inserted into the appropriate frames.

This is a two step operation. First the document is transformed into a string based on the `ShowXML.xsl` stylesheet, which we will examine in detail in just a moment. Then the string itself is inserted into the frame. We begin on line 42:

```
42: var s = XMLInput.transformNode(XMLDisplayStyle.XMLDocument);
```

The `transformNode` method takes as its argument a stylesheet. To understand the argument we provide, we must look at line 163:

```
163:   <xml id="XMLDisplayStyle" src="ShowXML.xsl" ></xml>
```

Here, in the body of the HTML document, we've declared an XML island whose `id` is `XMLDisplayStyle` and whose source document is `ShowXML.XSL`. When this XML island is created, `ShowXML.XSL` is read from the file and created in memory. We can get to it as an XML document by calling the `XMLDocument` property, as we do in line 42. It is this XML Document, from the island, that is passed in as a parameter to XMLInput's `transformNode` method.

In short, we've called the `transformNode` method on our input XML (source) document, passing in the ShowXML.XSL stylesheet. This stylesheet renders the XML document as HTML so that we can display it in the upper-left frame. We'll return to ShowXML.XSL later in this chapter, for now let's assume that what is returned is a string with valid HTML to render the source document. This string is put in the variable s, which on line 43 is then displayed in the upper-left frame:

```
43:        parent.frames.Input.document.body.innerHTML = s;
```

This is accomplished by setting the `innerHTML` property of the body element of the document from the Input frame.

We then repeat this process on lines 44–45 for the stylesheet so that it will be rendered in the upper-right frame.

> **Note**   Until now we have loaded our XSL files by creating a DOMDocument object and explicitly calling the `load` or `loadXML` methods. Here we are using an XML island both because this gives us the opportunity to show this technique, and also because we will be using this XSL file frequently and it is advantageous to load it only once.

Do the Transformations

Our next step is to apply the stylesheet to the XML source document, which we do on lines 48–52. We start by creating an output XML document on line 48:

```
48:        var XMLOutput = new ActiveXObject("Microsoft.XMLDOM");
```

After setting its `async` property to false, we call the source document's `transformNodeToObject` method, which takes two arguments: the name of the stylesheet for the transformation, and the name of the object in which to put the result.

```
50:        XMLInput.transformNodeToObject(XMLStyleSheet, XMLOutput);
```

We check for parse errors on lines 51 and 52, and if there are none, then `XMLOutput` now contains the result of applying the stylesheet to the source document. We are now ready to display this result.

Here we have used `transformNodeToObject` rather than `TransformNode`. `TransformNode` returns a string, and `transformNodeToObject` takes as its second parameter an object, in this case a DOMDocument, into which it places the results of the transformation.

Because this is a two-step operation, it is more convenient to keep the results in an object that we can then manipulate. Additionally, we can check the object for parse errors, which we do on lines 51 and 52.

Display the Results

On line 55, we create an HTML string for the result document, exactly as we earlier did for the source and stylesheet. On line 56 we display this string in the lower-left window.

```
55:        s = XMLOutput.transformNode(XMLDisplayStyle.XMLDocument);
56:        parent.frames.OutputSource.document.body.innerHTML = s;
```

Finally, on line 57, we call the `write` method on the lower-right frame, which renders whatever HTML we give it as it would be shown in a browser. The HTML we pass is the result of accessing the `xml` property on the output DOMDocument. This returns the string of XML, which in this case is HTML ready for display.

Displaying XML with HTML

In this discussion we've waved our hand over how the XML input document and XSL stylesheet are displayed in the browser. Let's go back and examine this in some detail.

Our task is to transform the XML into HTML format. No surprise, we'll use XSL. What we need is a stylesheet that will create HTML so that the browser will display the XML exactly as it would appear in a text editor. The stylesheet we'll use is `ShowXML.XSL`, as shown in Listing 9.3.

Listing 9.3 `ShowXML.xsl`

```
0:  <?xml version="1.0"?>
1:  <!-- XSL stylesheet to display arbitrary XML in an HTML browser -
    ➥similar to, but much simpler than, defaultss.xsl -->
2:  <xsl:stylesheet
3:      xmlns:xsl="http://www.w3.org/TR/WD-xsl"
4:      xmlns="http://www/w3/org/TR/REC-html40"
5:      result-ns="">
6:
7:  <xsl:template match="/">
8:      <html>
```

```
 9:            <body>
10:                <style>
11:                    * {font-family:'Verdana'; font-size:8pt;}
12:                    <!-- element container -->
13:                    .e  {margin-left:1em; text-indent:-1em;}
14:                    <!-- tag -->
15:                    .t  {color:#990000}
16:                    <!-- xsl: tag -->
17:                    .xt {color:#990099}
18:                    <!-- markup characters -->
19:                    .m  {color:blue}
20:                    <!-- text node -->
21:                    .tx {color:black;}
22:                    <!-- cdata -->
23:                    .di {font-family:Courier New;}
24:                    <!-- DOCTYPE declaration -->
25:                    .d  {color:blue}
26:                    <!-- pi -->
27:                    .pi {color:blue}
28:                    <!-- comment -->
29:                    .ci {color:green}
30:                </style>
31:                <xsl:apply-templates/>
32:            </body>
33:        </html>
34: </xsl:template>
35:
36: <!-- flag any unknown elements that make it this far -->
37: <xsl:template match="*">
38:     <div style="color:red"><xsl:apply-templates/></div>
39: </xsl:template>
40:
41: <!-- attributes -->
42: <xsl:template match="@*" xml:space="preserve"><span class="t">
    ➥<xsl:node-name/></span><span class="m">="</span><xsl:value-of/>
    ➥<span class="m">"</span></xsl:template>
43:
44: <!-- text nodes -->
45: <xsl:template match="textNode()">
46:     <div class="e">
47:     <span class="tx"><xsl:value-of/></span>
48:     </div>
49: </xsl:template>
50:
51: <!-- CDATA -->
52: <xsl:template match="cdata()">
53:     <div class="e">
54:         <span class="m">&lt;![CDATA[</span>
55:             <span class="k"><pre><xsl:value-of/></pre></span>
56:         <span class="m">]]&gt;</span>
```

continues

Listing 9.3   Continued

```
57:        </div>
58:    </xsl:template>
59:
60:    <!-- comments -->
61:    <xsl:template match="comment()">
62:        <div class="e">
63:            <span class="m">&lt;!--</span>
64:                <span class="ci"><xsl:value-of /></span>
65:            <span class="m">--&gt;</span>
66:        </div>
67:    </xsl:template>
68:
69:    <!-- Doctype - can't read it, so just say that it's there -->
70:    <xsl:template match="node()[nodeType()=10]">
71:    <div class="e">
72:    <span class="d">&lt;!DOCTYPE <xsl:node-name/><i> (Can't display...)
    ➥</i>&gt;</span>
73:    </div>
74:    </xsl:template>
75:
76:    <!-- PIs -->
77:    <xsl:template match="pi()">
78:    <div class="e">
79:    <span class="m">&lt;?</span><span class="pi"><xsl:node-name/>
    ➥<xsl:for-each select="@*"><xsl:node-name/>="<xsl:value-of/>"
    ➥</xsl:for-each></span><span class="m">?&gt;</span>
80:    </div>
81:    </xsl:template>
82:
83:    <!-- Elements without descendants (leaves) - these get empty tags -->
84:    <xsl:template match="*">
85:        <div class="e">
86:            <div>
87:                <span class="m">&lt;</span><span>
                ➥<xsl:attribute name="class"><xsl:if match="xsl:*">x
                ➥</xsl:if>t</xsl:attribute><xsl:node-name/></span>
                ➥<xsl:apply-templates select="@*"/><span class="m">
                ➥/&gt;</span>
88:            </div>
89:        </div>
90:    </xsl:template>
91:
92:    <!-- Elements with any kind of descendants-->
93:    <xsl:template match="*[node()]">
94:        <div class="e">
95:            <div>
96:                <span class="m">&lt;</span><span>
                ➥<xsl:attribute name="class">
                ➥<xsl:if match="xsl:*">x</xsl:if>t</xsl:attribute>
                ➥<xsl:node-name/></span>
```

```
           ➥<xsl:apply-templates select="@*"/>
           ➥<span class="m">&gt;</span>
  97:       </div>
  98:       <div><xsl:apply-templates/>
  99:           <div>
 100:               <span class="m">&lt;</span><span>
                   ➥<xsl:attribute name="class"><xsl:if match="xsl:*">x
                   ➥</xsl:if>t</xsl:attribute><xsl:node-name/></span>
                   ➥<span class="m">&gt;</span>
 101:           </div>
 102:       </div>
 103:   </div>
 104: </xsl:template>
 105:
 106: </xsl:stylesheet>
```

The best way to examine this file is from the bottom up.

Leaf Elements

Let's start, in fact, with line 83. Here we are going to match any elements that do not have descendents.

 Note
The XQL (XML Query Language) match however is on *. How do we know we'll match only those with no descendents? Because, as we'll see shortly, we match any with descendents on line 93. Remember that XSL works from the bottom up. Having matched elements with descendents on line 93, only those with none will match on line 84.

We assign an outer and inner `div`, the outer to control indentation, the inner to hold our contents.

Let's take line 87 apart, as quite a few things are going on in this one line of code.

```
<span class="m">&lt;</span><span><xsl:attribute name="class">
➥<xsl:if match="xsl:*">x</xsl:if>t</xsl:attribute><xsl:node-name/>
➥</span><xsl:apply-templates select="@*"/><span class="m"> /&gt;</span>
```

We begin with a `span` whose attribute is `class="m"` (which causes the text to appear in blue). We then write the letters `&lt;` which will appear in the browser as an open angle-bracket (<). Finally, as in all well-formed XML, the span is closed.

```
<span class="m">&lt;</span><span><xsl:attribute name="class">
➥<xsl:if match="xsl:*">x</xsl:if>t</xsl:attribute><xsl:node-name/>
➥</span><xsl:apply-templates select="@*"/><span class="m"> /&gt;</span>
```

We then create a new span whose attribute is either `class="x"` or `class="xt"` depending on whether this element is in the XSL namespace.

We determine whether or not we have an element in XSL namespace with the xsl:if element, which only produces its output (in this case the letter x) if the test condition is true. The test in this case is a match of the letters xsl: followed by zero or more letters. After this is accomplished, we close off the attribute tag, and use the self-closing XML node-name tag to copy in the node we've matched (that is, the element which matched on line 84), and we close the span.

```
<span class="m">&lt;</span><span><xsl:attribute name="class">
➥<xsl:if match="xsl:*">x</xsl:if>t</xsl:attribute><xsl:node-name/>
➥</span><xsl:apply-templates select="@*"/><span class="m"> /&gt;</span>
```

Next, we call apply-templates to match any attributes of the node. These will be handled by other lines in the XSL file, which we'll consider shortly.

```
<span class="m">&lt;</span><span><xsl:attribute name="class">
➥<xsl:if match="xsl:*">x</xsl:if>t</xsl:attribute><xsl:node-name/>
➥</span><xsl:apply-templates select="@*"/><span class="m"> /&gt;</span>
```

Finally, we end with yet another span, class="m", to hold the closing tag which we create with the /> which will translate into the html />. The div elements are closed on lines 88 and 89, and the template itself is closed on line 90.

We've now output the complete tag for this leaf element in HTML, so that when it is shown in the browser it will look exactly like the XML looks in our editor.

Elements with Descendents

We are now ready to consider the match for elements that *do* have descendents, as shown starting on line 92. The most interesting aspect of this template is the match statement

```
93:  <xsl:template match="*[node()]">
```

We've not seen the square brackets used like this before. These are called a filter, but here's how to understand them. If I were to write match="foo/bar" XSL would find any element foo with a child element bar and return bar. If, however I were to write match="foo[bar]" then XSL would find any element foo with a child element bar but return foo. That is, it says, "find any element which has a child."

* matches any element and node() returns any node, so this match is read "find any element which has any node as a child"—that is, "find any element which is not a leaf."

Once again we create an outer and inner div. In fact, line 96 is almost exactly like line 87, except that this time we don't create a self-closing tag; just an open tag.

We next create a second div to hold the contents (that is, the children) of the element we've matched. Finally, on lines 99–101 we create a third div to hold the closing tag.

Matching Processing Instructions

On line 77 we match on processing instructions, and we mark them for display in blue. Let's examine line 79 bit-by-bit, as this pattern is repeated for other elements as well.

```
79:   <span class="m">&lt;?</span><span class="pi"><xsl:node-name/>
      ➥<xsl:for-each select="@*"><xsl:node-name/>="<xsl:value-of/>"
      ➥</xsl:for-each></span><span class="m">?&gt;</span>
```

We begin with a span whose class is set to "m" (for markup characters) and hence which will be displayed in blue. In this we place <?, which will be rendered in HTML as <?.

```
79:   <span class="m">&lt;?</span><span class="pi"><xsl:node-name/>
      ➥ <xsl:for-each select="@*"><xsl:node-name/>="<xsl:value-of/>"
      ➥</xsl:for-each></span><span class="m">?&gt;</span>
```

We follow with a span whose class will be set to "pi" (for processing instruction) and this too will be blue. The first element we see in this span is <xsl:node-name/>, a self-closing element which places the name of the current node into the span. Thus, if we matched the first processing instruction in the file

```
<?xml version="1.0"?>
```

the effect of <xsl:node-name/> would be to write xml into the HTML span. We then begin an xsl:for-each loop, iterating over all the attributes (select="@*"). For each attribute found we see the following

```
<xsl:node-name/>="<xsl:value-of/>"
```

that is, place the (attribute's) node-name followed by the equal sign, followed by the value of that attribute. Again, if we are processing the element

```
<?xml version="1.0"?>
```

this will cause the string version="1.0" to be written into the HTML stream. When the attributes are in place, this span ends.

```
79:   <span class="m">&lt;?</span><span class="pi"><xsl:node-name/>
      ➥ <xsl:for-each select="@*"><xsl:node-name/>="<xsl:value-of/>"
      ➥</xsl:for-each></span><span class="m">?&gt;</span>
```

The final span creates the closing bracket, prepended with a question mark.

Once again, if we find the element

```
<?xml version="1.0"?>
```

the HTML we produce as a result of line 79 will be

```
<div class="e">
  <span class="m">
    <?
```

```
  </span>
  <span class="pi">
    xml version="1.0"
  </span>
  <span class="m">
    ?>
  </span>
</div>
```

The result of reading this HTML in a browser will be to display the line as

```
<?xml version="1.0"?>
```

Just as we hoped!

Matching Other Elements

On line 69 we do for DocType what we just did for processing instructions. Here the match is also interesting. Rather than matching on any element which has a child node, this matches on any node, whose node Type is 10: that is, a DocType.

The nodeType is the XML DOM NodeType that is defined by the DOMNodeType Enumeration. This is simply a set of names and (constant) values assigned as part of the XML standard. The enumerated value for the Document Type Declaration is 10.

On line 61 we match XML comments and write them out on lines 63–66 as HTML comments.

On lines 51–58 we match and display CDATA sections. Note here that we surround the actual CDATA itself with <pre> and </pre> tags, so that the browser will not attempt to reformat.

On line 44 we match and write out all textNode elements. Here we simply enclose the text in spans with the "tx" class attribute.

Matching Attributes

On line 42 we match attributes (as we promised earlier we would). Let's take this line apart.

```
42:  <xsl:template match="@*" xml:space="preserve"><span class="t">
     ↪<xsl:node-name/></span><span class="m">="</span><xsl:value-of/>
     ↪<span class="m">"</span></xsl:template>
```

We begin by instructing the XSL parser to preserve the space between attributes.

```
42:  <xsl:template match="@*" xml:space="preserve"><span class="t">
     ↪<xsl:node-name/></span><span class="m">="</span><xsl:value-of/>
     ↪<span class="m">"</span></xsl:template>
```

We create a span to hold the attribute's name. For example, if the attribute were `foo="bar"` this span would hold `foo`.

```
42:    <xsl:template match="@*" xml:space="preserve"><span class="t">
    ➥<xsl:node-name/></span><span class="m">="</span><xsl:value-of/>
    ➥<span class="m">"</span></xsl:template>
```

We then create a span just to hold the equal sign and the open quotes (into which we'll write the value, `bar`).

```
42:    <xsl:template match="@*" xml:space="preserve"><span class="t">
    ➥<xsl:node-name/></span><span class="m">="</span><xsl:value-of/>
    ➥<span class="m">"</span></xsl:template>
```

The `xsl:value-of` element writes out the value (for example, `bar`) and we create a final span to hold the closing quote.

The Top of the Stylesheet

On line 37 is our match for unknown elements. We believe it is impossible to get here (we already match all elements later in this file) but we have it here to prove our assumption (good programmers wear both a belt *and* suspenders).

The root element is matched on line 7, and it is here that we create the `<html>`, `<body>`, and `<style>` elements, providing the styles that will be used throughout the resulting HTML document.

Examining the Results

If you refer to Figure 9.2, you find that we are, in fact, able to display the XML file, in the upper-left frame, inside the browser. This is the visible result of calling `ShowXML.xsl` on that frame.

How do we know what the underlying HTML looks like? Because these pages are loaded dynamically, we can't just examine the source. If you choose View source from the browser, you'll see only the source for the frameset. If you right-click on the upper-left pane and choose "view source" the results are disappointing indeed—only the `<html>` tags are visible. Remember that this frame was filled in dynamically, using `innerHTML`.

We do have a solution, however. We can feed `chap3.xml` into XSL Helper, and ask it to process the file not with `story2html.xsl` but rather with `ShowXML.xsl`, as shown in Figure 9.3.

Figure 9.2

The XML file.

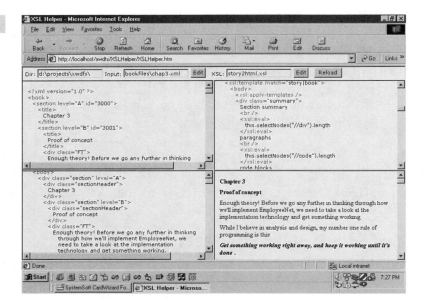

Figure 9.3

Using ShowXML.xsl.

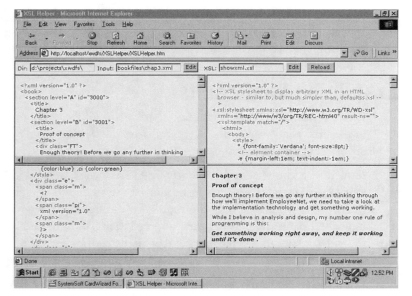

What you see here is that chap3.xml is still shown in the upper-left window. The upper right now shows ShowXML.xsl as we'd expect. The lower left, however is where the real interest is. This is the HTML created by ShowXML.xsl—the very same HTML that is created to create the view in the upper-left window!

Look closely, and you'll see that after the style element is the outer div (class = "e"), the inner div (class = "m"), and then a span (class = "m") with the characters <?. This is followed by a span (class = "pi") with the letters xml version="1.0".

This is all exactly as we predicted from reading the XSL!

Note

Does your head hurt yet from all this recursion? Try this one on for size: How do we render the HTML shown in the lower-left frame of Figure 9.2? After all, if we just show this file as it is written, we won't see the tags. In fact, that is what is being shown in the lower-*right* frame.

So how do we accomplish this magic? Easy. The HTML we produced is valid XML, so we hand the contents (produced by ShowXML.xsl) right back to ShowXML.xsl. It creates the HTML to render this page as we see it! Sometimes programming is very much like falling down a rabbit hole.

Editing and Saving Changes

XSL Helper also supports the notion of editing either the XSL stylesheet or the input XML document. To see how this works, we return to lines 71–92 of Listing 9.2 where the Edit function was defined, reproduced here as Listing 9.4.

Listing 9.4 `XSLHHeader.htm`

```
71:     // allow the user to edit the contents of the specified frame
72:     function Edit(n)
73:     {
74:         // get a reference to the specified frame
75:         var d = parent.frames(n).document;
76:
77:         // read the contents of the file as a string
78:         var s = ReadFile(document.all(n).value);
79:
80:         // now set the contents of the frame to be one large <textarea>
81:         d.body.style.margin=0;
82:         d.body.innerHTML = "<textarea id=EditText style='width:100%;
➥height:98%;border:0;font-family:Verdana;font-size:8pt;'>
➥" + "</textarea>";
83:
84:         // set the contents of the text area
➥to the contents of the file
85:         d.all("EditText").value = s;
86:
87:         // display the Save and Cancel buttons and hide the Edit button
88:         var prefix = n.substr(0,2);
89:         document.all(prefix + "Save").style.display="";
90:         document.all(prefix + "Cancel").style.display="";
91:         document.all(prefix + "Edit").style.display="none";
92:     }
```

9

The parameter is passed in when the button is clicked, as was shown on lines 168 and 173 of Listing 9.2:

```
168:    <input type=button id=InEdit value=Edit onclick="Edit('Input')">
173:    <input type=button id=StEdit value=Edit onclick="Edit('StyleSheet')">
```

Thus, the value of n will either be Input or StyleSheet. We use that to retrieve the document in the appropriate frame, stashing it in the local variable d, on line 75.

```
75:             var d = parent.frames(n).document;
```

We then read in the contents of the file as a string, using the ReadFile method, shown in Listing 9.2. On lines 81–82 we transform the contents of the frame into a single text area

```
81:             d.body.style.margin=0;
82:             d.body.innerHTML = "<textarea id=EditText style='width:100%;
        ➥height:98%;border:0;font-family:Verdana;font-size:8pt;'>
        ➥" + "</textarea>";
```

and on line 85 we use DHTML to set the value (contents) of that text area to be the string we read from the file.

```
85:             d.all("EditText").value = s;
```

All that is left is to hide the Edit button and show the Save and Cancel buttons; this is accomplished on lines 89–91.

When the user saves the file, it is written out to disk, and whether it is saved or cancelled, we hide the Save and Cancel buttons, and show the Edit button.

Next Steps

This concludes our tour of XML and XSL. In the next chapter I'll briefly review the techniques we've used and I'll point out resources for continuing study. Thank you for traveling with us, and please remember to remain seated until the book comes to a complete stop.

Chapter 10

Review of Technologies and Techniques

In this brief chapter, we'll review the technologies and techniques used to create BiblioTech and XSL Helper, and then we'll attempt to provide pointers to resources for continuing study. XML is an exciting and rapidly evolving standard, and while no book can remain 100% current for very long, we are confident that the material provided in this book will be relevant and, we hope, helpful for many years to come.

A Look Back at What We've Done

Although XML is a method of structuring information for storage and interchange, working with XML is really all about transformations. If you consider the work that went into creating BiblioTech, just about everything we have done involves transforming information from one format to another. The power of XML and XSL is that they make it very easy to accomplish this.

In the course of building our applications we've used many different techniques to accomplish these transformations. This, of course, was intentional. We tried to show the flexibility of this toolset by doing things in lots of different ways. In a production application, we might have tried harder to be more consistent in technique, but for the purposes of this book, we wanted to demonstrate many different methods. This will hopefully allow you, as you design your own applications, to choose the most appropriate and natural techniques.

Transforming from HTML to XHTML

Our first transformation is one we didn't write, and can't even explore except indirectly. We began, as you recall, with Word documents, but we used the built-in facilities of Word 2000 to transform the documents into "Web" format. This format amounted to HTML with a little XML mixed in. While this didn't get us where we wanted to go, it was a necessary first step and saved us a fair amount of custom programming.

Because Word 2000's HTML output is not well-formed XML, we needed to transform it first to XHTML so we could begin using the XML tools. We wrote custom VB code to transform the file into XHTML format—still a valid HTML document, but also well-formed in the XML sense.

 **Note**

If we look one level down in the HTML to XHTML transformation process, we'll see it is actually comprised of two "sub-" transformations.

First, we used the MSHTML IE parser to convert an HTML text stream into an in-memory object representation of the HTML. Then, second, our custom VB component walked that in-memory object tree and converted things back to a string representation of the XHTML.

We see this pattern often. One of the strengths of XML (and HTML) is that its on-disk representation is a human readable string format, but it is much more convenient and efficient to manipulate the structure in memory via the object tree.

Transforming from XHTML to XML

With this accomplished, we had well-formed XML (XHTML), but the document is still basically HTML: oriented for display and with much of its inherent structure implicit. At this point we wanted to transform the document into our "canonical" XML format, which is how we stored the content and from which we derived all our other versions.

This transformation was actually accomplished with the use of three techniques. First, we took advantage of what will become a very common tool: using an XSL Stylesheet to transform one version of XML into another. This allowed us to get rid of some HTML stuff we no longer needed and to change the HTML-specific tags and structure into the format that we wanted.

We then applied two other transformations using custom VB code, working on in-memory XML DOMDocuments. One of these worked essentially by copying every element of the source tree to a new DOMDocument, placing them in the desired structure, and then discarding the original DOMDocument. The other moved elements around within one DOMDocument, rearranging the structure.

Our next task was to split up the chapter-sized documents into "stories", the atomic units we would store in the database. Here again we read the XML string representation into an in-memory DOMDocument. This time we didn't change the source, we just created several DOMDocuments—one for each story—built by copying elements from the source. As we built each one, we used the `.xml` method to extrude a string version of the XML to save in the database.

Using XML and XSL to Display the Stories

Having created stories, we wanted to be able to display them. So we built another XSL Stylesheet which converted the XML for a story into HTML which could be rendered by a browser. The XML string was retrieved from the database and loaded via `loadXML()` into a DOMDocument. The XSL was loaded directly from its file via `load()`. The resulting HTML was returned as a string to the ASP, which wrote it to the `Response` object. This again is a common pattern for the display of XML.

To build the table of contents, we took a different tack. Rather than working from an existing XML file or object, we built up an XML document by concatenating strings based on database content. In our implementation, we used script code in an ASP; in production, we might have used a stored procedure in the database, or a separate object. Once we constructed the XML string, we then used the familiar pattern of transforming it to HTML via an XSL Stylesheet.

To further demonstrate the flexibility of XML, we then used two other techniques to produce the same table of contents. In the first alternative, we reproduced the identical XML document, this time not using string concatenation but rather by applying an XSL transform to the canonical chapter XML file. The resulting XML was identical to the XML produced from the database, and so we were able to use the same XSL Stylesheet to transform it into HTML.

The second alternative technique was to combine the two XSL transforms into one. Here we created an XSL Stylesheet that went directly from the chapter XML file to the desired HTML.

10

We then implemented variations on how stories could be displayed—one for down-level browsers, and another that enhanced the output with a mechanism for copying unformatted code blocks to the Windows clipboard. These showed how, by simply changing the XSL Stylesheet, we were able to produce different forms of output to suit particular needs.

Client-Side XSL

Up to that point, all our work had been done on the server. We used the browser only to display the results.

This might actually be hard to see if you were running everything on a single machine. The model, however, was to manipulate the files either on a back-office editorial system and/or on the Web server before sending HTML to client browsers.

In the server-side work, we did not take advantage of the capabilities of the browser to directly handle XML. With XSL Helper, however, we did use some of the client-side facilities. Here we used XML islands within an HTML page, and took advantage of the browser's built-in support for loading XML and performing XSL transforms.

The advantage to client-side processing is that you don't need special administrative privileges; in fact you don't need a server at all! Note also that even though we're now working on the client, we still use the same XML objects and methods as we used on the server. The manipulation of XML is location-independent.

The disadvantage of client-side processing is that, at least for today, you are tied to exactly one browser type, Internet Explorer 5, and you do have to cope with the various security restrictions that are part of that browser. That said, XSL Helper was a good example of some of the things that can be done at the client in a suitable environment.

You Ain't Seen Nothin' Yet

Now that we finished our retrospective tour, you may feel that you've been inundated with all of the things you can do with XML. But wait, there's more! Even though this is a relatively new technology, it is being expanded in a number of ways at a very rapid pace. No book can describe all these ways in detail because the wheel is still in spin, but we can point you in the right direction for further exploration.

Evolving the Spec

Although XML itself has reached Recommendation status at the W3C, there is much work going on to extend and evolve the spec. The XSL dialect we have discussed in this book was only a draft recommendation when implemented by Microsoft for IE5, but the transformation piece of XSL (now called XSLT) has recently been issued as a Recommendation. Progress also continues on the formatting part of XSL.

Complying with the Spec

In addition to the specification work, there is the continual effort on the part of vendors to bring their products into compliance with the spec, while also adding proprietary extensions and features. We recommend that you check in frequently at www.w3.org as well as the various vendors' sites to keep track of this rapidly evolving technology.

Client-Side Features

Although we touched briefly on client-side manipulation with XSL Helper, there are many other client-side features implemented in IE5. XML can be viewed directly, with a built-in default stylesheet. XML can also be directly viewed by using an adaptation of CSS to specify the styling of elements. The XML page can refer to an explicit XSL Stylesheet or manipulate its contents via client-side script. For an environment where the browser choice can be specified, this opens up many possibilities.

DTD

This book used a DTD to specify the schema of the XML documents. DTDs are familiar to those who have used SGML, and there are tools that have the capability to work with them. But working with DTDs in an XML environment can be awkward: The syntax of the language is quite different from XML, DTD information cannot be accessed or manipulated from the DOM, XSL has no way of accessing or specifying DTD information, and many of the restrictions of the language itself are obscure or seem arbitrary. Even for the simple uses of DTDs in this book, we've had to jump through hoops to get the functionality we wanted.

A Schema Specification Language

There are several proposals and Draft Recommendations for a schema specification language that is more natural to XML. IE5 implements XML Schema, which is based upon XML-Data and DCD (both are W3C Notes). XML Schema gives you the opportunity to express schema information in a much more flexible and consistent manner, but with the risk that the details of the specification will change as it evolves.

Other SQL Server Capabilities

We stored our XML data in a conventional SQL database, in a string representation. We really didn't take much advantage of the relational or other capabilities of SQL Server. In fact, we could have stored our entire data set as one large XML document and used the "querying" facilities of XSL (for example, `<xsl:for-each>`) or the DOM (for example, `selectNodes()`) to extract from the file the elements we wished. Of course we would then forgo the advantages of indexing, backup, database tools, and so forth, but for small datasets, this might be a reasonable approach without the overhead of a full-fledged database.

10

XML Integration with Other Products

Many database vendors have announced plans to marry XML more tightly with their products. For example, the forthcoming SQL Server 7.5 (codenamed "Shiloh") is expected to be "fully XML-enabled". At the time of this writing (the last days of 1999), Microsoft has released a Technology Preview that demonstrates some of the ways it intends to couple the technologies. For example, it allows you to specify a query in a URL and thereby receive a recordset formatted in XML. Clearly we can expect some exciting developments in this arena.

ADO 2.1

ADO 2.1 includes built-in facilities for saving and restoring recordsets in XML format. This can be used, like the previously available proprietary binary format, for persistence, but because the XML is accessible, this is a handy way of getting information into or out of recordsets from other applications or systems.

XMLHTTP

Included in the IE5 XML implementation is an object called XMLHTTP. This object allows you to send and receive messages in XML format between machines via HTTP. Using HTTP as the transport helps in dealing with the myriad issues of firewalls, routers, and connectivity in general. Because the messages are in XML, we can use any of our growing bag of XML tricks to format and manipulate the content.

Next Steps

While you may want to supplement what you've read here with many other resources, our best advice is to dive into the Microsoft Developer Network. This powerful compendium of information is available online or on CD. Here you will find massive reference information as well as updates on the Microsoft-specific implementation of the specification.

Another significant resource is of course the World Wide Web Consortium Web site (www.w3.org). There are, as well, many Web sites devoted to XML techniques and discussions, including http://www.xml.com/, http://architag.com/xmlu/, and the various newsgroups and mailing lists.

In addition, this book will be fully supported, including updates, errata and source code, on http://www.LibertyAssociates.com—just click on Books & Resources.

Appendix A

Recommended Reading

Along the way we have used a number of technologies such as Visual Basic and ASP that you might not yet feel you have mastered. This brief reading list will point you to books which can help flesh out your understanding of these topics.

Visual Basic

There are a number of good books on Visual Basic, most notably *VB from Scratch* (Que, ISBN: 0-7987-2119-8, 1999, by Robert P. Donald and Gabriel Oancea) and *Beginning Visual Basic 6* by Peter Wright (Wrox, ISBN: 1-861001-05-3, 1998). People I know who are VB experts have a lot of respect for *HardCore Visual Basic* by Bruce McKinney (Microsoft Press, ISBN: 1-57231-422-2, 1997).

ASP

The single best book I've read on ASP is *Professional ASP 3.0* (Wrox Press, ISBN: 1-861002-61-0, 1999). The *from Scratch* series published by Que has recently released *ASP from Scratch (ISBN 0-7897-2261-5, 1999)*, which walks you through a complete ASP application.

JavaScript

By far the best I've read on this subject is *JavaScript, the Definitive Guide* by David Flanagan (O'Reilly & Associates; ISBN: 1-56592-392-8, 1998). This is a magnificent book and it is no surprise that it has been a runaway best seller. Again, our Que series has published *Java 2 from Scratch* (0-7897-2173-2, 1999), which uses Java to create a complete application.

ADO

I usually keep the *ADO 2.1 Programmer's Reference* by Dave Sussman (Wrox Press, ISBN: 1-861002-68-8, 1999) by my side, and I recommend it highly.

Transact SQL & SQL Server

The best book I've seen on SQL is *Transact SQL Programming* by Kevin Kline (O'Reilly & Associates; ISBN: 1-56592-401-0, 1999). This terrific book takes you through all you need to know about SQL but are afraid to ask.

Inside Microsoft SQL Server 7.0 by Soukop & Delaney (Microsoft Press, ISBN: 0-7356-0517-3, 1999). This book is less about teaching you how to use SQL Server and more about why it is built the way it is. This is truly a great book.

MTS, COM & COM+, Enterprise Applications

One of the most ambitious works on large-scale Web application development may be *Enterprise Application Architecture* by Joseph Moniz (Wrox Press, ISBN: 1-861002-58-0, 1999).

MTS MSMQ With VB and ASP (Wrox; Alex Homer and David Sussman, ISBN: 1-861001-46-0,1998) and *Professional VB 6 MTS Programming* (Wrox; Mathew Bortniker, ISBN: 1-861002-44-0, 1999) are wonderful in-depth examinations of MTS.

ActiveX and ATL

This is a difficult topic and there are many good introductions, but the books which stand out in my mind are the matched set of *Beginning ATL Programming* by Richard Grimes (Wrox, 1-861001-20-7, 1999), et al and *Professional ATL COM Programming* by Richard Grimes (Wrox, 1-861001-40-1, 1998). These are *wonderful* books.

Web Design and User Interface Design

If you are going to read one book on UI design, take a look at Philip and Alex's *Guide to Web Publishing* (Philip Greenspun, published by Morgan Kauffman, ISBN: 1-5586-0534-7, 1999). This is an incredibly creative book and well worth your attention, though it is not strictly a programming book.

The Inmates Are Running the Asylum by Alan Cooper (Sams Publishing, ISBN: 0-6723-1649-8, 1999) and *The Design of Everyday Things* by Donald Norman

(Doubleday Books, ISBN: 0-3852-6774-6, 1990) ought to be required reading for every developer in the United States. These are wonderful books about everything wrong in how we design software (and many other things!) and they are a delight to read. Put these at the top of your reading list.

XML

If you'd like to flesh out your understanding of XML and XSL, I highly recommend *Professional XML Design and Implementation* (Wrox, Paul Spenser), *XML Applications* (Wrox, Frank Boumphrey et al, ISBN: 1-861001-52-5, 1998), and *Professional Style Sheets for HTML & XML* (Wrox, Frank Boumphrey, ISBN: 1-861001-65-7, 1998).

Distributed Internet Applications

Designing Component Based Applications (Microsoft Press, by Mary Kirtland, ISBN: 0-7356-0523-8, 1999) is a wonderful introduction to the Microsoft DNA architecture. I've had the pleasure of talking with Mary briefly in the past, and she is simply a brilliant engineer. Her book is exceptional and I recommend it highly.

Designing Distributed Applications (Wrox, Stephen Mohr, ISBN: 1-861002-27-0, 1999) is a great overview of the issues involved in designing for distributed applications.

Object-Oriented Analysis and Design and Patterns

This field is suddenly awash in good books, though many are a bit academic for my taste. Certainly the flagship books must be *The Unified Software Development Process*, *The Unified Modeling Language User Guide*, and *The Unified Modeling Language Reference Manual* all by the "Three Amigos": Grady Booch, Ivar Jacobson, and James Rumbaugh.

I have written two books in this category: *Beginning Object-Oriented Analysis and Design* (Wrox Press, ISBN: 1-861001-33-9, 1998) and *Clouds to Code* (Wrox Press ISBN: 1-861000-95-2, 1997). *Beginning Object-Oriented Analysis and Design* is a tutorial, and covers the UML as well as analysis, design, and architectural mechanisms including persistence, concurrency, and distributed objects. *Clouds to Code* is a detailed case study, written as it happened, of the development of a real-world application.

A

Once you've read a book or two on object-oriented programming, be sure to pick up *Object-Oriented Design Heuristics* by Arthur J. Riel (Addison Wesley, ISBN 0-201-63385-X, 1996). This wonderful book helps you understand the difference between great designs and mediocre ones. It is filled with world-class advice and guidance and I recommend it highly.

Perhaps the hottest and most interesting trend in software development of the past decade is the advent of design patterns. These are an attempt to capture, name, and describe design solutions that can be reused in a variety of situations. The seminal work is *Design Patterns: Elements of Reusable Object-Oriented Software* by Gama et al (Addison Wesley, ISBN 0-201-63361-2, 1995).

Index

JESSE LIBERTY'S
from scratch
PROGRAMMING SERIES

Best selling C++ author, Jesse Liberty and accompanying authors teach novice programmers how to program in today's hottest languages in the context of building a complete application. Learn how to architect efficient and scalable projects before you start coding and then see when and how to apply critical programming concepts and techniques to bring your application to life.

OTHER UPCOMING *FROM SCRATCH* TITLES INCLUDE

In *Active Server Pages 3.0 from Scratch*, Nicholas Chase takes novice Web programmers through the process of planning, designing, and building a Web site using Active Server Pages. You will create an online magazine that has news, interviews, archives, a small memorabilia store, person-to-person auctions, and personalized start pages. Topics include VBScript, connecting to databases, HTML, and planning and designing a Web site.

ACTIVE SERVER PAGES 3.0 FROM SCRATCH
ISBN: 0-7897-2261-5
November 1999

Java 2 from Scratch walks you through the analysis, design, and implementation of a functioning application using Java 2. Learn all the critical programming concepts and techniques associated with the language in the context of creating a functioning stock market tracker and analyzer. Each chapter builds on the previous with a casual tone, in-depth examples, and detailed steps to ultimately create the application.

JAVA 2 FROM SCRATCH
ISBN: 0-7897-2173-2
November 1999

Jesse Liberty's WebClasses from Scratch is designed to teach Web database programming in the context of building EmployeeNet, a robust and scalable human resources intranet application. The sample program shows readers how to create and deploy Web databases by using key technologies such as Visual Basic 6, HTML, ASP, WebClasses, MTS, COM+, and SQL Server 7 in the context of creating a working, deployable intranet application.

WEBCLASSES FROM SCRATCH
ISBN: 0-7897-2126-0
September 1999

Meghraj Thakkar, author of *e-Commerce Applications Using Oracle 8i and Java from Scratch*, takes the novice Web programmer through the process of creating a Web-enabled database application. The reader will learn about the requirements, analysis, design, implementation, testing, and deployment of an online coffee shop. Topics covered are database objects, populating the database, SQL, PL/SQL, and Java.

E-COMMERCE APPLICATIONS USING ORACLE 8I AND JAVA FROM SCRATCH
ISBN: 0-7897-2338-7
April 2000

The IT site
you asked for...

It's Here!

InformIT is a complete online library delivering
information, technology, reference, training, news,
and opinion to IT professionals, students,
and corporate users.

Find IT Solutions Here!

www.informit.com